WIN THE RACE OR DIE TRYING

Uncle Earl's Last Hurrah

Jack B. McGuire

University Press of Mississippi / Jackson

www.upress.state.ms.us

The University Press of Mississippi is a member
of the Association of American University Presses.

Photos courtesy the author unless otherwise noted.

Manufactured in the United States of America

First printing 2016
∞

Library of Congress Cataloging-in-Publication Data

Names: McGuire, Jack B., author.
Title: Win the race or die trying : Uncle Earl's last hurrah / Jack B. McGuire.
Description: Jackson : University Press of Mississippi, 2016. | Includes bibliographical references and index. | Description based on print version record and CIP data provided by publisher; resource not viewed.
Identifiers: LCCN 2016018901 (print) | LCCN 2016005804 (ebook) | ISBN 9781496807649 (ebook) | ISBN 9781496807632 (hardback)
Subjects: LCSH: Long, Earl Kemp, 1895–1960. | Governors—Louisiana—Biography. | Louisiana—Politics and government—1865–1950. | BISAC: HISTORY / United States / State & Local / South (AL, AR, FL, GA, KY, LA, MS, NC, SC, TN, VA, WV). | HISTORY / Social History. | BIOGRAPHY & AUTOBIOGRAPHY / Political.
Classification: LCC F376.3.L67 (print) | LCC F376.3.L67 M375 2016 (ebook) | DDC 976.3/061092 [B] —dc23
LC record available at https://lccn.loc.gov/2016018901

British Library Cataloging-in-Publication Data available

For Sue, Again and Always,
and the grandchildren who
are our joys—Mackenzie, Liam,
Jack, Charlie, Alex-Anne, and
Madeleine Rose

CONTENTS

PREFACE

A "last hurrah" is defined as a final appearance or effort or final moment or occasion of glory or achievement, especially at the end of a career, or a "swan song," such as a politician's last campaign. The word *hurrah* has been around for several centuries, defined as an excitement, fanfare, or cheer. The term *last hurrah* was popularized by a novel by Edwin O'Connor, *The Last Hurrah*. The book was published in 1956, followed by a movie adaptation that starred Spencer Tracy.

O'Connor chronicled the final campaign of a legendary but fictional politician, Frank Skeffington, who served as governor of his state once and mayor of his city for multiple terms. O'Connor's book won the Atlantic Prize for Fiction and is regarded as an iconic novel of American politics. It was based on the legendary but very real politician James Michael Curley, mayor of Boston and governor of Massachusetts, who had many characteristics in common with Governor Earl Kemp Long of Louisiana. A book review said that "the novel portrays Skeffington as a flawed great man with many achievements to his credit." The reviewer noted that O'Connor gave an insightful view of politics, following his subject "through rounds of campaign appearances and events, thereby showcasing a dying brand of politics and painting a broad picture of political life in general."

The story is told through the eyes of Skeffington's nephew, Adam Caulfield, whose uncle has asked him to take an insider's seat for his final race for reelection. "Well, Adam," Skeffington tells him, "my guess is that the old-fashioned political campaign in a few years will be as extinct as the dodo. It'll be all TV and radio, it'll all be streamlined and nice and easy. Oh, mind you, I use the TV and the radio sometimes, but I also get out into the wards. I speak in arenas, armories, street corners—anywhere I can gather a crowd. I even kiss babies. But that's the way I've always done it, and I must say it's usually paid off. But there's no use kidding myself about it. It's on its way out, just as I am. Yes, yes, this is my last campaign, Adam, the last hurrah."

When I read Jack Beatty's marvelous biography, *The Rascal King: The Life and Times of James Michael Curley, 1874–1958*, I was struck by several similarities between Curley and Long.

Beatty wrote that "He never built a machine; such organizations as he put together were no more than temporary platforms to assist his climb." Curley, Beatty said, "had no ideas of handing on his political inheritance to the next generation. He was in politics for life."

"Throughout his career, Curley had to contend with rough editorial comment," Beatty noted. "But the sort of people who read editorials were already lost to Curley anyway."

In the novel, and in life, Skeffington and Curley lost their "Last Hurrahs."

Earl Long won his.

ACKNOWLEDGMENTS

Two high school classmates, Byron Unkauf and Jerry Jacobs, went with me to Alexandria to follow Earl K. Long's runoff campaign for the Eighth District seat in the US House of Representatives. It was mid-August 1960, the summer before we entered college. We stayed at the Bentley Hotel and over a three-day weekend went to a dozen of the stump speeches of Uncle Earl, as he called himself, in such towns as Effie, Echo, and Mansura. Some of the photographs of that "Last Hurrah" included in this book were made by us. It was an unforgettable experience following, watching, and listening to Earl Long at his "speakings," with music, singing, giveaways, and old-fashioned oratory by masters of the trade like Bill Dodd and Joe Arthur Sims, and above all, Uncle Earl.

I did not intend to write the story of *Uncle Earl's Last Hurrah.* I had hoped that Robert Gentry, his youthful "p.r man" would do that, and eleven or twelve years ago I sent him copies of all of the material I had gathered on that campaign, including my correspondence with Congressman Harold McSween, state representative W. K. Brown, and others. I lost most of my own files when our home in Mandeville, Louisiana, flooded in Hurricane Katrina in 2005. Three years ago, I asked Robert for copies of what I had sent him, and he said he would bring them to me at an upcoming induction banquet of the Louisiana Political Museum and Hall of Fame in Winnfield. Robert brought me not only my own papers but several boxes of his own files as well and said that I was welcome to copy everything in them. He said it was unlikely that he would ever get around to writing the story of the campaign, but he wanted to see it done, so he urged me to do so and to use any of his papers that would help me.

Robert's files included many newspaper clippings, circulars, and other materials, but their real treasures were his notes about his experiences with Earl Long and the texts of speeches that he, Robert, had given over the years about the campaign. While I did an enormous amount of research and had my own papers and memories of it, this story about Uncle Earl's last election could not have been written without the assistance and support of my dear friend Robert Gentry, to whom I am most grateful.

Dr. Edward F. Haas, who has written extensively on New Orleans and Louisiana politics, including histories of the administrations of Mayor deLesseps S. Morrison, in which my father served, and Mayor Victor H. Schiro, in which I served, read the original manuscript and made valuable suggestions. I am grateful for his friendship over more years than either of us want to count.

I am grateful to the anonymous reader for the University Press of Mississippi who recommended publication of the manuscript if the text was reorganized and a number of revisions made. I wish I could thank him or her personally for the critique. My friend Mike Stagg, a fine journalist and political consultant, reworked the manuscript for me, following the reader's comments, and edited and vastly improved it. I was very happy that when the Press sent the final manuscript back to the reader, he had the same opinion and it was accepted for publication.

Mike Stagg has assisted me throughout the process, including a search for photographs during trips to Alexandria and Winnfield. He was determined to find a photograph of the so-called Battle of Florien, when Long and McSween confronted each other in a name-calling contest, and he did with the assistance of Jim Smilie, the engagement and community content editor of the largest circulation newspaper in Eighth Congressional District, *The Town Talk* in Alexandria.

The *Winn Parish Enterprise* told Mike they did not have photographs he wanted, but that their retired pressman, Raymond Carpenter, might. Carpenter was delighted to provide one of Long with his sisters.

Linda Huffman Cox, Long's beloved Shug, provided a recent photograph of herself because she had none with Mr. Earl. She said that he was such a familiar presence in Winnfield that folks there didn't take pictures with him. She has wonderful memories of him, and her stories in a series of interviews of her that James Ronald Skains did for the *Piney Woods Journal* were invaluable sources for me. Skains also contributed an interview with Clem Huffman, manager of the Pea Patch Farm, and ran down a photo of Mr. Clem holding a painting of it. I am grateful to him and to Tom Kelly, editor of the *Piney Woods Journal*, a publication I look forward to receiving each month.

Leon C. Miller, head of the Louisiana Research Collection (LRC), and Sean C. Benjamin, Public Services Librarian for the Special Collections of the Tulane University Library, provided photos of Huey and Earl together both before and after they made up. The LRC is an incredibly valuable resource, and I am proud that the collection of city and state political memorabilia that I placed there is in such capable hands.

Charlene Bonnette, head of the Louisiana Collection at the State Library of Louisiana and Tara Z. Laver, curator of manuscripts for the Special Collections of the Louisiana State University (LSU) Libraries, gave permission for use of their photographs of Long that had previously appeared in my book, *Uncle Earl Deserved Better*, in 1995. I was very tardy in again contacting those collections and explained that I was on a deadline to obtain permissions. They both responded immediately, and I appreciate their help.

I cannot imagine what the Louisiana Political Museum and Hall of Fame would do without its longtime director, Carolyn Phillips. I have been a member of its Friends board for many years and have enormous respect and admiration for her leadership. The Museum, under the office of the lieutenant governor, gets its funding from the legislature, and it is disappointing that in a state known for its politics, the Museum struggles on hand-to-mouth, begging for support each year. The Museum's collections and displays are fascinating, and I am grateful to Carolyn for locating the photograph of Uncle Earl blowing a horn to start a hog hunt.

My search for a photograph of Uncle Earl and Dick Davis, the aide who befriended and then betrayed him, took me to the Cammie G. Henry Research Center of the Watson Library at Northwestern State University of Louisiana in Natchitoches. University Archivist Mary Linn Wernet and University Libraries webmaster, Sonny Carter, provided the image that I sought.

When I asked Mary Linn Wernet about photographs of Earl Long and Bill Dodd campaigning on the riverbank in Natchitoches that

Robert Gentry had told me about, she directed me to the family of John Curtis Guillet, who took the photographs on August 20, 1960, one week before the runoff. I put Mike Stagg on this and he contacted J. Chris Guillet, the photographer's grandson. Chris located digital contact sheets of the images and sent Mike scans of them, graciously making the photographs available. They are an important part of this book, including its cover. I was also delighted that there was a photo of Uncle Earl handing out quarters to kids, as I had hoped to find a picture of that. I was fascinated to learn about John Curtis Guillet (1922–2014) and his sixty-year photography career. A collection of his negatives is in the Cammie G. Henry Research Center and his work can be found on the website for The Guillet Gallery LLC: The Photography of Curtis Guillet. It has many wonderful images; next to Uncle Earl speaking, my favorite is an iconic color portrait of the renowned folk artist Clementine Hunter holding a rooster.

I became acquainted with the superb staff of the University Press of Mississippi when it published *Louisiana Governors: Rulers, Rascals, and Reformers*, which I coauthored with Walter G. Cowan in 2008. Craig Gill, assistant director and editor-in-chief, is a pleasure to work with. I am grateful to Craig and to Katie Keene, editorial associate; Steve Yates, marketing director; Courtney McCreary, marketing assistant; and John Langston, production manager and art director for their great work.

In one of his stump speeches, Earl K. Long pointed to the heavens and thundered, "They keep records up there. And you write them yourself." This book is my story of Uncle Earl's Last Hurrah, but he wrote the record of that incredible campaign himself, determined to win the race or die trying. Fifty-five years have passed since I heard him speak, but I can see and hear him still as I write these words. My wife Sue has been with me for most of my journey with Uncle Earl since then, and I am certain that she is as happy as I am that it has now found closure.

Jack B. McGuire
Mandeville, Louisiana
October 2015

WIN THE RACE OR DIE TRYING

INTRODUCTION

"If they ever tell you that Ol' Earl Long is dead," Louisiana folklore went, "you just ask them to call a governor's race. If Earl don't git up and run, he's dead sure enough."[1]

Earl Kemp Long, younger brother of the Kingfish, Huey P. Long, was a candidate for governor or lieutenant governor in every state election but one between 1932 and 1959. In campaigns for governor in 1940, 1948, and 1956, he crisscrossed the state, making hundreds of stump speeches as he appealed to and campaigned among people at crossroads and creek forks who had never seen a governor before. On June 26, 1939, serving as lieutenant governor, he took the oath of office as governor for the first time in a brief governor's mansion ceremony following the resignation of Governor Richard W. Leche. Exactly twenty years later, on June 26, 1959, he was released from confinement at the state mental hospital at Mandeville. In his long political career he succeeded to the governorship once, won it twice, lost it once, won the lieutenant governorship once, lost it three times, and was congressman-elect when he died. He put it best when he said, "I've had ups and downs all my life, just more ups than downs."[2]

He was probably the most approachable governor Louisiana has ever had. In his final term, from 1956 to 1960, he disdained attending many ceremonial functions, sending Lieutenant Governor Lether Frazar instead, but he loved to stop at rural cafes, gas stations, and feed stores to talk with farmers in a language they understood. His shopping trips for bargains were legendary, and if there was a limit on a purchase at a supermarket, he would go through the checkouts several times and have his state police driver do the same. He loved to haggle, and while many purchases, particularly those in quantity, sounded strange, he bought things for the farm and gifts for friends and poor people. A dozen straw hats would go in the trunk of his limousine, and he would put one on and then give it to an old-timer at the next stop, frequently signing the hatband for the recipient, who was delighted to brag that Uncle Earl had given him his own hat. He took enormous pleasure from giving things to people and would sit on the back seat of his car shelling peas and putting them in small sacks to give away. Dupre Litton, his executive counsel, wrote that "Long spent most weekends at his beloved Pea Patch Farm, and upon returning on Sunday night his car was often loaded with vegetables, corn meal, buttermilk, and pork. This was a major portion of the Mansion menu." He hunted wild hogs and said that when he did, "Uncle Earl always brings home the bacon."[3]

Al Mechana, one of the state troopers who drove Long, said that they sometimes had chickens and pigs in the Cadillac limousine and on occasions had more animals at the end of the day than they started with. "He'd get a hamper full of chickens and there'd be feathers flying out of the trunk like we'd just come out of Mexico," Mechana recalled. "He'd give somebody a chicken and they'd give him a little pig. Into the trunk the pig would go. By the time we got to Winnfield, we looked like Ringling Brothers."[4]

At heart, he was a country boy from over in Winn Parish who knew how to talk to the common people, and he knew how to look when he talked. Iris Kelso, the dean of Louisiana political columnists for many years, said he was "irascible, unpredictable, earthy, and brilliant in his deliberately rural ways."[5]

He asked listeners at his stump speeches to "vote for a man who looks like you, thinks like you, talks like you, works like you, acts like you, and smells like you on Saturday night." In his final campaign, he told stump audiences, "I've always tried to stay with the people that made me. I could have gone with the big shots, sold out the poor people and the schoolchildren and the old agers, and the papers and the fat cats would all be saying that Earl Long's a great man, that Uncle Earl's a statesman. But I'm not a high hat and never have been. I'm a country boy from over here in Winn Parish, a farmer like you, and I like my Pea Patch more than anything else. Vote for one of you, not a big shot who wears fancy clothes and talks ten dollar words."[6]

"I'm just an old ordinary gazebo," he said. As for a socially elite men's club in New Orleans, "I don't belong to the Boston Club. You could look at me and tell that. There's two reasons—they don't want me and I don't want them." He said, "I don't know how to get in Antoine's," a legendary New Orleans restaurant, "or get out. I was led in there once in my life and led out." With the menu in French, he said, "They didn't have a thing on the bill of fare that I could read. Commme-ca-ca-silvouplait, poly pea pot in the bag, and it cost about eighteen dollars. I could go to the cafeteria and eat for six bits or ninety cents."[7]

He told candidates on his ticket, "Don't write anything you can phone. Don't phone anything you can talk face-to-face. Don't talk anything you can smile. Don't smile anything you can wink. And don't wink anything you can nod." He also warned, "Don't ever take too big a campaign contribution. I did once and the sonofagun was in my outer office every day for four years."[8]

Until television caught up with, and regrettably surpassed, his style of fire-and-brimstone politics, he put on a marvelous show every four years, bringing the sound and fury of Longite politics to every nook and cranny of the state's sixty-four parishes. It was as much fun as when the circus came to town.

"There you would find him, in any of a score of backwoods parishes in the heat of an election campaign," Thomas Martin wrote in *Dynasty: The Longs of Louisiana*. "The steaming Louisiana sun would heat up and Earl would get hot with it. Hands jammed into his hip pockets, coat off, sleeves rolled to the elbows, the galluses showing, he would roar his message with a gravel-tinged voice that took on a tremulous falsetto when he became excited."[9]

Audiences roared at his assaults on political enemies, some good-humored, others daggers to hearts. "He doesn't have enough sense to get out of the rain" was how he characterized one opponent. "He's in every skin game, and he's bald-headed too," was his description of another. "No question but that man is a confirmed alcoholic. He's a wife-beater. He's been shooting at his wife, and he has diabetes," he said of another. One opponent was "the biggest shyster that God ever let live," others were "smooth as a peeled onion" and "so bad he couldn't get elected dog catcher." He chuckled that a legislator was "too big a liar. You know, sometimes you want a reasonable liar that can make it stick."[10]

Marshall Frady wrote in his book *Southerners: A Journalist's Odyssey* that their supporters "loved Earl but they feared Huey." He said that

> Earl was a somewhat more antic and skirling spirit, an obstreperous jaybird of a man even well into middle age, one watery eye usually squinting feistily and waggishly, attired in black mohair suits with flowered ties, with the sober swankiness of a funeral parlor director or prosperous Baptist parson. Sitting, though, he would cross his legs to disclose drooping white cotton socks. He was disposed to a cuisine consisting of Vienna sausages, salted watermelon, and buttermilk. Whenever he was out on his campaign circuits, it was his habit, while perched restlessly up on the platform among the other candidates on a hotly flaring afternoon, to produce from his suit pockets an inexhaustible succession of handkerchiefs, like a magician endlessly flourishing forth scarves, each of which he would sop in generous splashes of Coca-Cola and then swipe bracingly over his flushed face. After that, with an air of abstract earnestness, he would absorb himself in grabbing at the flies mumbling about him.
>
> He was, on the whole, an open-hearted and affable soul, finally innocent of Huey's capacity for a mongoose-eyed ferocity. . . . In his constant peregrinations by limousine over the map of Louisiana, he would repeatedly pause along the roads to purchase such random commodities as post-hole diggers, hams, pitchforks, forty-four cases of cantaloupes once and seven hundred dollars' worth of cowboy boots, occasional livestock like goats and chickens, cases of 7-Up and Dr. Pepper, fifteen pounds of okra—he once suspended a press conference at the mansion over two hours while he lingered beside some highway haggling over guinea hens.[11]

Frady said that "his mornings as Governor usually commenced with an exhaustive meditation on racing sheets arrayed over a conference table, after which he would place his bets by phone, later dispatching a state trooper over to his bookies to collect if he had fared handsomely. That out of the way, he would then studiously consult the supermarket ads in that day's paper."[12]

The cantaloupes and cowboy boots Frady wrote about were purchased on a celebrated western trip as gifts for allies after talking his way out of one mental hospital and firing his way out of another by dismissing the people responsible for his confinement. One legislator said that Long sent him a crate of Texas cantaloupes collect and the freight charge alone was more than what the cost would have been at his local market. As for his election bets, rather than two-dollar ones he bet hundreds on some races, keeping a fund of cash in a safe in his mansion bedroom. One story went that a Baton Rouge bookie whom he bet with on credit always had to pay the winnings when a state trooper showed up to collect them, but Long never sent money to cover the bets he lost. When Uncle Earl got deeply in the hole, the bookie pestered him for his money. Annoyed, Long said the bookie was operating an illegal gambling operation and he sent State Police to raid it.[13]

He had a lot of fun lambasting the big daily newspapers, calling the *Times-Picayune* the "Times Pick-On-You" and the Alexandria *Daily Town Talk* the "Alexandria Blabber." He saw the value of pouring it on them in rural areas — and he did. "You can tell a man by the enemies he has made," he shouted. "The Times-Picayune is one of my biggest enemies and I don't propose to lose it by any act of mine." He told one stump audience, "The only way Uncle Earl can tell the people what's going on is with this big mouth of mine. You can't believe what you read in the newspapers. They don't tell the truth. But how are you going to fight people who buy paper by the boxcar and ink by the tank car? You need to come out and hear the truth."[14]

In a 1948 cover story, *Time* magazine described him as "shifty-eyed" and wrote that

> he has none of Huey's wild, magnetic appeal. At 53 he is a soft, dumpy man with a mushy voice, a flaccid handshake, a venomous temper, and the general bearing of a small-town pool hall operator. But he has the "Long Look" and a shrewd insight into the mind of Louisiana's tobacco-chewing common man. He calls himself "Old Earl," gets up as early as 5:30 in the morning to let visitors wander into the governor's mansion. He appoints "colonels" with a lavish hand and presents lesser fry with penknives, after first extracting a penny so "a friendship won't be cut." He enjoys the feel of clean white suits, but he never allows his interest in the finer things to interfere with a certain honest vulgarity. On the day he was elected governor, he asked friends to his house, spread out a copy of the anti-Long New Orleans *Item*, and spent the afternoon spitting on it.[15]

Long was not only happy to let visitors into the mansion to show them around, he often invited supporters with whom he kept up correspondence to spend the night. He wrote one Cloutierville couple that "you have always been considered among my very best friends" and said, "Mrs. Long and I will be very happy to have you visit us at the Mansion at any time convenient to you. We have plenty of room and would be happy to have you spend the night" so we "can see and talk with you in the near future."[16]

Uncle Earl said that "the deadliest politics in the world is no politics at all. Mighty few politicians ever seemed to learn that. They all want to corkscrew, sidestep, and do fancy footwork. When a man never opens his mouth except to say what he means; when he never breaks a promise; when he keeps in touch with his people and doesn't let the hangers-on and sucker-ups surround him so the people can't get to him, that man has ninety-nine percent of the professional politicians licked from the jump, because they can't figure out anything as simple as that." He said "I've got one language—the truth!"[17]

Earl Long did not simply pose as a friend and champion of the common man and a benefactor of the "little people" of Louisiana. He was motivated by a genuine desire to improve the lot of the state's poor people.

"My opponents fought the old age pension," he sneered. "Now they tell you they can give you a better old age pension themselves. They fought our hospital program. Now they say they can run the hospitals better. They opposed the good roads program, and now they claim the ability to build good roads, better than those who made them possible. A minimum pay scale for teachers was obtained over their opposition, yet they now pose as the teachers' friend." Several months before he left office, Long was asked in an interview what he considered his greatest achievements. He named the old age pension first, then school hot lunches and good roads.[18]

In stump speeches, he loved to recall his own school days, when children of poor families would go behind the schoolhouse to "eat an old cold biscuit and old cold greens. Those biscuits were so hard you could knock a mule out with one." He was proud, he would say, to have provided "a good hot meal and cold, sweet milk for kids" whose school lunch was the only full balanced meal of the day they received.[19]

Long equalized the pay for schoolteachers, ending the longtime practice of paying white teachers more than black teachers with the same seniority. With the exception of a bond issue to pay a World War II veterans' bonus, he did not increase the state debt; he proposed a $140 million bond issue for roads and bridges as a constitutional amendment in 1950, but it failed. Southeast Louisiana Hospital in Mandeville, planned as a custodial facility, was changed to a treatment venue by Long after state hospitals director Jesse Bankston recommended that it be a state-of-the-art institution.[20]

While there were noteworthy "good government" aspects to many things he did, Long was a master of the art of spoils politics. "Those who are with us in the first primary will get the jobs, contracts, and favors, and those who come aboard in the runoff will get just what they deserve—good government," he chortled. When a green reporter saw the governor in the capitol building and asked how many people worked there, he said "about half of them." A rookie legislator told the governor how thrilled he was to be representing his people and said, "Governor, I'm going to be with you when you're right, and I'll have to be against you when you're wrong." Long snarled, "Understand this, boy, I don't *need* you when I'm right." Asked what to tell a delegation that said they had not gotten a road he had promised, he answered, "Tell 'em I lied." The Louisiana legislature, he said in a moment of anger, "is the best bunch of lawmakers money can buy." Asked if he bought them, he said, "Hell no, I don't buy them. Huey bought them, but I just rent them, it's cheaper that way."[21] As for Attorney General Jack P. F. Gremillion, he laughed, "If you ever want to hide anything from Gremillion, put it in a law book."[22]

Diehard anti-Longs viewed the Long administrations as periodic doses of evil visited upon the state, yet the survival of their faction was largely dependent on the excesses of their opponents and the extent to which they adopted the Long programs as their own. If indeed the Long versus anti-Long fights were contests of Good versus Evil, then in Earl's three major elections, for governor in 1940, 1948, and 1956, the final score was Evil 2, Good, 1.

1.

THE LONGS: A POLITICAL FAMILY

Earl Kemp Long loved to tell crowds in stump speeches that he grew up poor but had no regrets about that because it made him understand those who had few advantages and made him want to provide benefits and a better life for them. In his famous speech by the Evangeline Oak in St. Martinville, Huey Long said that generations had cried bitter tears there, waiting for the roads and bridges, schools and hospitals that they had been promised but had never come. Huey asked his listeners to give him the opportunity to dry those tears, and once he had the power to do so, he pulled Louisiana out of the mud and into the modern age. His younger brother, Earl, built on that legacy during a long and storied political career

In his monumental biography of Huey Long, Dr. T. Harry Williams wrote that Huey created a myth that the Longs were abjectly poor and lacked education, culture and opportunity. It was accepted not only by his own generation but also by later ones as well, and finally by history. Writings about the Longs almost universally depict them as representing the very lowest strata of Southern white society, the poor white or hillbilly type, crude, coarse and comic. So plausible did Long make the myth that only a few have challenged it. The most violent dissenters are the feminine members of the Long family, Huey's sisters, who survived him and have to live with his legend.[1]

Huey P. Long Sr., known as Old Hu, provided well for his family, at least by the standards of Winn Parish. He bought a tract of several hundred acres with a large log house in 1886; the cabin was replaced by another house, and in 1907 he built a colonial-revival house with two stories, ten rooms, and a balcony. He had four sons and five daughters; one daughter, Helen, died in infancy. The sons were Huey P. Long Jr., the Kingfish, who dropped the diminutive from his name; Julius T. Long;

Earl K. Long; and George S. Long. The surviving daughters were Charlotte, Clara, Lucille, and Olive.

Their father prospered during the lumber boom in the hill country of north central Louisiana. The town of Winnfield grew, and Old Hu profited by selling property he had acquired for home sites. Few Winn Parish families owned more land than the Longs, "nor did any family live any better or more proudly. Old Hu and his wife were proud that they had a big house, that they set a good table, and that they were financially independent. They were even prouder that they were people who had genuine intellectual pretensions, who read books and magazines, and who talked about things they read." There was no public library in Winnfield, and while books were not common in many households, the Longs boasted shelves of the classics and subscribed to magazines. They were, Dr. Williams said, "among the literary elite."[2]

While Huey and Earl both played the rube when it suited them, they were not the uneducated boys they led people to believe. Old Hu "was insistent that every one of his children got some kind of college education and helped each on the way as much as he could," Williams wrote. "Julius attended Louisiana Polytechnic Institution at Ruston and Tulane University. George received a dental degree from an institution in Quincy, Illinois. Huey spent brief interludes at the University of Oklahoma and Tulane. Earl, who came of college age when his father had more money than when Julius and Huey were young, went to Polytechnic, Louisiana State University [in Baton Rouge] and Loyola University in New Orleans. All the girls took the two-year teacher training course at the state normal school at Natchitoches, and all taught in secondary or grade schools for varying periods. One, Olive, eventually received a master's degree from Columbia University and became a member of the faculty of the normal school" now known as Northwestern State University.[3]

Because they owned land and had a relatively large home, the Longs stood high in Winn Parish. That was a relative term, however. In a richer, plantation parish, the Longs would have been on a lower, middle-class rung; in Winn, they were on a top rung because "farmers in Winn, with its thin soil, had a rougher time than those in most other parishes. Winn was poor—pathetically, almost sensationally poor—but they did not accept their lot as something ordained by higher economic law or by people higher on the economic scale; they did not see it as something to be endured without complaint."[4]

Voters in Winn Parish did not support secession during the Civil War and instructed their delegate to the state convention to oppose leaving the Union; he was one of 17 dissenting votes out of 130, and he refused to sign the Ordinance of Secession. In the 1890s, the Populist Party appealed to the sense of class identity of farmers in the South and Midwest with its "radical remedy for the ills of the time—a program of national governmental control over the economy." The farmers in Winn embraced its ideology and became its strongest supporters in the state.[5]

The Long children grew up with a keen understanding of their roots in the backwater area known for poverty and dissent. They became a remarkable family that produced governors, US representatives, and US senators, and they divided Louisiana for decades into two political camps—the Longs and the anti-Longs.

The oldest of the Long children, Julius Tison Long, was born in 1879. He practiced law and in 1912 was elected the district attorney for the Fifth Judicial District of Winn and Jackson Parishes. He served for eight years. Rather than stand for reelection in 1920, Julius ran for state district court judge against the incumbent Casimir Moss, a former political ally, and lost in a heated campaign.

Julius moved to Shreveport in 1921 and continued to practice law until his death in 1965. Thomas Martin said that Julius would "write scathing articles denouncing his brother as a thief and a liar." One, published in *Real America* in September 1933, was titled "What I Know About My Brother, Senator Huey P. Long." Julius supported Huey in his first race for a seat on the Railroad Commission in 1918 and backed him in both campaigns for governor.

Julius was "the early organizer, the money raiser, the political horse trader and detail man without whom no political organization flourishes." When Huey did not support Earl for governor or lieutenant governor in 1932 and a defiant Earl ran for the latter office against Huey's candidate, Julius and most of the family rallied behind Earl. Julius and Earl both testified against Huey at a US Senate subcommittee hearing into election fraud in Louisiana after Huey's candidate, John H. Overton, unseated US Senator Edwin Broussard. Julius described how Huey received big rolls of cash from utility lobbyists. He called Huey a drunkard surrounded by a gang of gunmen and said that he should be forced out of public life.[6]

In 1934, Huey and Earl made up, and Earl supported Huey's candidate, Lieutenant Governor John B. Fournet, for a seat on the Louisiana Supreme Court. Julius supported Fournet's opponent, and they almost came to blows when Earl taunted him at a political meeting. In later years, Julius and Earl were not close. When Earl was sworn in as governor in 1948, he had Judge Casimir Moss, the man who had thwarted Julius's judicial ambitions, administer the oath of office. The enmity lingered a decade later. Julius had nothing public to say about Earl Long's breakdown while the latter was serving as governor in 1959, which was brought on in part by the stress Earl experienced fighting segregationist voter purges that swept the state in the wake of President Dwight Eisenhower's use of federal troops to integrate Little Rock High School. Julius supported the segregationist ally of Leander Perez, Willie Rainach, for governor in the primary election that year and eventual winner Jimmie Davis in the runoff against New Orleans Mayor deLesseps Morrison.[7]

George Shannon Long, known as Shan or Doc, was regarded as the handsomest of the Long men. He practiced dentistry in Oklahoma City and served in the Oklahoma state legislature, but he eventually returned to Louisiana. He was elected to Louisiana's Eighth District seat in the US House of Representatives in 1952 and served until his death in 1958.

Charlotte Arabella Long Davis, born November 11, 1876, was the oldest of the clan. In addition to teaching school in Winn Parish, she was a tutor for many children. She married Robert W. Davis, a lumberman, and after his death she was president of Davis Bros. Lumber Company in Ansley in neighboring Jackson Parish. Active in civic and charitable work in Ruston, she sang in the First Baptist Church choir and was a member of the Colonial Dames, the Daughters of the American Revolution, and the National Society of the Sons and Daughters of Pilgrims. She died on May 15, 1961.[8]

When Lucille Long Hunt died in Ruston on February 28, 1985, at age eighty-five, she was the last survivor of the Long children. Born on January 31, 1898, she taught school in Shreveport and was widowed by Stewart Smoker Hunt, a prominent lumberman. Her son, John S. Hunt II, was an attorney and served on the Louisiana Public Service Commission from 1964 until 1972.[9]

Olive Ray Long Cooper lived the longest of the Long siblings, passing on at the age of ninety-five on January 8, 1982, in Natchitoches. Born in Winnfield on April 17, 1886, she earned a degree in art. She married Edward Cooper and they moved to Natchitoches so she could head the Art Department at what is now Northwestern State University. Her own work was exhibited in a number of galleries. Active in civic affairs, she founded the Natchitoches Art League and the St. Denis Spring Arts Festival and was a charter member of the Association for the Preservation of Historic Natchitoches.[10]

Clara Long Knott joined her sister Lucille Long Hunt in campaigning for Earl in the 1960 race for Louisiana's Eighth District seat in the US House of Representatives. Born October 5, 1888, she taught in public schools for ten years and in 1914 married William M. Knott of Many, a cashier at Sabine State Bank and Trust. Knott became president of the bank in 1916 and served in that capacity until his death in 1952. Clara prevailed on Earl in 1956 during his final term as governor to make old Fort Jesup a state park.

Fort Jesup was founded by Zachary Taylor in 1822 as an outpost to protect US interests against Mexico. The fort was located within ten miles of Many and had been under the care of locals until Clara convinced her brother to make it a state park. In 1961, Fort Jesup was designated a National Historic Landmark. Clara was president of the Children of the American Revolution and Louisiana vice regent of the Daughters of the American Revolution as well as a member of the United Daughters of the Confederacy, Daughters of the Republic of Texas, and the Daughters of Pilgrims. She died on January 27, 1973, and is buried in the Fort Jesup Cemetery.[11]

Charlotte and Clara were proud to be accepted into membership in patriotic organizations based on colonial and revolutionary ancestry, presumably through Longs who were in the Baltimore area before the Revolution. The Maryland Longs were people of substance. Old Hu's father, John Long, was born in Ohio, but John Long's father James was an Episcopalian minister and physician from Baltimore. James Long devoted himself to the ministry, and a preaching call took him to Springfield, Ohio, and then, in 1841, to Smith County, Mississippi, from which three of his sons (including Hu) went to Louisiana.[12] Charlotte did the extensive genealogical research required on application for membership and shared her files of church, legal, and census records and the family tree with T. Harry Williams for his biography of Huey.[13]

Huey and Earl would not have been caught dead bragging about colonial ancestors and revolutionary patriots. Nor did they tap into Confederate traditions in their politics. Winn Parish had two hundred slave owners and one thousand slaves in 1860, but most of the white farmers operated small patches. They also saw the Civil War through the traditional southern agrarian lens of "a rich man's war and a poor man's fight." Many Winn Parish farmers dodged conscription into the Confederate army while hoping for a Union victory. John Long did not serve; his two brothers were in the Confederate army for a limited time.[14] Earl never referred to the Civil War. Huey spoke of Confederate legend in mocking terms during a speech in the US Senate. Williams wrote that Huey had "boasted of his ancestors who had been Southern patriots. They got to be patriots, he said, because the sheriff arrested them and forced them into Confederate service." Huey and Earl had other ancestors who fought for the Union. Huey also said that he had relatives who wanted to fight on both sides.[15]

Earl never conjured up memories of Pickett's Charge or the burning of Atlanta, and he made no claims of his ancestry other than that they were poor but that his parents had raised him right and worked him hard. He spent hours under a hot sun picking cotton, Earl claimed, and there were days when he was so exhausted that he had to put a watermelon in his bag to make the weight for the day's picking.

Earl Kemp Long was born in Winnfield on August 26, 1895, the eighth of nine children. He and Huey were very close during childhood, and he was the only family member to remain close to Huey during adulthood.

Earl dropped out of school to take to the road as a traveling salesman. When Huey ran for railroad commissioner in 1918, Earl covered the district for him, nailing up posters and nailing down votes. Huey won. When he ran for governor in 1924, Earl worked for his brother's strong third-place finish, which laid the groundwork for Huey's successful 1928 campaign. As a reward for his work on Huey's behalf, he was named state inheritance tax collector for Orleans Parish.[16]

Earl did not receive a college degree, but he took law courses at Loyola University of the South in New Orleans and passed a special bar examination. "If it wasn't for the Catholics I wouldn't be a lawyer," he said. "I went to Loyola University. I'm a Baptist but the Catholic Fathers there gave me a free scholarship." He wore a Loyola ring and would hold his hand up and point to it on the stump, telling audiences to be tolerant as he was. He told one rally that he was "sixty percent Baptist and forty percent Catholic," which was the makeup of the state then. His gravelly voice was the result of a childhood accident, when he mistook a jar of lye water for plain water and swallowed from it. In later years, when his throat was sore after stump speeches, he liked to sip from a jar of pure honey.[17]

He also had a stump story about how he got up at five o'clock Sunday mornings to get the surrey ready to take his Baptist grandparents to church. He would come back, rest and feed the horses, and then he would take his Catholic grandparents to Mass. Riding back from a political meeting, his driver said, "Governor, I didn't know you had Catholic grandparents." Laughing, he said, "Hell, boy, we didn't even have a surrey."[18]

Palmer R. Long of Shreveport, one of Huey's three children, said that his uncle liked to have a good time and made the campaign caravans of sound trucks and cars a lot of fun. "I was around on the campaign trail with him lots of times," Palmer said. "It was hilarious. You know, giving away, hell, you name it, at his speeches. Finally he was giving away everything from watermelons to kids, just anything to get a vote, I mean anything." Palmer said that Earl was not as smart as Huey, but country folks identified with him. "See, Daddy had to more or less act the country boy," he explained. "Earl was the country boy. That was what the difference was. He was country through and through. Wasn't nothing but."[19]

David Bell was a cousin of Long's; his grandmother, Delia Tison, and Earl's mother, Caledonia Long, were sisters. He was forty-seven when Long died and said he was with Earl for thirty-two years, working in campaigns, driving him, and holding state appointments. He was director of Veterans Affairs in 1959, when Earl fired him after public reports that he had been extravagant with expense accounts, but they stayed together personally. Bell reminisced that he was "12 or 14 years old when Huey first started in politics and I started out hanging on a sound truck putting out handbills and tacking up pictures. After Huey got elected I was in Baton Rouge. I used to get apples for Huey every day. Somebody would come and stick their head out the door and say 'the Governor wants an apple.' So I had to run out to a fruit stand and get him some apples."[20]

Bell said that while he drove Earl, he served more as an alter ego than chauffeur. "Earl was a very careless driver," he said. "I did all the driving when I was there. I was scared to let him drive. He probably wouldn't get us there." Comparing Huey and Earl, he said that "in politicking, Earl was the best politician of the two brothers. Huey was an organizer and he could put a campaign together faster than anybody I ever saw and knew how to do it. But Earl was the best head-to-head politician that ever lived. Earl identified more with the common people. Earl was loved more. Earl knew so many people in Louisiana. He knew their backgrounds, their Ma and Pa, and could call them by their names when he would see them. He had a fantastic memory. Earl was much quieter than Huey. Huey was flamboyant. I don't know whether Earl was much quieter though because Earl was pretty busy talking all the time himself. It would be hard to get a word in edgewise with either one of them. They all loved to talk."[21]

Clem Andrew Huffman was born in 1917 on Cypress Bayou in LaSalle Parish. He was seventeen when Earl Long hired him in 1934. He managed the Pea Patch after Long bought that property and was with him until the end.

"I first met Earl K. Long when he brought a bunch of wild hogs down to French Forks in LaSalle Parish to fatten them up on over-cup acorns," Huffman recalled. "We got them wild hogs penned up and carried them back to the Pea Patch where we butchered them. Earl sold the meat to the paper mill commissary in Hodge." Earl took him on then, and Huffman said, "I was just barely a grown boy when I started working with Earl. I hadn't even finished school at the time." He said a few months later he was with Earl at the farm when he got the news Huey had been shot, which "really devastated Earl." He recalled that as a salesman, "Earl had a very good selling business going that he just gave up after Huey got into politics" in order to help his brother. "After Earl saw what kinda worker I was and decided that he liked me, he carried me down to Baton Rouge to show me around. He bought me a new pair of boots and some clothes."[22]

All the Longs were high-strung people, with Huey and Earl more so than the others," Huffman said. "Huey was so energetic that he was something else to see in action. The big difference was that Earl was really just a country guy who loved hog hunting. Hog hunting was his passion and relaxation. When Earl was at the Pea Patch he would start seeing people real early in the morning. Usually after four or five hours of talking to people he would holler at me to saddle up his horse. I knew that meant he was ready to go look for some hogs. Earl's favorite horse was a dark red gelding that he called 'Ole Prince.' His favorite hog dog of all time was an almost all white Catahoula Cur that he called 'Whitey.' Earl never had less than three or four hog dogs around the Pea Patch. On his statue, there are dogs, but those weren't his type of dogs. He was a Catahoula Cur man."

Several writers have suggested that Earl's wife Blanche avoided going to the Pea Patch, but Huffman said that during his twenty-five years with Mr. Earl they averaged going hog hunting at least once a week and that Blanche was sometimes there. He recalled that "even Miss Blanche, who was as true a city girl as Earl was a country boy, would get into the act sometimes in making sausage."[23]

Huffman said that "after Earl really got going in politics we didn't sell any meat from the wild hogs we caught. Earl gave away all the hams and bacon while he was campaigning. We'd be out in the woods with the dogs and hogs and Earl would see a big fat boar hog and he'd holler 'there's a bacon hog.'" Huffman said that "Frank Long from over around Georgetown" would hunt with them, as well as "two of Earl's cousins, the Long twins that were known as 'Little Brother' and 'Big Brother.'"[24]

In 1957, the *Times-Picayune* ran a story about him headlined "Clem Huffman, state civil service employee, manages Long's farm," suggesting that he was carried on the state payroll as a livestock inspector but spending much of his time working at the farm. Long responded that Huffman spent most of his time on the road doing inspections and the state got full value for what he was paid; the farm was a part-time job on his own time, Long said.[25] As a civil service employee, Huffman was under the civil services' prohibitions on political activities, so he could not travel with the stumping group, but he was well-known and highly regarded, and he was effective in voicing his personal opinion to many people. At one of the speakings, when Long was drawing for prizes,

Clem Huffman's daughter Linda had the winning ticket for a big bucket of lard. Clem told her to give it back so that it could be redrawn, telling her that someone else in the audience would be happy to win it.[26]

Many years later, Mr. Clem, at eighty-three, was overseeing the annual Uncle Earl's Hog Dog Trials in Winnfield. The dogs would grab a hog by the ear to bring it down. Huffman said the only thing wrong with the show "is that Earl ain't here to enjoy it himself." Huffman said that Long loved to hunt hogs and would butcher them himself.[27]

Harley B. Bozeman, who knew both Huey and Earl and wrote about them in the Winnfield newspaper in many columns over the years, said in 1957 that there were "many other wild hog hunters in this area besides Governor Long who enjoy listening to their Catahoula hog dogs bay a bunch of wild hogs and then lead—not drive—the swine into a pen." He said that for the past 150 years the woods between the Red and Ouachita Rivers had been full of wild hogs, and they were "the source of financial income and pleasure to many natives."[28]

Bozeman said that when the governor was a boy, "he always went with his father to pen up the wild hogs during hog killing time in the late fall and winter, and again, in the spring, when the animals were rounded up for 'marking.'" Bozeman said Huey and Julius did not like hunting and slaughtering the hogs, but Earl loved it. He explained that the dogs would bay a bunch of hogs, the hogs would take after them, the dogs would lead them into a pen, and the dogs would jump over the fence while the hunters dropped the gate. The hogs would be fed corn to fatten them before they were killed for meat.[29]

Huffman said that he remembered "one time I was at the Pea Patch by myself when up came a big black limousine. It was Governor Jimmie Davis. He asked me if Earl was around and I said no. He said good because all he wanted to see at the Pea Patch was them hogs that Earl kept talking about that could drink milk out of a bottle. Those hogs were just plain ole Piney Woods rooters." Huffman said Davis asked for a cup of the coffee he fixed for Earl before they went to the hog pen; "he took one swallow and said, 'Man, that coffee is alive.'"[30]

Discussing Long on the stump, Huffman said, "With his sense of humor and his gravelly rough voice, he could really tear up his opponent on the campaign stump. As a kid, Earl had got some lye water in his throat which gave him a rough sounding voice."

Clem Huffman told a story about a man who had spoken harshly about Long in his presence. Long said he was going to see the fellow and took Huffman with him. Richard McCaughan, who interviewed Huffman for his book *Socks on a Rooster: Louisiana's Earl K. Long*, wrote, "Arriving at the critic's home, Long began inquiring about the man's chickens and cows, while gradually edging through the gate into the yard. After telling Huffman to get them some cool well water, the ex-Governor asked the father of the family if he had any coffee. Finishing their refreshments and conversation, the congressional aspirant gave one of the children a quarter and bade good-by. This brief social sojourn resulted in the whole family supporting Long, which meant about twenty additional votes."[31]

Long, who did not have children, was very fond of Linda Huffman, daughter of Clem Huffman. She spent a lot of time at his farm as a teenager, recalling "one thing that Mr. Earl liked to do that always ended up to my liking was that he liked to go visiting in the afternoon. He would say something like this to my Dad, 'Clem, I want to go up and see Joe Jones.' Mr. Earl would say, 'Clem, you remember how to get there, you go up 499 through Sikes and turn left at that old barn. You go down that road about a half mile and turn right at that big ole hickory tree. His house is down about a quarter mile. You remember he's got a picket fence that has pickets missing off the front gate.' Mr. Earl had a fantastic memory which I guess you needed if you were going to be successful in politics like he was. On those afternoon trips, we would usually visit three or four families before heading back to Winnfield." Called Shug for sugar by Long, she said the best part of the rides was that "Mr. Earl always wanted to go to Dick Porter's Drug Store when we got back to town. That was the part I liked best because Mr. Earl would always buy me a big ice cream cone. Mr. Earl would also pick up a bunch of daily newspapers that Mr. Porter got for him every day. Mr. Earl probably stayed up half the night reading the papers."[32]

Linda said that "Mister Earl and Miss Blanche wanted to adopt me. I was born on January 31, 1942, and Mister Earl and Miss Blanche were at the clinic in Winnfield with my Mom and Dad that night. They had been talking with my Mom and Dad for several weeks about adopting me," and she said that her parents told her that the Longs "kept telling them ya'll are young and will probably have several other kids while we don't have any. Mister Earl was 47 at the time and my Dad was 26 and Mother was 23. Ironically, my parents did not have any more children so I was an only child." She said that her parents would not part with her, but "they let Miss Blanche name me and she chose Linda Lois. Lois was also my Mother's first name."[33]

Linda Huffman said many years later that "all the work on the Pea Patch was done by trusties from Angola," the state prison. "Usually the trusties were very well-behaved. It seemed like a new group of trusties would come up each year. When one misbehaved or had a bad attitude, my Daddy would make a phone call and a car would show up the next morning with a new trustee and take the old one back to Angola."[34]

She remembered that "just about everything we ate at the Pea Patch was grown or raised on the farm. Mr. Earl loved field peas, okra, tomatoes, sweet potatoes, corn, and fresh pork. He loved just about every kind of fruit, especially peaches. When they would go hog hunting, Mr. Earl's cook, Sadie, would always pack them a lot of food so they could have a picnic lunch in the woods. Mr. Earl always carried along some Vienna sausage and crackers when he traveled around the state but he always insisted on eating his sausage directly out of the can."[35]

She reminisced that "when Mr. Earl would come to the Pea Patch without Miss Blanche she called him quite often. Their conversation always went along about the same line for about the first ten minutes or so. Miss Blanche was always pressuring him about his health. After about fifteen minutes, Mr. Earl would get aggravated at her and would holler out real loud to my Daddy, 'Clem, come over here and talk to Misses Blanche—eee!' I can close my eyes and still hear my Daddy's side of the conversation. 'Yes, m'am the Governor is eating well. No, m'am, the Governor is not over doing it. Yes, m'am, I'm taking good care of the Governor.'"[36]

With a touch of nostalgia, she said that "one of my fondest memories of my time with Mr. Earl was when we would be sitting out on the back porch and he would be reading his papers and making phone calls. In between papers and phone calls, he would talk to me. After a while he would say, 'Shug, let's take a walk and see what's going on.' He loved to see how the crops were growing or how the harvest was coming along if it was that time of year. He also loved for him and me to gather the eggs in the hen house and barn. I would hold the egg basket and he would reach in and pick up the eggs in the nest. One time he reached into a nest and touched a chicken snake. From then on, Mr. Earl always looked before he reached for an egg."[37]

She said that it was an exciting time at the Pea Patch

> when Mr. Earl would come in from Baton Rouge. His car would be crammed full of stuff that he had bought or people had given him along the way. Clothes, vegetables, live chickens and you name it were in the car. Most times the windows were down and stuff was hanging out the windows. He would give away all the clothes and most of the other stuff to needy people in Winn Parish. I remember many times that Mr. Earl would tell people who got sick and couldn't afford to go to the doctor to go see Dr. Moseley and tell him to put it on his bill. He'd do the same thing on medicine: "Go to Sam Brian's pharmacy and tell him to put it on my bill" Mr. Earl would say. Whenever Mr. Earl was giving something away or helping someone, it seemed to put him in high spirits. It may have had something to do with his Christian faith. I don't ever remember him going to church while he was in Winnfield but he talked about tithing and loved to listen to gospel music, especially the song "In the Garden." I've heard him say numerous times that you don't have to put tithes in a collection plate. You can use your tithes to help other people.[38]

"Another thing that got Mr. Earl excited was when people would talk about the Old Age Pension that he had got passed," she remembered. "He loved to hear that people were saying Earl got me my pension. When Mr. Earl came out to our place on the Tullos Highway, which was quite often, he always wanted to go visit my grandparents who lived in a little house on our property. My grandmother had known Mr. Earl since he was a little boy and drank the lye water. She would always make teacakes when Mr. Earl visited. He would always ask her about her pension and if it was enough money to help her out. Mr. Earl would tell my grandmother 'I gotta make sure that you are getting enough pension money to keep buying the stuff you need to make these teacakes.'"[39]

Linda said that for her first few years, they lived with Earl and Blanche "in what they called the Cotton House which is now part of the Crawford Ranch on the Possum Neck Road, now known as the Horseshoe Road in Winnfield." The Longs then moved to the Pea Patch and took the Huffmans with them for a short time before Linda's family moved to a house east of Winnfield. They spent a lot of time at the Pea Patch, and Long would have Clem fix coffee and then bring the baby in to them, and he and Blanche would put her in bed with them and play with her.[40]

If Uncle Earl treated Linda Huffman like a daughter, then Ellis "Easy Money" Littleton, a driver and "go-fer," was the son he never had. Long took him under his wing when Littleton, who completed the third grade, was seventeen. Littleton was working at James McLemore's cattle auction barn in Alexandria in 1947 when Long visited it. Long walked into the ring without realizing that a gate was open, and Littleton, sitting on a rail, saw several bulls coming toward the chute. They would have run over Long, but Littleton ran to the gate and slammed it down before the bulls could get out. Littleton said that "a number of bulls had broken out of their pen when Uncle Earl came into the arena. I ran and pushed him into the pen and kept the animals from killing us both." Long believed that Littleton had saved his life and took him on. For the next thirteen years, Littleton worked for him. He drove Long, helped at the farm, acted as a handyman, and did "anything Mr. Earl needed doing." Littleton said Long was "like a father to me," and he worshipped Long. He recalled that "if Mr. Earl met you one time, 20 years later if he saw you he could call you by your first name." Long was down-to-earth, he said, despite being governor. "Uncle Earl was no big-time operator. He wore his old straw hat, overalls, and suspenders. He put on no airs."[41]

Easy Money said there was a hog pen in the left corner of one of the three barns at the Pea Patch, and "Mr. Earl told me to jump over and grab 2 or 3 of them. I said 'Who's gonna pay the doctor bill?' I caught two, turning around, trying to bite me. Caught the blue striped one and it went to squealing. The sows went wild. One grabbed me by my calf. Red Harkins got me and kicked the sow off me." Long gave Littleton a pocket watch engraved "E. K. Long" because Littleton couldn't tell him what time it was when he asked. "I don't have no watch, Mr. Earl," he said. "When I want to know the time now, you can tell me," Long replied.[42]

Littleton said that when he went to work for Long, they did not have any agreement on salary then or later during a thirteen-year relationship: "He just from time to time would give me $50 or $100 or $500. When somebody would ask him for money, he wouldn't have any, so he would ask to borrow $50 or so from me. He always made sure I had money, and, of course, he paid all the expenses. I was never on government payroll."[43]

2.

EARL KEMP LONG: A POLITICAL LIFE

Huey and Earl had been very close, sleeping in the same bed as youngsters, but Earl's ambitions brought them into conflict as adults. Huey appointed him to the lucrative position of state inheritance tax collector for Orleans Parish. Earl's duties were light in New Orleans. In his biography of Huey Long, T. Harry Williams wrote that Earl "was in Baton Rouge more than he was in New Orleans, and when in the Capitol, he was generally closeted with Huey. He employed Earl as a contact man with legislators and with Long leaders in the state as an organizer of Long machines in the parishes."[1] But Earl wanted more, and he asked Huey to support him for governor in 1932. When Huey refused, Earl asked for lieutenant governor but was again rebuffed. Huey had been elected US Senator in 1930 but delayed taking his seat until he could install a friendly successor. He maintained in his 1933 autobiography, *Every Man a King*, that it would have been a political mistake to have more than one Long in high office, but his real concern was that he knew he could not control Earl, and he wanted a loyal puppet in the governor's chair.[2]

Breaking with Huey and supported by most of the family, Earl ran for lieutenant governor and allied himself with the anti-Longs. The brothers crossed paths several times during the campaign, when Huey stumped for his candidates on the O. K. Allen ticket; on one occasion, Earl challenged Huey to a fist fight. He never hesitated to fight; when Huey was impeached by the state house in 1929, he tangled with an anti-Long legislator and bit him. Several supporters claimed or have been given credit for blocking conviction by the state senate by persuading the requisite number of its members to sign a round robin stating they would not vote to remove Huey from office, but there is no doubt that if Earl did not suggest the strategy, he helped execute it.[3] "I really cinched that business," Earl said of the round robin. "Huey was pretty worried. But we got those signatures. In fact, we could have got more if we needed them."[4]

During the controversy, another anti-Long was confronted by Earl on the capitol steps. "I bet Earl bit him," Huey said, referring to Earl's fights.[5]

When they were boys, Huey ran from fights but Earl took up for him and fought his battles. Friends and family said that Earl actually enjoyed fighting, regardless of the cause. He loved the passion unleashed in the fights, where every weapon—including teeth—could be put to use. Earl brought the same passion he found in fighting to his politics. It defined his style.[6] Dupre Litton wrote that "Huey dodged fights. Earl never hesitated, jumping into one, and the rougher the better."[7]

The ticket called "Complete the Work of Huey P. Long" won a smashing victory. Earl was given a job by the Roosevelt administration, which was directing patronage to the anti-Longs after Huey broke with FDR, but he continued to nurse the wounds inflicted by his brother's treatment of him. When a Senate subcommittee held hearings in New Orleans to investigate fraud in the election of Huey's candidate, John Overton, to the US Senate in 1932, Earl showed up to testify to ballot box stuffing in elections and said a utility company lobbyist had given Huey $10,000 for the 1928 campaign. Huey, acting as Overton's counsel, denounced Earl as a liar, but Earl said that he had opposed construction of the new state capitol building because "there was going to be graft in the cement and architects and other things." The subcommittee concluded that there had been vote fraud on both sides but not enough to change the outcome.[8]

Earl knew that he had no political future without Huey, and Huey valued Earl's political skills, particularly in dealing with legislators. They reconciled in 1934, and Earl was an adviser to him during a series of special sessions of the legislature that consolidated Huey's control of the state and gave him dictatorial powers. In the jockeying for position by administration leaders after Huey was assassinated, Earl emerged as the candidate for lieutenant governor on a ticket headed by Judge Richard W. Leche of the Court of Appeal in New Orleans. Earl was not trusted by many of the leaders, but his name was valuable to the ticket, and it won in a landslide.[9]

Earl was never in the inner circle of the state administration. Leche resigned as the Louisiana Scandals of 1939–1940 unfolded, revealing widespread corruption by Huey's political heirs. Earl took the oath of office on June 26, 1939. The investigations and prosecutions that followed saw many political figures convicted and sent to prison. "It's a terrible thing when a man shows up crooked," Earl said, "but when Jesus Christ was on earth he picked twelve men, and one of them was a son-of-a-gun." Denying any involvement in the misdeeds, he said "they would have indicted me if I'd spit on the sidewalk," and he ran for a full term in 1940. The Long vote was split when James A. Noe, a state senator close to Huey who had served briefly as governor after O. K. Allen died in office, also ran for governor. James H. "Jimmy" Morrison, attorney for the strawberry farmers in Hammond, entered the race as an independent candidate. He denounced Long as corrupt and mounted a nighttime Convicts' Parade on Canal Street in New Orleans, viewed by over one hundred thousand people, that featured truck floats with Leche, Long, and other administration officials in prison stripes.[10]

Long was attacked by Noe, who had given Huey his first transfusion and on several occasions cried as he talked about their political and personal friendship. "He carries around an onion in his handkerchief to cry about Huey," Earl snapped. Morrison took an organ grinder's monkey with him, calling it Earl Long. When the monkey ran away, Morrison said that it went crazy from being called that. Long shot back that the monkey fled because Morrison was too cheap to pay it, "even though it was working for peanuts."[11]

The anti-Long standard-bearer, Sam Jones, a corporation lawyer from Lake Charles, charged that either Long was part of the Scandals, or if, as he claimed, he did not know what was going on, then he was too dumb to be governor. Jones, who was state commander of the American Legion, charged that Long was a World War I draft dodger. Long responded that he had an exemption to support an ill sister, and he said Jones never left the state to go overseas. "He spent his time at Camp Beauregard and his momma brought him cake every day," Long claimed. Jones, Earl charged, "never wears the same underwear twice, and whistles and lies at the same time." When the administration paper, the *Louisiana Progress*, ran a picture of Jones with a big diamond stickpin added in, and took it out in a subsequent one, Jones said "this gang even steals from photographs."[12]

"They're calling me Earl Kangaroo Slickum Crookum Long," Earl said. "That don't hurt me at all. I don't want to rob a man of his good name just to win an election. I don't want to be governor that much."[13] He then poured it on Jones.

In an appeal to a North Louisiana audience, Earl thundered that Jones was not "one of our rural kind. He's High Hat Sam, the High Society Kid, the High-Kicking High and Mighty Snide Sam, the guy that pumps perfume under his arms." He urged them to "vote for one of your own kind. Don't you vote for that high-hat, sweet-smelling little thing from Lake Charles. You vote for a good old country boy from over here in Winn Parish that thinks and smells like you on Saturday." He had, Long proclaimed, "been carrying on like Huey P. Long, Oscar Allen, Jesus Christ, and God Almighty would have me do."[14]

Earl garnered a substantial lead in the primary, but Jones won a narrow victory in the runoff after Noe endorsed him in return for Jones's promise to split the state patronage with him. Most observers wrote Earl Long's political obituary, failing to recognize that he had received 40 percent of the first primary vote and 48.2 percent in the runoff, losing by only nineteen thousand votes despite all of the bad baggage of the Scandals.[15]

Long announced for governor for the 1944 election, but when he failed to obtain support from Mayor Robert S. Maestri of New Orleans, one of Huey's intimates, and other leaders, he ran for lieutenant governor on a ticket headed by former US Representative Lewis Morgan of Covington. Public Service Commissioner James H. "Jimmie" Davis of Shreveport took a big lead over Morgan in the primary, while Long led for the second spot. Davis won in the runoff, and Long narrowly lost his race while running well ahead of Morgan. State law provided that if a runoff candidate for governor withdrew, the high man for each office would be declared the winner. Earl, correctly seeing that Morgan could not win, had tried to get him to pull out of the runoff, and they campaigned separately for a few days before getting back together. Had Morgan withdrawn, Long would have become lieutenant governor again.[16]

3.

EARL LONG'S FIRST FULL TERM AS GOVERNOR: 1948–1952

With the 1948 election nearing, people were bored by eight years of reform rule under Jones and Davis. Davis had let the Jones organization fall into disarray and had appointed some Long adherents to positions in his administration, along with members of his band. He was absent from the state for a number of months making movies, including one about himself. Jones sought to rekindle the reform zeal of the Scandals, but that was in the past for most voters. He attacked Earl for testifying against Huey in circulars, advertisements, and speeches, but Russell Long, Huey's son, took the stump for his uncle and made a statewide radio broadcast for him that was also distributed as a circular titled "Why I Am for Earl Long."[1]

Russell said the New Orleans newspapers were "desperate" to elect Jones: "On the one hand they scream that Earl Long and Huey Long had some differences back in 1932, and on the other hand, they attack and vilify the reputation of my late father, who is not here to defend himself. As for the differences which arose between Earl Long and my father, we know that these differences lasted less than a year before Huey and Earl patched them up, and Earl went back to helping my father. When Huey Long and Earl Long made up their differences that was the end of it as far as my family was concerned and that is how it has been since that time. It is too bad that brothers sometimes have a quarrel or a spat. When it happens, all they can do is shake hands and forget it. That is what Huey Long and Earl Long did sixteen years ago, and my family doesn't care to hear any more about these differences." Russell told rallies that "every family has differences from time-to-time. My father and my uncle did, but they got back together. The family is satisfied and you should be too."[2]

Earl declared early, foreclosing the candidacies of any other Longites. He said that "when I started out as a candidate for governor practically every politician in this state gave me the cold shoulder." He brought William J. "Bill" Dodd on the ticket for lieutenant governor, and they made hundreds of stump speeches throughout the state. He attacked Jones as a "do-nothing" and said Davis had been merely a "banjo-picking song-and-dance man." Long pledged a broad program of benefits, including an increase in the old-age pension, free hot school lunches, a higher homestead exemption, increased salaries for teachers, and many public improvements. Long had a big lead in the primary over Sam Jones, Judge Robert F. Kennon, US Representative James H. Morrison, and several other candidates and took 66 percent of the vote in the runoff, defeating Jones 432,528 to 223,971. "Happy days are here again," he exulted. "The Longs are back in the saddle. We'll improve on everything Huey did."[3]

In the runoff, he sent a postcard to voters with his picture on one side and an invitation to the inauguration on the other, indicating his contempt for Jones's chances. Celebrating his victory, he said, "When I go into office I'm going to have an inaugural party for anybody who wants to come. When they arrive we'll just add another plate to the table, and tell them to come on in. We'll give them all the soda pop and hog dogs and buttermilk they want, if I have to kill every hog I can raise." When it became clear how great the response was going to be, the ceremony was moved from the capitol steps to the LSU Stadium. Thousands came, consuming tens of thousands of hot dogs, cold drinks, and cups of buttermilk. Wearing a crisp white linen suit on the platform, he chuckled, "Looks like they all came."[4]

Reflecting on his loss in 1940, Long said, "I think maybe the Lord decided I could make a better Governor at 52 than 44." Asked if he liked being governor, he said, "Sure I want to be Governor. Only one person in more than two million can be Governor. Think about that. Ain't that an honor? And then every time you answer the door at the Mansion somebody's bringing you a turkey or a ham or a basket of something. I like that free stuff."[5]

In a study of state politics, Allan P. Sindler wrote that Jones lost because "the reform forces tried to re-create the good fight of 1940. Unfortunately for their purposes, the Scandals no longer fed the flames of an incensed morality, and the reforms so dear to the heart of Jones appeared to many voters to have less value than the welfare-state pledges of Earl Long. Good government, as defined by the actions of

Sam Jones and Jimmie Davis, had failed to win the allegiance of a majority of voters."[6]

In his first legislative session, Long pushed through $200 million of new and increased taxes, among them unpopular levies on cigarettes, beer, wine, liquor, and gasoline that affected the "little people." Reminded that he had promised not to increase taxes, he snarled, "Where the hell did people expect these benefits to be paid from?"[7] Slot machines were illegal, but that didn't stop Earl from convincing legislators to pass a tax on them. He had pledged to continue the civil service system enacted by Jones but instead pushed through a bill to repeal that reform. When reminded of his promise, he claimed that he did not sign the pledge; shown a copy of it, he claimed his signature was a forgery.[8] When the session adjourned he said, "I don't think I've ever seen a Legislature with less drunkedness and less rowdyism." Sindler wrote that "On state taxation and expenditure Earl Long rose well above the past, and on spoils politics he returned happily to the past, though scrupulously avoiding any repetition of the Scandals."[9]

Earl declared war on New Orleans, sponsoring legislation to reduce its sales tax to deprive it of revenue and redraw the Commission Council to have members elected from the assessment districts rather than council districts. With the assessors being members of the Old Regular faction that had dominated city politics until deLesseps S. "Chep" Morrison was elected mayor in 1946, Long anticipated that the Council members in the next election would be Old Regulars who would take over the city government. Morrison, who had been elected a state representative on the Jones ticket in 1940 and reelected in 1944 while in the army, fought back, and several measures that had to be voted on as amendments to the state constitution were defeated. Morrison won overwhelming reelection in 1950, defeating a Long-backed Old Regular candidate, and he called for a home rule charter for the city that would free it from many restrictions in state statutes.[10]

When Senator Overton died in 1948, Earl supported Russell in a special election for the remaining two years of the term. He had appointed Russell as his executive counsel and said in endorsing him that he would be a fine US senator. Russell, however, had played an instrumental role in Earl's legislative program, and Mayor Morrison and other anti-Longs got behind Judge Robert K. Kennon, who had run third in the governor's race. Russell defeated Kennon by only 11,000 votes in a rebuke to Uncle Earl and his tax increases. Long changed his ways and backed off his domination of the legislature, which a newspaper editorial had denounced as Earl's "trained seals." He had called on Morrison to resign but gave up that fight and supported home rule for the city after Kennon received a big majority there.[11]

Long suffered a severe heart attack in 1950 while hunting wild hogs at his farm, and he spent several months recuperating there. He supported Russell for a full term in the 1950 election, saying that Russell "has two years seniority and has a good record. He is a good boy. The fact is, I say, not because he is my nephew—I have several nephews—he is one of the most conscientious, tolerant, uncontrollable young men I have ever known in my life and is most respectful of the rights of other people." With his disarming candor, Uncle Earl said, "He will vote for what he thinks is right, regardless of what I say—I have already tried him—and what you say or what any pressure group says. He is an improvement on his uncle and his father, Huey P. Long. He is better educated and respects the other man's opinion more." Russell, for his part, said "the day of the demagogue is over. I have no apologies to make for being the son of Huey Long or the nephew of Earl Long. They have both helped the people of our state."[12]

Buoyed by Russell's overwhelming victory, Earl resumed bossing the legislature, which put a constitutional amendment for a $140 million bond issue for roads and bridges on the November 1950 ballot; however, it was defeated by a margin of fifty thousand votes. In 1951, he proposed a constitutional convention to update the lengthy 1921 document but was criticized when it appeared that his plan would provide for extensions of terms for current statewide elected officials and would not require popular ratification. To make matters worse, he intended to appoint a majority of the delegates. Opposition to his scheme was so great that he gave up on this maneuver.[13]

Allan Sindler wrote that

> Earl Long's administration from 1948 to 1952 taught the voters to appreciate good government in a manner more dramatic than could a dozen Jones-Davis administrations. The uglier manifestations of Longism reappeared, including a controlled Legislature, a war against New Orleans, and tendencies toward

> dictatorial power. Most shocking of all, taxes kept pace with expanding benefits, which undermined Longism's persuasive propaganda that its liberalism was somehow free of charge. But Earl Long was to discover, as Jones had before him, that factional victory was not a mandate to turn back the clock. The curious spectacle of Earl Long's candidate affirming his loyalty to civil service in 1952 thus must be understood in terms of the Long-induced popular comprehension of the importance of certain reform principles, notwithstanding popular repudiation of Jones in 1948.[14]

Sindler said that "Earl Long, though an adept rural politician, skilled in personalized politics, was no second Kingfish." Despite the similarities in their fights with the urban newspapers and the New Orleans municipal government, "Earl outstripped the Kingfish only in the magnitude of state taxation and expenditures. Huey's younger brother never scaled the dizzy heights of adulation and dictatorship that the Kingfish did."[15]

4.
THE 1951 ELECTION

Long fielded a ticket headed by Judge Carlos G. Spaht of Baton Rouge for governor and State Representative John J. McKeithen of Columbia for lieutenant governor in the 1951 Democratic primary. He later said, "I thought the way for Spaht to win was for me to run for lieutenant-governor on his ticket," but Spaht did not want that and many of his own leaders were opposed. Lieutenant Governor William J. Dodd, elected with Long in 1948, had expected to have his support, but Long declined to back him, claiming that Dodd had tried to "take over" while he recovered from his 1950 heart attack. US Representative Hale Boggs of New Orleans ran with the support of Russell Long and Mayor deLesseps S. "Chep" Morrison of New Orleans but was edged out by Judge Kennon, who went into the runoff with Spaht. It was generally understood that Earl could get Spaht in a runoff, but whoever was in it with him would win. Russell and Earl traded barbs on the stump. Earl said that his nephew and Boggs were "two squirts from Washington." Russell shot back that his uncle was "not nearly as bothered by his heart trouble as by Mansionitis—a strong desire never to leave the Governor's Mansion." Earl had approached Boggs about running for lieutenant governor with Spaht, but the congressman declined. The split between the Longs led the Kennon and Dodd backers to charge that Spaht and Boggs were a "double-entry" and that the governor would be happy with either of them.[1]

Despite claims by some later observers that Long did not want Spaht to win and had not given him full support, Earl campaigned with him, raised money, and attacked his opponents. Spaht later felt it hurt him when Long took charge of the campaign, but he acknowledged that with little name recognition, he had to run as Long's candidate in the first primary. In the runoff he tried to create some distance between Long and him on issues and said Long was unhappy with his independent streak coming out, but it was to no avail.[2]

Long enjoyed stumping even when he was not a candidate, and he put on a show on the hustings with Spaht. He loved to take after Kennon, who was perhaps the only politician of his era whom he genuinely feared. Kennon had a homespun way of talking and charm much like Long and, while he thought he would win a head-to-head fight, Long would just as soon not have it. Appearing with Spaht, Long said that Kennon's blood was "sixty-five percent champagne and thirty-five percent talcum powder." Kennon was a nice-looking man, but he had big ears. Long called him "jug ears" and said "if you drop a dollar bill on the ground in Ville Platte, Kennon can hear it fall in Opelousas." Kennon, he cracked, "has such an open mind, if he leaned over his brains would fall out."[3]

Lucille Mae Grace, Register of the State Land Office for many years, was the first woman to run for governor. She was backed by Leander Perez, the racist district attorney for Plaquemines and St. Bernard Parishes. Perez had her charge that Boggs was a Communist on the basis of his alleged role in a student organization at Tulane University whose members, prior to World War II, pledged not to fight in any war and which was cited by the House Un-American Activities Committee during the Red Scare of the 1950s as being a Communist organization. Grace sought to have the State Democratic Central Committee refuse to put Boggs on the ballot on the grounds that its rules prohibited Communists from qualifying as candidates. At a special meeting of the committee, Long engineered defeat of the Grace motion, but he let the attack hang out there. "Boggs is no communist," Long said on the stump. "He's a Catholic and we all know the Catholic Church is opposed to the communists. His brother is a Catholic priest. He goes to the cathedral down in New Orleans and kneels down and kisses the Archbishop's ring. No, Boggs is no communist, he's too Catholic for that." This left-handed defense of Boggs played well in Protestant North Louisiana and cost the congressman dearly. While a copy has not been found, there were reports that a flyer there carried a picture of Boggs genuflecting and kissing the pope's ring on a visit to Rome.[4]

Spaht led in the primary with 173,987 votes to 163,434 for Kennon, who edged Boggs out to make the runoff. As expected, Kennon overwhelmed Spaht by a vote of 376,232 to 242,518 in the second primary.[5]

Kennon ran a "civics book" administration with an independent legislature and reform program that enshrined civil service in the state constitution and required a two-thirds vote in each house to increase taxes or levy new ones. While he had substantial accomplishments, Kennon neglected his politics and many supporters were disappointed at his failure to reward them.

Mayor Chep Morrison appealed for Kennon's support in the 1956 primary, but Kennon backed Fred Preaus, his Highway Commission chairman. Kennon was unwilling to forgive Morrison for reneging on an agreement they had made in 1950 that Kennon would run in 1952 with Morrison's backing, and Morrison would run in 1956 with Kennon's support. Morrison could not keep the deal when Boggs entered the race in 1952. They had been law partners and Boggs's wife Lindy was the mayor's first cousin, and so he reluctantly supported Boggs.[6]

Russell Long, after joining with Morrison to support Boggs, wanted a new generation to take over, led by the three of them, all of whom saw active duty in World War II. He wanted an end to the Long versus anti-Long factionalism that had defined state politics, and he, Boggs, and Morrison envisioned a political climate in which they would take turns as governor and US senator. Russell considered running for governor in 1956. He wanted his uncle to retire from politics, but Earl would have none of that. When Russell, with Earl's heart condition in mind, said, "Uncle Earl, you can take it easy and be an elder statesman," Earl snapped, "I'd rather be dead."[7]

Politics was Earl Long's life, and he had no intention of sitting on the sideline. "This is a game of survival of the fittest," he had said in 1940. "I'm the fittest and I'll survive."[8] In a stump speech for Spaht in 1951, Earl declared that "I am going to stay in politics until I am taken from this earth."[9] Campaigning in 1959, after having taken a physical examination, Earl said his doctors had told him to slow down and rest more. He roared his response from the stump: "I won't quit until I die. I'll die fighting for our people whether you vote for Uncle Earl or not."[10]

5.
PEAK EARL: 1956

There had been speculation that Russell Long would run for governor in 1956, but Earl made it clear that he was running. In a letter to a supporter, Earl said that he had worked hard for the people in his prior term, and "my reward for this is the overwhelmingly favorable response that my announcement as a candidate for 1956 has received. When the date for filing has come and gone, I believe you will find one Long in the race—and that will be Earl K. Long for Governor."[1] In seeking another term, Earl said that "out of a sorry bunch of candidates, I stand head and shoulders above 'em."[2]

Long said that he hoped Morrison would run. "I'd rather beat Morrison than eat any blackberry or huckleberry pie my mama ever made," he said. "Oh, how I'm praying for that stump wormer to get in the race. I want him to roll up his fancy cuffs, get out his little tuppy, and make himself up." When he announced, he exuded confidence, declaring that no matter how many candidates ran, "there will be no second primary."[3]

Long said he made between five hundred and six hundred stump speeches in the primary campaign. There were only two or three television appearances because, he said, "television makes me look like a monkey climbing a stick." He ridiculed Morrison as "a high-flyer who wears four hundred dollar suits. Put one of those on Uncle Earl and it'll look like socks on a rooster, it won't go on." Morrison, he claimed, was "so high and mighty he has to get on a stump to spit." He did an imitation of Morrison putting on makeup, powdering his face, and covering the balding top of his head with a toupee. "Uncle Earl don't need no tuppy," he told rural crowds. "I'm happy with the hair God gave me." As for Kennon's man, Long attacked him in his home town: "Fred Preaus is a fine man, a fine man. He has a Ford Agency just down the street there. If I needed a car, I'd trade with him. But if I needed two cars, I couldn't do business with him. He couldn't handle the deal." Long said, "How can I compete with Della Soups on television? I ain't even got one of them make-up kits." He claimed that the mayor was listed as "one of the ten best-dressed men in America." In addressing segregation, he asked blacks in his audiences, "What is more important—to ride on the front seat of a bus or to have a full belly."[4]

Shug Huffman said that she got her first real taste of politics in the 1956 election. "At night we would go out in my Dad's truck to put up signs," she said. "I got to where I could jump out of the truck and nail up a sign as fast as anyone. It was also tradition back in those days that while you were putting up signs for Mister Earl, you took down any signs of his opponents. I also got to ride in the sound truck and play the records for Mister Earl on the days of his campaign speeches. He let me keep all the records after the campaign so I had a very large collection for that time. However there was one record that was never played during a Mister Earl campaign and that was 'You Are My Sunshine,' by Jimmie Davis. In fact, I was prohibited from ever playing that record when we would be at the Pea Patch or Mister Earl and Miss Blanche were visiting our house on the Tullos Highway."[5]

Morrison led a large field of Earl's opponents, but Long won an astounding first primary victory, with over 51 percent of the vote, beating Morrison 421,681 to 191,576. Earl carried sixty-two of the state's sixty-four parishes. "Huey never done that," Earl crowed.[6]

Resting from the rigors of the campaign, Earl said he had recovered from his 1950 heart attack but had been cautioned to lead a "normal life," free from stress and strain. That might be hard to do now, he said. "The next time I get sick, it'll probably be from talking too much with my big mouth."[7]

Governor Earl K. Long was joined on the inaugural platform in front of the capitol building by US Senator Russell B. Long and US Representative George S. Long in what *Time* magazine called "Louisiana's monumental living tableau to the memory of Huey." The governor's wife, Blanche, was the state's Democratic national committeewoman, and the party's national chairman, Paul Butler, joined them on the stand with Camille Gravel of Alexandria, the state's Democratic national committeeman and Earl's supporter. Several politically ambitious cousins were also there, including newly elected State Senator Speedy O. Long of Jena and Gillis W. Long. Speedy said that the Longs usually tried to get together at the capitol, "especially every four years."[8]

A few days after his inauguration, Earl disclaimed any interest in supporting a constitutional amendment to allow a governor to succeed himself. Even if it was adopted, he averred, it should apply only to his successors and not himself. He had no desire, he said, for a following term because "I just want to last this one out in good health."[9]

Reflecting on his election, Long said that "the pioneering that Huey did had a lot to do with my victory. We were more or less opposite types, however. I'm the slow, plodding type, and Huey was quick and ready at all times. He was kind of on the style of Alexander the Great. Alexander conquered the world before he was 21 and cried because he didn't have more worlds to conquer. Huey was like that. I've often wondered how Huey would have made out physically if he had lived to be an old man. He died when he was 42. I'll be 61 next August."[10]

Long was scheduled to deliver a thirty-minute address to a joint session of the legislature to open its 1956 meeting, but he spoke for two hours and sixteen minutes, discussing state needs; lamenting the influence lobbyists had on members; and criticizing his opponents, including Leander Perez. When Perez offered to meet him "man-to-man," Long bellowed "I ain't got no medals for running, you know." After Perez held meetings of the White Citizens' Council to oppose integration, rail against "the burr heads," and claim that Negroes were genetically an inferior race, Long ran into him in the Capitol lobby and sneered, "Whatcha gonna do now, Leander? The Feds have got the atomic bomb."[11]

Long removed a number of Kennon's appointees to state boards by having the legislature address, or move, them out of office by declaring the seats vacant.[12] He engaged in a feud with Secretary of State Wade O. Martin Jr. that culminated with the governor having the legislature strip Martin of his ex officio offices as custodian of voting machines and insurance commissioner and making those functions elective offices. At a committee hearing on the bills, they fought for control of the microphone, snatching it back and forth from each other. Long roamed the floors of both chambers, often sitting in a member's seat, and he followed the voting on a board in his office. Spying a red light for a "no" vote on a bill, he ran from his office to the house chamber and stood over a cowering representative until he changed his vote.[13] "I was governor this time from scratch," he thundered, "and whether you like the way I scratch or not, I've done my damnest."[14]

6.
THE EIGHTH CONGRESSIONAL DISTRICT FORESHADOWING: 1958

When Earl's brother, U.S. Congressman George Long, died in 1958, there were ten candidates for the open seat from Louisiana's Eighth Congressional District. The strongest appeared to be Alexandria attorney Harold McSween, with his base in the district already established. McSween had served on the Rapides Parish School Board and in 1956 defeated Earl's sister, Clara Long Knott of Many, when she sought reelection to the state Board of Education from the Eighth District. The other two major candidates were State Senator Speedy O. Long and Alexandria attorney and State Representative Lloyd Teekell, the governor's candidate.

Speedy was born in 1928 in Tullos, which straddles the border between Winn and LaSalle Parishes. Speedy got his nickname from his premature birth.[1] A distant cousin of Earl's, described as a third cousin, he graduated from Winnfield High School, served in the navy, and graduated from Northwestern State College at Natchitoches in 1951. He was elected to the state senate in 1956, graduated from the LSU School of Law in 1959, and opened a practice in the town of Jena in LaSalle Parish.[2]

McSween and Teekell went into the runoff. Speedy, finishing third, carried Winn and LaSalle Parishes in the primary. He had sought Earl's support but was told he was young and had time to wait. Disappointed, he declined to endorse either candidate in the runoff publicly, but many years later McSween said that Speedy worked behind the scenes for him and was very helpful. Ironically, McSween believed that "had Earl supported Speedy instead of Lloyd, a fine man but not named Long, Speedy might have defeated me in the first primary."[3]

McSween made capital of the governor's intervention and campaigned on the slogan "Vote for the Man, not the Machine" in the runoff. Long attacked him as "a smart brat" who lived in a luxury home with gold-plated bathroom fixtures. McSween, he charged, was "very resourceful, very energetic, the most successful double-talker, double-dealer, flim-flammer that's been on the public scene in years."[4] Long put his political reputation on the line, saying that a McSween victory would be a personal slap at him. At an Alexandria rally two days before the election, he claimed that only a catastrophe could prevent a Teekell victory. A news story said "the Governor staked much of his political prestige on the McSween-Teekell fight, stumping more vigorously than he ever did for himself. He also brought into the fracas all of his legislative backers from the Eighth District, a large number of them from outside the district, and a bevy of appointed officials from all parts of the state." Long, Teekell, and their surrogates blasted the Alexandria *Daily Town Talk* and other McSween supporters. Long attacked his former associate, Camille Gravel, with whom he had parted ways over Gravel's support of McSween. He also broke with other former allies who backed McSween, including Avoyelles Parish sheriff F. O. Didier and Winn Parish assessor John Bell.[5]

McSween defeated Teekell by 7,749 votes, carrying five of the eight parishes, including Winn, in an election with a voter turnout of 72 percent. An analysis of the results said "Teekell could lead only in Sabine, Vernon, and Natchitoches Parishes, but even in these Long strongholds, his plurality was far less than had been conceded to him. In Natchitoches, he topped McSween by only eighty-two votes. LaSalle, Avoyelles, and Grant, which along with Winn are usually strong for a Long-backed candidate, gave McSween large majorities. McSween's victory was sealed in Rapides Parish, which includes Alexandria, where he won 14,341 to 7,967."[6]

McSween later said that he probably would have lost not only if Earl had supported Speedy instead of Teekell, but if Earl had stayed out of the race as well. The governor took over Teekell's campaign, stumping with him, and made himself an issue, and many voters resented his role. McSween said he benefited from "Mr. Earl's unpopularity of the moment" after he tried to raise taxes and from the racial issue, where McSween was viewed as stronger on segregation than Long and Teekell. McSween said his victory was due in large part to "the mean and dynamic racial issue that played out in my favor, ironically, even though I did not own spurs as a racist, having refused to join the White Citizens' Council, to which I was invited when a school board member but rejected."[7] In an interview thirty years after the election, Mrs. Jewell Long, George's widow, said that "Mr. Teekell was supported by both Earl and myself, and he would have beaten Mr. McSween if it hadn't turned into a race between Earl and McSween."[8]

McSween said that he also had behind-the-scenes support from a number of influential politicians who had fallen out with Long for various reasons. They included Camille Gravel; Louisiana Auditor Bill Dodd; Superintendent of Education Shelby Jackson; Commissioner of Agriculture Dave Pearce; Harvey Peltier, who was Earl's running mate in 1940; and Public Service Commissioner John J. McKeithen, who ran for lieutenant governor with Spaht in 1952.[9] These were all men who had benefited from their association with Long, and their defection was surprising but welcomed by McSween.[10]

Gravel, with Long's support, had ousted Governor Kennon's Democratic national committeeman in a battle before the Democratic State Central Committee in 1954 and played an important role in Long's 1956 campaign, joining him on the inaugural platform. Long said that they fell out over Gravel's independence, but Blanche Long had a different story. She said that Earl put Gravel and Judge Edmund Reggie of Crowley out of his inner circle after the 1956 election. She said that "Judge Reggie and Camille Gravel took their seats out there in the reception room of the Governor's office, and nobody could see the Governor unless they went through Camille and Reggie. When Earl found out about that, he told Camille to move out of the governor's mansion, where he was staying for the legislative session, immediately, that when he got ready to be governor he'd have to run and get elected. He said 'Now get out! And on your way, take that little Arab friend of yours, Reggie, with you. And don't either of you ever come to my office again.' I heard Earl tell him that. So they fell out right then and he fought Earl from then on."[11]

Gravel also believed that Earl was upset at him for persuading the Louisiana delegation to the 1956 Democratic National Convention to support Senator John F. Kennedy for the vice presidential nomination after Adlai Stevenson threw the choice open to the convention rather than picking his own running mate. Long was for Senator Estes Kefauver, the eventual nominee, and Gravel and Reggie worked the delegation in Kennedy's behalf. Reggie said that they brought it up for a vote while Long was at the racetrack. Louisiana operated under the unit rule, so a majority for Kennedy gave all of the votes to him. Reggie had been appointed to a vacancy as Crowley City judge by Long in 1950, when he was only twenty-two. He served until 1976 and played an important behind-the-scenes role in several administrations.[12]

Regardless of what happened in 1956, Long became aware that Gravel was supporting McSween against Teekell and sought revenge. He called a special meeting of the Democratic State Central Committee to oust Gravel as national committeeman. The governor had ready allies in segregationists dissatisfied with Gravel's support of the civil rights platform plank at the 1956 convention. They had already tried to replace him but were not successful when Long backed him. This time, working with them, Long and his supporters voted Gravel out by a two-to-one margin. The Democratic National Committee, however, claimed that only it could change national committeemen once they were seated, and Gravel's status remained in dispute.[13]

In mid-1959, when Long was asked about Speedy and the Eighth District race, he chuckled, "Speedy's O. K. He's an independent little booger, but he's all right. I didn't oppose Speedy for Congress. I supported Teekell because I figured he was the best shot. The biggest mistake the district ever made was electing McSween, and you'll see it before the two years is up. He's already voted against REA [Rural Electrification Administration], and you know why? His daddy is head lawyer for the Central Louisiana Electric. McSween shouldn't have even voted. He had a personal interest in the thing."[14]

Long would later help the district rectify that error.

7.
RACE, RAGE, AND RAINACH

Louisiana State University in New Orleans was opened in 1958, without incident, as an integrated campus. Long had supported and signed legislation to establish the school as a commuter branch of the Baton Rouge campus. Its establishment had been opposed by the flagship institution and the LSU Alumni Association. New Orleans mayor Chep Morrison proposed that it be located in Gallier Hall, the old city hall, which would drastically limit its size. Long was determined to put a state university in New Orleans, and a committee he appointed sought a site from the Orleans Levee Board, which had reclaimed a large swath of the lakefront and had a 178-acre tract that had been leased to the federal government for a Naval Air Station that closed. Louis Roussel, the board's chairman, wanted to subdivide the parcel into four hundred home sites. Long sent Theo Cangelosi, whom he had appointed to the LSU Board, to tell him that he wanted that site made available. When Roussel responded that if the governor wanted it, he would have to get a "new Levee Board," Long did just that. Members served at the pleasure of the governor, so he replaced Roussel and three other members appointed by Governor Kennon. Roussel told the press that Long had "fired" him, but Long rejoined, "I didn't fire them. I simply notified them they would be replaced. Their terms have been up since I took over as Governor. They were holdovers."[1]

Claude W. Duke, a friend and supporter, was named chairman of the Levee Board and acted quickly to lease the property to the university for ninety-nine years at one dollar per year. Eight months later the school, making good use of a number of military structures there, opened with 1,500 freshmen. At the opening convocation, Long criticized opponents of the school, including the *Times-Picayune*, that said he had made a "fancy gift" of property for the university because the revenue from sales of four hundred lots was lost. "I did my duty," he shouted. "I never backed up one iota to make this college a success."[2]

In 1983, on the twenty-fifth anniversary of the founding of what had become the University of New Orleans, Andrew Flores, a member of its first class, said, "without UNO, without Earl Long, I wouldn't have been able to afford an education. Uncle Earl, wherever you are, God bless you!"[3]

Long did not hesitate to veto special appropriations and other legislative acts that he thought unwarranted. He vetoed 326 bills from 1956 to 1960, a record that still stands. By contrast, Governor Edwin W. Edwards, in four terms, vetoed 295 bills.[4]

He also warned that mineral lease payments should be managed carefully, with a portion going to a rainy day fund. In February 1959, he denounced a proposal by legislators to use an oil lease windfall for teacher salary raises, stating that it was foolhardy to use nonrecurring income to fund a recurring expense. Previous legislatures, he said, had "acted like a sailor in town on payday" in spending oil and gas money. "Just because we've got that lease money is no reason to go wild and throw it away," he warned. "Anything extra ought to be saved for a rainy day." His advice has not been followed over the past half-century, and the state still uses nonrecurring funds to pay recurring expenses, resulting in yearly budget controversies and crises and raids on other state funds. Long was intimately familiar with his state budget, and it is ironic that the so-called liberal Long was much more conservative in managing state fiscal matters than governors and legislatures are today.[5]

While he wanted to increase some taxes, particularly on wine, luxury cars, and the Fair Grounds Racetrack in New Orleans, the constitutional amendment requiring a two-thirds vote of each house to increase existing taxes or levy new ones was a problem. Long was stymied in the house by the 34 Club, a group of members who banded together to oppose any tax measure. With thirty-four members in the club, they only needed to pick up two more votes to block a two-thirds vote in the 105-seat body. Acknowledging frustration, he snorted that "during the campaign I said I still had snap in my garters. Now some of it has snapped out." But he would persevere, he grinned, because "I'm the last of the red-hot poppas in Louisiana politics, just like Sophie Tucker is the last of the red-hot mommas. When I'm gone, there won't be any more."[6]

Until his final term as governor, Long did not have to deal with race as a divisive social and political issue. In a number of other southern states, political demagogues had waved the tarbrush and waged campaigns based on white supremacy, appealing to poor whites who may have been at the bottom of the economic ladder but, to them at least, were still above blacks. Huey Long's Louisiana was spared the racism practiced by Theodore Bilbo in neighboring Mississippi and Gene Talmadge in Georgia. There, and across the South, as Allan Sindler noted in discussing the Dixiecrat movement in 1948, "The conservatives were able to stampede their class opponents into support of conservative objectives by arousing racial anxieties. Earl Long's Louisiana, welfare-prone and uncommitted into Negro-baiting, proved vulnerable to that hoary tactic when preservation of segregated schools became a dominant issue."[7]

Only a handful of blacks were registered to vote in Huey's day, when the so-called white primary prevailed, making the state Democratic Party a "white man's club" to which blacks could not belong. Democratic nomination was tantamount to election with the very small Republican Party ("they can meet in a phone booth," wags said) controlled by attorneys and others who were more interested in federal patronage when a Republican was in the White House than they were in building a party. The result was that virtually everyone registered as Democrats so they would have a vote in their local and state elections. When Earl lost the 1940 runoff to Jones by a slim margin, fewer than one thousand blacks were registered to vote in Louisiana.[8] In 1944, the US Supreme Court prohibited racial discrimination in state primary elections, and by 1948 there were 28,177 black voters. By 1956, that number had increased to 161,000. The greatest increase came during Long's 1948–1952 term as governor. Earl Long actively encouraged black voter registration during that period.[9]

In a study of the civil rights struggle in Louisiana, Adam Fairclough wrote that with white political leaders committed to maintenance of segregation, blacks had to decide who was moderate and who rabid and choose between the two evils. "Earl Long was plainly the lesser evil," Fairclough wrote. "As the civil rights issues became more prominent the most ardent white supremacists were increasingly found to be in the anti-Long camp." Long not only encouraged black voter registration, but "blacks were attracted to Long's program of expanded public services."

In his 1948–1952 administration, "he raised the state old age pension to $50 per month, paid hefty bonuses to returning war veterans, built hundreds of new schools, and not only increased but equalized teachers' salaries," ending the practice of paying black teachers less than white ones. "It was scarcely surprising that Long received the lion's share of the black vote," Fairclough concluded.[10]

While the race issue had not been a factor in his previous administrations, it moved to center stage in Earl Long's final term as governor. His opponents recognized his vulnerability to charges of being "soft" on segregation and moved to exploit it.

Earl's appeal had always been to poor people regardless of race. His programs of benefits carried blacks along with whites, with little or no dissent. But now, with the 1954 *Brown vs. Board of Education* decision, the Supreme Court of the United States found the doctrine of separate but equal to be inherently unequal, and it declared school segregation unconstitutional. White southerners were faced with the fact that black children would now be allowed to attend public schools with their children. The regime of racial segregation as the core of the southern social and political order was now threatened.

Poor and rural whites became targets of appeals to their presumed racial superiority, and Long—with his longtime support of black voting rights—was attacked for failing to defend the southern way of life. It quickly became an emotional issue that was wrapped in social status. As one rural white put it, "I may not have much and be much, but at least I am better than a nigger."[11]

Robert Kennon was serving as governor when the *Brown* decision was handed down by the Supreme Court. The governor and the legislature jointly denounced the decision as "intolerable, impractical, and in the ultimate sense, unenforceable." The Joint Legislative Committee to Maintain Segregation was created. State Senator William "Willie" Rainach of Claiborne Parish, which is northeast of Shreveport near the Arkansas state line, was named chairman. Rainach was assisted by Claiborne Parish representative John Garrett, who had succeeded Rainach in the state house when he won election to the state senate.[12]

They were joined by Leander Perez, the racist district attorney of Plaquemines and St. Bernard Parishes. Perez had supported Long in 1948 but broke with him later in the year when Long failed to support the Dixiecrats against Harry Truman. Rainach and Perez coordinated the formation and activities of the Citizens' Councils to lead the fight against the National Association for the Advancement of Colored People (NAACP) and its push for school integration. Rainach cynically acknowledged that the opposition to integration would be "merely a delaying tactic," with the federal courts eventually striking down all legislation to preserve segregation. Rainach said that voter registration would be the key to maintaining white political power, and the way to accomplish that was to cleanse the registration rolls of black voters.[13]

"The entire battle is one of political power," Rainach told his confederates. "Political power is made up of votes. Therefore the key to victory lies in the polls."[14]

Rainach, Garrett, Perez, and their cohorts hatched "an elaborate plot to smash the NAACP, decimate the black electorate, and destroy the Long machine." They coordinated their plans with Governor Kennon and Attorney General Fred LeBlanc in a series of secret meetings. Their strategy was to prosecute the NAACP under a law enacted by the Fuqua administration in 1924 that enlightened Louisiana leaders designed to smash the Ku Klux Klan. It required organizations to file lists of their members with the secretary of state. The segregationist leaders knew that the NAACP would fear that members would be harassed or submitted to punitive actions such as job loss if their names were made public.[15]

Attorney General LeBlanc filed suit against the NAACP and a state district court judge enjoined it from operating in Louisiana until the membership lists were filed. With LeBlanc defeated for reelection in 1956, Attorney General Jack P. F. Gremillion, who was elected on the Long ticket, continued the prosecution of the NAACP. The organization complied with the injunction but lost many members and closed all of its branches in the state except for those in New Orleans, Lake Charles, and Shreveport.[16]

Rainach formed the Association of Citizens' Councils of Louisiana in January 1956 and turned his attention to suffrage. "Earl Long emphasized bread-and-butter issues, downplayed race, encouraged black voter registration, and forged political alliances with black political leaders," Fairclough wrote, but his opponents were going to move race to the forefront now. With the South embracing massive resistance to integration, using all means available to forestall mixing, Long tried to be careful by insinuating himself "in the political center, criticizing both the NAACP and the Citizens' Councils as extremists. But the nearly universal unpopularity of school integration among southern whites—who were far more numerous than black voters—posed an enormous problem for racial moderates."[17]

Preferring to choose his battles and knowing that federal courts would strike down the measures that Rainach and Garrett were pushing through the legislature, Long signed a series of bills designed to preserve segregation passed in the 1956 session. They "mandated segregated waiting rooms, toilets, eating facilities, and water fountains in train and bus stations" and banned interracial participation in "any dancing, social functions, entertainment, athletic training, games, sports, and other such activities involving personal and social contacts."[18]

With Long having to support segregation, Rainach took on voter registration in a strategy intended to "halt, and then reverse, the growth of the black electorate." Perez, Rainach, and Garrett not only wanted to limit the franchise but sought to purge the rolls of blacks, expecting that the fewer the number of black voters, the less attention white politicians would pay to them. With blacks comprising a third of the state's population, but only one-third of that number registered to vote, Louisiana white supremacists were determined to stop the black vote from growing larger. Rainach's target was the 160,000 black voters and his goal was to remove as many of them from the rolls as he could.[19]

The method Rainach adopted was to challenge the registration of blacks whose registration cards contained any errors or misspellings and have them removed from the rolls. Then they would be subjected to difficult tests to reregister.

In April 1956, the Citizens' Councils began conducting voter purges in the northeast Louisiana city of Monroe in Ouachita Parish. There were approximately 4,000 black voters on the rolls in Ouachita Parish when the campaign began. When the Citizens' Council was done, only 921 black voters remained registered to vote there. The challenges were led by anti-Longs who succeeded in ousting the moderate mayor, John E. Coon, a Long supporter who enjoyed black support. Coon was defeated and replaced by W. L. "Jack" Howard, an anti-Long. When wealthy former governor James A. Noe, Monroe's leading citizen, found out that his cook, maid, and gardener had been scratched from the rolls, he confronted the counsel for Rainach's committee, William Shaw, at the Ouachita Parish courthouse. Noe warned Shaw that if the Citizens' Councils were successful in removing blacks from the rolls, "They will, as well, disenfranchise our Italians, our Jews, our Catholics, or even our Protestants."[20]

Rainach, in promoting the purges of black voters, drew a line in the sand for Long for a battle that lasted for three years and culminated in the 1959 session of the legislature. Long sought to derail the purges by liberalizing the registration requirements to keep blacks on the rolls, while Rainach sought to make it more difficult for them.[21]

"It's far-fetched to ask a man to interpret the Constitution," Long said of a requirement parish registrars of voters were now being pressured to follow as a test for applicants to register. "Why, if you turn around and ask a man who asked you the same question, chances are he couldn't answer it." The 1921 constitution had instituted the requirement that a registrant be able to read and interpret a section of the state or federal constitution to the satisfaction of the local registrar. In practice this requirement had not been enforced, and Rainach claimed that one hundred thousand blacks were illegally registered to vote. Long announced that he would introduce bills in the next session that would abolish the requirement that an applicant be able to read and interpret the state and federal constitutions and that would allow elderly voters to receive assistance in casting their ballots, which was designed to help illiterates.[22]

Rainach responded with his own proposals to further restrict the franchise. Neither man got his way, with a wary legislature declining to take them up. The voter purges, however, gained momentum. "The elimination of black voters represented a direct attack upon supporters of Earl Long and, by extension, upon Earl himself," Fairclough said. "That Rainach was taking aim at Earl Long became unmistakably clear when, on September 4, 1958, he and William Shaw turned up at Winnfield, in Winn Parish, Earl Long's home town," to help members of the local Citizens' Council challenge black voters.[23] They even tried to remove Long's cook at the Pea Patch Farm.[24]

Purges were undertaken in ten North Louisiana parishes. In Bienville Parish, 552 of the 587 black voters were disqualified, while in Red River Parish, only a dozen blacks were left after the registrar accepted 1,500 challenges. Black registration was reduced from 1,773 to 79 in Webster Parish.[25]

While Long had encouraged black registration, and it had grown enormously in his prior term, his influence on the black voter purge issue was limited. As the governor, he appointed only one registrar of voters, in Orleans Parish. In the other sixty-three parishes, registrars were appointed by their local governing body, which were called police juries. The State Board of Registration, composed of the governor, the lieutenant governor, and speaker of the house, could remove parish registrars. When police juries dismissed registrars who were not cooperating with the purges and replaced them with registrars who did, Long had the board reappoint them. The courthouse gangs composed of the sheriff, district attorney, assessor, and clerk of court generally set the policy on registration, with some actively supporting the purges and others blocking them. In Tangipahoa Parish, District Attorney Joe Arthur Sims, a friend and political ally who was Long's unsuccessful candidate for attorney general against Fred LeBlanc in 1952, ended a longtime ban on black voters there and encouraged registration.[26]

At the end of 1958, the purges moved to South Louisiana. Rainach's method was to hold meetings with local officials and registrars to explain how to disenfranchise blacks for errors and omissions on their forms and to apply constitutional interpretation tests of twenty-four questions drawn up by Leander Perez to reregister. One question required an applicant to explain the procedure needed to remove a president from office.[27]

Some registrars in South Louisiana opposed the purges and were replaced. The East Feliciana Parish registrar, who refused to enforce the interpretation test, was dismissed by the police jury there. His replacement, working with the Citizens' Council challengers, slashed black registration from 1,276 to 50. In Washington Parish, 1,377 black voters were removed from the rolls. Others fought back. In St. Landry Parish, Sheriff D. J. "Cat" Doucet told Rainach that as fast as his voters were scratched, he would put them back on.[28]

Long became convinced that he was the only person who could guide the state through the segregation and voter rights fights. "It's easy to say nigger and scare everybody in the state," he said, "but, I think you should have a kind feeling toward the Negro." Earl said he could not oppose segregation but he believed that in opposing the Citizens' Councils on voting rights he would have the backing of the many whites who would not favor disenfranchising thousands of blacks through voter purges. "A lot of people are following you not because they agree with you, but because they are scared not to," Long told Rainach at a 1958 legislative committee hearing.[29]

Rainach and Long clashed repeatedly during the 1958 legislative session. "Every time you say nigger, you scare everybody in the state to death," Long growled at Rainach in one confrontation. "I'm 1,000 percent for segregation, but I don't think you should run for office on it," Long said on another occasion. "I'm willing to state my position anytime, anywhere. I don't believe in sleeping with them, or going to school with them, and I don't believe it helps a colored person any to sit in the front of the bus."[30]

"I love the nigger," Rainach told the Legislature, "but I know he can't run this country. The breeding in him does not allow him to run a civilization, and I won't allow our civilization to go to ruin."[31] Claiming that he was not a racist, Rainach said, "I do not feel that the two societies should mix. I wish it were possible for whites and blacks to live together but it just isn't."[32] Leander Perez put it more blatantly when he incited a rally during the New Orleans school desegregation crisis: "Don't wait for your daughter to be raped by these Congolese. Don't wait until the burr-heads are forced into your schools. Do something about it now."[33]

Estimates vary, but one professor concluded that between 1956 and 1958, thirty-one thousand blacks were stricken from the rolls in Louisiana, more than half of those in northern parishes. "Racism was brought back into Louisiana politics, weakening the foundation of the Long faction," Dr. Perry Howard wrote.[34] During the purges, twenty-one parishes began requiring the interpretation test and a new citizenship test mandating that an applicant be "of good character." In 1960, after Long was out of office, the US Supreme Court ruled both of those tests unconstitutional.[35]

Long drew up bills for the 1959 legislative session with the intent of halting the purges. One would prohibit challenges for minor errors on the forms. The other would prohibit removing any voter who had been registered for one year or more.[36] Long expected to have broad support, but for once he misjudged the mood of the legislature. He failed to recognize that with the state election looming that December, none of the legislators, including his own leaders, could afford to be seen as soft on segregation, and support for black voting rights had become equated with support for integration.

Removal of blacks, who had voted for him in record numbers, threatened Long's political base, and he was caught between defending their right to vote and alienating rural whites opposed to integration and civil rights. In the end, Long opted to fight a battle to preserve the voting rights of blacks. In doing so, he was not necessarily the liberal statesman that an admiring northern writer, A. J. Liebling, characterized him as in *The Earl of Louisiana*. He feared that if blacks were scratched from the rolls, rural whites would be next.

Historian T. Harry Williams wrote that

> Negroes, supported by the federal government, were demanding suffrage and an array of other rights, and white opposition to these demands in Louisiana and most Southern states was almost universal. The race issue could no longer be subordinated. Earl still attempted to keep it within bounds. But he was caught in a vise. His strongest supporters, the rural whites, were bitterly opposed to greater rights for blacks and might not be held in line by Earl's promises of additional social benefits or his verbal tributes to segregation. But he also had strong Negro support. Largely as a result of his influence, the registrars in many Louisiana parishes had enfranchised numbers of Negroes, and the black vote now constituted approximately 15 percent of the electorate. Earl commanded most of this vote, but it is not clear that he had brought it into being solely for reasons of personal profit. He seemed to feel that qualified blacks deserved the right of suffrage, and he possibly thought that the grant of the vote might blunt Negro militancy on other issues. Whatever the case, he did not want to see the Negro vote eroded.[37]

Long, Williams said, "always contended he did more to preserve the basic fabric of segregation than all the segregationists—and that the way to do it was by turning the attention of both races to normal political issues."[38]

With the gathering storm of the race issue, inflamed by the White Citizens' Councils, Long believed that he was the only reasonable political leader who could guide the state through the controversy. Instead, Long lurched toward political downfall. He recanted on an earlier pledge not to seek consecutive terms as governor. Instead of a constitutional amendment, Earl floated a ploy whereby he would seek another term by resigning just before the primary and letting Lieutenant Governor Frazar succeed him. In this scheme, he would then be a candidate to become Frazar's immediate successor rather than his own.

At the dedication of a bridge in Grand Ecore in Natchitoches Parish on April 30, 1959, before a crowd of over five hundred, with dozens of local and parish officials present, Long was in full campaign mode. "You know I'm running, don't you?," he shouted. "Sounds like it, don't I? Only the Good Lord or the law could stop me." Described as affable and "in high good humor, his gravelly voice occasionally ranging into the well-known squealing falsetto, the master campaigner dusted off his political opponents, boosted his local friends," and covered many topics. Among others in the audience he recognized was former State Senator Lester Hughes, who had signed the round robin to block Huey's conviction on impeachment. "If it hadn't been for Lester Hughes there probably wouldn't have been any Longs," he chuckled. "He was a charter member of the Robineers."[39]

Acknowledging his interest in removing voting machines from precincts with fewer than one hundred registrants, he yelled, "They say I don't want voting machines. The only time I ever won an election in the first primary in my life was when we had voting machines" in 1956. But asked if voting machines would stymie him, Long chortled, "If you have five commissioners all working together they can play 'Home Sweet Home' on a voting machine."[40]

Long said he was "not making any promises this time that taxes won't be raised if necessary, but they should be distributed so everybody pays a part, and not come out of the back and sweat of the poor man and woman like sales tax does. I tried to tax wine fifty cents a gallon—it's twenty cents now and some of it will make you drunk quicker than whiskey. We have a three dollar car license, the same amount for a little old pickup and a Cadillac. We get our share of the race track tax in New Orleans like a calf sucking on a hind tit."[41]

He ridiculed opponents. Attacking Wade O. Martin Jr., Long said with his usual candor that "there are more deadheads in the Secretary of State's office than I got in the Governor's office."[42]

Calling for understanding on the racial issue, he said most Negroes did not want to socialize with whites but wanted to be treated right.

"We've been inadequate, we haven't provided as the Lord wants us to," he stated, but "they don't want to associate with us any more than I want to be a member of the Boston Club. Once I talked to a man by there and they fumigated the place when I left."[43]

"I'm a gifted promiser and a fair performer," he said. As for civil service, he believed in it but didn't think it ought to "freeze in nincompoops and deadheads." Laughing, as if the idea had just come to him, he said, "Maybe we ought to put Old Earl under Civil Service, and I'll just keep on being Governor."[44]

As the May 1959 session of the legislature neared, Long was not sleeping well, smoking again after stopping following his 1950 heart attack and drinking more than the occasional highball he had previously enjoyed. His wife Blanche was pressuring him to retire when his term ended and be an elder statesman. She was building a luxury home for them on millionaire's row, as it was called, on Capitol Lake, and he was worried about that as well. While they kept an apartment in Baton Rouge, he had always campaigned out of his Pea Patch farm in Winnfield. Friends described the small house there as "a shack," and he thought that a luxury home would make supporters think he had gone "high hat" on them. To make matters worse, the Internal Revenue Service was investigating his taxes for the prior three years.[45]

Blanche was worried about how he was driving himself and saw changes in his behavior, as did his office staff. Dupre Litton, his executive counsel, later wrote in *The Wizard of Winnfield* that Earl was taking uppers and downers and that he found him in his office with a bucket of ice water, making compresses to put on his head. Litton was concerned when Long told him to draw up bills to liberalize the registration laws, which would provoke a fight with the rabid segregationists, but Long said that he was determined to fight the voter purges.[46]

Earl had always joked about his "big mouth" and temper and chuckled that he might be locked up one day because of it. In 1940, denouncing opponents for out-promising him, he shouted that "if you believe Sam Jones and Jimmy Noe can do what they say about old age pensions, there's a screw loose in your head, looser than in mine. I'm going to have a checkup made when this campaign is over, and maybe they'll find I'm crazy." One radio speech was cut off when he lapsed into profanity. In a New Orleans speech opening his runoff campaign against Jones, he denounced "big shot, blackguarding, smart aleck, High Hat Sam" and said "I told some of my good preacher friends, my good priest friends, and some of the fine Christian ladies supporting me that I wouldn't say 'hell' and 'damn' and such words in my speeches. But you don't know how it incapacitates a man to leave those words out when you have to discuss such a slanderous, blackguarding outfit as the Jones gang." He told his ticket candidates not to say damn or hell north of Alexandria and to be careful of vulgarity elsewhere, but he often broke that rule himself, noting that "I had an uncle who joined the church and he lost half of his vocabulary."[47]

Throughout his career, Long was noted for his fiery campaign oratory and harangues before the legislature and its committees. Appearing before the legislature in 1956, he complained that one of his bills failed because lobbyists had employed blondes and brunettes in the dark hours of the night to sway votes. Asked to explain his intemperate remarks, he acknowledged that he got carried away sometimes, but "I'm told that holding these things in doesn't contribute to longevity. I'm told it's best to just belch 'em up." He then added, "This is the best Legislature that money can buy."[48]

As he hurtled toward the expected confrontation with the arch segregationists in the legislature, Earl began to lose control. "Always a garrulous politician with a quick sense of humor," Thomas Martin wrote, "Earl now began to tirade at the drop of an imagined slight. Close political friends, who had been accustomed to the rasping, gravel-coated voice that took on an adenoidal twang when Earl became excited, began to detect a new quality when the Governor spoke. Before, the voice had been full of humor, the words usually punctuated with a low, rasping chuckle. Now the voice roared out harshly, the words cut indiscriminately. The closer the friend, the sharper the epithet. Few escaped the gubernatorial wrath as a sensitive Earl fancied himself hemmed in by political plotters and conniving traitors. In this group he included, especially, members of his own family."[49]

8.
UNCLE EARL'S VERY PUBLIC FALL

In a May 13, 1959, address to a joint session of the legislature when it convened, Long said that his floor leaders would introduce bills to liberalize the registration laws. "I am one million per cent for segregation," he said, "and will do everything to maintain it in the future. We have done it from 1956 to 1959. There are 160,000 colored people who will vote on election day in December and, frankly, I don't intend to belittle or chastise the colored people. Their votes count just as much as mine or any white person's vote." From the standpoint of Rainach and his allies, that was the problem—those colored votes counted just as much as theirs. "We cannot do with Earl Long in office," Rainach, wearing a Confederate flag tie, snarled. "His days are over in the State of Louisiana. We will see to that."[1]

The session, in an odd-numbered year, was a fiscal one that could deal only with money matters. Long sought to halt the voter purges by introducing bills to grandfather in voters who had been on the registration rolls for one year and to prohibit removal for minor mistakes in applications. He had two bills introduced in the senate, where under the rules, the Judiciary Committee would have to report them to the floor as fiscal. Without that label they would require a three-fourths vote for introduction. Long appeared before the committee on May 19 to support his bills. In the back-and-forth that followed, Rainach taunted him for "turning his back on the white people of Louisiana" by favoring voting rights for Negroes. Glaring at him, Long said, "After this is all over, you can go home with your mind at peace, and go out on your porch, take off your shoes, put your feet up on the rail, look at the moon, and talk to your God. And when you do," and now his voice became a shout, "you'll know that Niggers are human, too! There's no longer any slavery!" he roared. "But this is not a Nigger bill. I'm as much for segregation as you are. But some of our finest, oldest citizens now stand disqualified.

There are poor old men and poor old women who have been told they are too ignorant to vote."[2]

With a majority of the committee standing behind Long, the bills were labeled "fiscal" and sent to the floor, but the senate rejected the committee report 19-13, and under its rules the bills were dead in that chamber. Long was in New Orleans to address the Young Men's Business Club when the vote was taken, and hearing of it, he was visibly upset. In recent speeches to the Police Jury Association and the Louisiana Council, AFL-CIO, according to a news story, "the Governor had spoken so violently and vehemently against political opponents as to excite considerable comment among spectators and TV listeners and viewers." Now, turned down by the senate for the first time since his term began, a news story said, "He returned to Baton Rouge in a rage, and administration leaders, summoned to his office, quailed before the violence of his temper."[3]

Long sought to bring his bills to the house, which was considering an inconsequential measure to authorize appointment of deputy registrars of voters in all parishes, regardless of population. The bill had been reported favorably by the Judiciary B Committee in the house and was awaiting final passage. Long's strategy was to send it back to the committee and to attach the bills killed by the senate to it as amendments. He anticipated it would then go to the house floor with committee approval.[4]

Rainach and his allies learned of Long's plan, and when the house reconvened on the evening of May 24, the innocuous registration bill that he wanted sent back to committee for amendments was laid on the table by a 46-45 vote. Under house rules it was dead for the session. Long's leaders called for a recess, and several members who had voted to lay the bill on the table were called to the governor's office for one of his "prayer meetings." The committee reconvened, called up the bill again on reconsideration, and a majority then returned it to the Judiciary B Committee for further hearing. Historian Williams wrote that Long's legislation "would have been difficult to pass if he had been at his political best. Unfortunately he was at his worst," and the stage was sent for a confrontation between Long and the segregationist leaders. They recognized that Long was under tremendous strain and were aware of his outbursts at the speaking engagements. They deliberately sought to goad him into an explosion.[5]

When Long appeared before the Judiciary B Committee meeting in the house chamber to speak for the bills on May 26, he lost control. He was interrupted and baited by opponents of his proposals. The counsel for the Joint Legislative Committee on Segregation said that he now knew what was wrong with Long—the governor had "constipation of the brain and diarrhea of the mouth." Long berated legislators for over an hour, exchanging insults with several. He said that he was going to live on millionaire's row in the house Blanche was building. "You wouldn't look at me and think that," he chuckled. He announced the Internal Revenue Service was investigating him but said he would "beat the rap." One legislator, he said, was "in league with the wineheads," and a parish official was "a Dillinger in disguise."[6]

"My brother Huey once told me you couldn't believe what a man would do to be governor," he told the shocked legislators. "He would do almost anything short of murder. I have the experience to be Governor. I know how to play craps. I know how to play poker. I know how to get in and out of the Baptist Church, and ride horses. I know the oil and gas business. I know both sides of the street."[7]

Liberally sprinkling his tirade with "damns" and "hells," he spoke for over an hour. When someone pointed out that a group of Catholic schoolchildren in the balcony with their teaching nuns were being treated to this spectacle instead of a civics lesson, he roared, "I sent for my Bible and I'm going to swear off cussing. Let's all the children, the good nuns, and me all swear off profanity as long as it's possible."[8]

The committee called a vote and rejected the amendments. His floor leaders finally persuaded him to leave the podium. "Yes, I've talked long enough," he said. "God bless you. The only way Ole Earl can get people on his side is by talking. If anything happens to close my big mouth, God help Ole Earl."[9]

He met with his leaders afterward, and not a single one was willing to offer the amendments from the floor. Lieutenant Governor Frazar and others urged him to apologize for his conduct before the committee, and he advised his house and senate leaders that he wished to address a joint session. He was invited to speak the next day. A brief apology was prepared for him by his office, but after the first paragraph he dropped it on the floor and let loose again. For an hour and thirty minutes, worn and haggard, sweating profusely, wiping his brow, swigging vodka and grape juice from a Coke bottle, he carried on, lambasting enemies, denouncing the failure to approve his bills, and assailing the White Citizens' Councils for their pressure on legislators.[10]

"They called all night long," he shouted. "They harassed people in every part of the state. Send those sapsuckers a telegram! Wire him! Call him! Tell him the woods are on fire! Oh, it's awful! The Niggers are fixing to take over! You never heard such claptrap in all of your life." He denounced whites who kicked Negroes in the daytime and slept with them at night, saying that an old uncle of his had gone into the colored quarters and climbed into bed with a woman. Her husband found them there "and shot my old uncle and he died." He shouted, "That's all they want. They want their womenfolk to be left alone."

Led from the chamber, he went to the mansion. There he announced he would leave on a stumping tour over the weekend to carry his case to the people.[11]

T. Harry Williams, discussing Long's breakdown, wrote that "for a time Earl Long was not a normal or pragmatic politician. He threw caution and compromise aside and fought for his bill with everything he had. He lost in the end and went into seeming eclipse. But he said some brave things that needed to be said and in so doing he opened a new vista in Louisiana and Southern politics—he showed that the segregation issue could be and should be frankly discussed."[12]

Blanche Long wrote a behind-the-scenes account several weeks later that appeared as "His Wife's Story of the Commitment" in *Life* magazine's extensive coverage titled "A Portrait of Earl Long at Peak of Crack Up." She said that she "knew this was coming eight months ago, it was just as plain as day. Suddenly Earl started talking about a fourth term as governor and it got so that was all he would talk about. He stopped eating and even though he had given up smoking years ago because of a thrombosis condition, he started to smoke cigarettes again. He started to drive himself unmercifully. After a long hard day at the capitol, he would come home and go to bed. But he couldn't sleep. After an hour or two of tossing and turning he would get up and walk around the bedroom or perhaps sit up in a chair with a light on. I was so sick with worry over him that I called the family together and warned them that we would have to do something or Earl would drive himself to the grave."[13]

Blanche said that "little things started to worry him. Last August we started to build a new house, the first one we had built on our own. He was all for it at first, but then he started to worry that the people would resent his living in such a grand manner. He said that the people liked him because he was one of them, and that he had always campaigned out of that little shack of his in Winnfield. He was called on for several conferences with the internal revenue people and that worried him too. Every little thing began to build up on his mind until it was obvious that he was getting sicker every day. He even admitted to me that he was a sick man and needed to go away to a hospital for a long rest, but he always had something more important to do. It got so that I would have to cry myself to sleep at night."[14]

"About six weeks ago I noticed that his condition was getting much worse," Blanche said. "He began to abuse his closest friends. He was irritable all the time and his temper kept getting shorter and shorter. His friends knew he was not a well man and they began to avoid him. Hundreds came to me and told me what I already knew: that he needed medical attention."[15]

She said that "it finally had come to the point where he wasn't walking anymore. He was just shuffling around where he used to walk proudly. He knew he had to get medical attention, but he insisted he had to stay for this last session of the legislature. I'd watch him go out in the morning and then sit around the mansion waiting for the telephone to ring. Any day I expected them to call me to tell me he had dropped dead in the street."[16]

Blanche said that when Earl spoke at the committee hearing she was sitting with some friends at the mansion, listening to the radio broadcast of it "when I heard him start in. I knew then that the end had come. My heart went out to him and I was so sick I wanted to cry. I wanted to go over there and get him, but I couldn't force myself to do it because I knew my heart would break if I saw him carrying on like that." She said that his rant before the joint session the next day "only confirmed what we knew. Then we found out that he had scheduled a speaking campaign through the state for that weekend. We all realized that he would never live through it if we let him go."[17]

How much *Life* paid Blanche for her piece is not known, but a report at the time said it was $5,000. Earl later said she should have split it with him.[18]

It was obvious that Long was suffering a breakdown. Blanche Long feared for his health and was worried the stumping tour would precipitate a heart attack and kill him. Russell Long, who had come home from Washington to help deal with the situation, was afraid that the speaking tour would cause further embarrassment, and he and Blanche felt that Earl's mental health and his physical well-being were affected. They brought in other family members and doctors and consulted with State Hospitals Department director Jesse H. Bankston, who had also held that position in Long's prior term and was a close associate. Bankston brought attendants from Southeast Louisiana Hospital in Mandeville to the mansion. Blanche said that when they told Earl they were not going to let him take to the stump, "he got very belligerent and said he was going anyway." He tried to break away from them and get to the elevator, but they blocked his way. He threw a big jar through a window and tried to fight his way past them again.[19]

They confined Long to his bedroom, where Bankston stayed with him. Dr. Arthur Long, a cousin, shot him up with sedatives, and the family determined that the only way he could receive rest and care would be at a facility out of state, where he could not exercise his powers as governor. Bankston recommended the Harris Clinic at John Sealy Hospital, a unit of the University of Texas Medical Branch at Galveston, and arrangements for his admission there were made by Dr. Robert Bernhard, an old friend. Long was strapped to a gurney, carried from the governor's mansion against his will, and put in a station wagon used for mansion errands by the attendants. "He resisted them all the way," Blanche said. "I didn't go with them to the airport because he was pretty violent to me and his two sisters."[20]

Long was flown on an Air National Guard plane to Galveston, where Dr. Titus Harris had been told he was coming as a willing and voluntary patient. Dr. Harris said he was deceived on that score after Long said he had been kidnapped. Blanche drove to Galveston and visited him in his room several hours after he was admitted. "He pleaded with me to take him home," she said, "but I knew I had to leave him there because I wanted him back in good health first." The hospital could not hold him for more than three days without a legal commitment, which would require that Blanche sign the papers. She said that "the decision to send him to Galveston was maddening enough, but now they were asking me to sign a restraining order to keep him there. It was terrible. I knew I had to sign it and it was the saddest thing that ever happened in our lives." After Blanche signed the commitment papers as next of kin, the Galveston County Probate Court ruled that "for the best interest and protection of Earl Long, a mentally ill person, because his mental illness is likely to cause immediate injury to himself or others, if not immediately restrained, it is ordered that the said Earl Long be, and hereby is, detained in protective custody."[21]

Journalists descended on Baton Rouge and Galveston to cover Long's collapse. Louisiana historian Williams believed that most of them, particularly those from "liberal Northern organs," failed to understand what had happened at the legislature. He said that while it might be expected that most of them would have been "sympathetic to Earl" because "he was fighting on the side of the angels," nearly all of them missed the issue at stake—preserving and expanding black voting rights. "Here, ran the accounts, was another comic Southern politician playing the usual part of the clown, acting as a Southern demagogue was supposed to act," Williams wrote. He said that Long's fight against the voter purges should have "qualified him for a place in the liberal heaven" and that "whatever Earl Long should have been criticized for, he was subjected to ridicule beyond his meed."[22]

Louisiana political reporters had a better understanding of the context of the events. A group of them that included Emile Comar of the New Orleans *States*, Iris Kelso of the New Orleans *Item*, Bill Lynch of the *Shreveport Times*, Margaret Dixon, managing editor of the Baton Rouge *Morning Advocate*, and Jim McLean, capitol correspondent for the Associated Press, gathered beneath Long's second-floor window at the Galveston hospital and called to him. He had his back to them, talking to an attendant, but hearing them call he shouted, "I'm no more crazy than you are. They led me in here in handcuffs. They wanted to kill the loan shark bill. They wanted to pass the sales tax. They wanted to kill my election bill."[23]

Bill Lynch later wrote that he would "never forget that Sunday night standing beneath the window, where Long was ensconced behind a heavy metal screen. There we were talking to the world's most famous person incarcerated in a psychiatric hospital shouting back and forth about loan sharking legislation." Reflecting on this many years afterward, he said, "For Earl Long, 1959 was a topsy-turvy world. He displayed a boundless energy, looking for the world like death warmed over, that left reporters and his personal entourage breathless. It was a period of high jinks, low drama, and God-awful politics."[24]

Mrs. Long received hundreds of messages of concern for Earl's health and well-being. On June 11, 1959, she responded to one from their old friends Mr. and Mrs. A. A. Fredericks of Natchitoches. Writing on governor's office stationary, she said, "It certainly is comforting to hear from good friends such as you, and I know that Earl will be glad to know that you are thinking of him and praying for his early recovery."[25]

On that same day, Willie Rainach wrote a friend that "I clashed head-on for the first time and we gave him the worst drubbing ever administered to the chief executive in the history of the state."[26]

Long was ordered held for a sanity hearing before the 122nd District Court in Galveston on June 16, 1959, but he obtained court-appointed attorneys and filed a habeas corpus petition for authorities to produce him in court to show cause why he was being held. He signed his petition, "Earl K. Long, Governor in Exile by force and kidnapping."[27] The hearing on his petition was set for June 15, 1959, so the sanity hearing was postponed for a week. At the hearing, he talked with legislators and friends who had come to support him and obtained money from several, claiming that he had no cash. One was Bankston, who gave him a hundred dollars. After taking testimony that included the circumstances of his removal, the judge said he would rule in several days.

Blanche anticipated that the court would hold him and that a sanity hearing would rule that he needed treatment. She wrote, "They say that when Earl gets out of the hospital he will take his certificate of health out on the campaign trail with him. Then he can say he is the only man in the race who can actually prove he is sane. The people will laugh and be happy again because they know he is the only man in the state who really knows their wants and needs. And I'll be happy again, too. I will know in my heart of hearts that he is well again. I've lived with this turbulent character for 27 years and I love him very much."[28]

Things were not going to be as prosaic as Blanche Long envisioned. Russell Long appeared before a joint session of the legislature to advise that the family would see to it that the governor received needed medical care. He said that Lieutenant Governor Frazar was "now your Governor, and may be for some time," and the unflappable Frazar, loyal to Earl, was a calm and reassuring presence, but Blanche and Russell underestimated Earl. While their concern for him was genuine, they failed to appreciate that politics was his life and committing him to a mental institution was going to have a devastating effect on his career. Earl and Blanche had been a wonderful team politically and personally for many years, but she made a critical error in thinking that they could work through this crisis, that he would understand she had acted in his best interests, and that he would forgive her. Instead, he acted to secure his freedom.[29]

In the interval before the hearing, Earl told Blanche and Russell that if they did not have him released, he would file a federal criminal complaint against them for kidnapping by carrying him across a state line by force and against his will. He told them that if they relented, he would agree to go to Ochsner Foundation Hospital outside New Orleans and not file charges against them. Russell was sufficiently concerned about the threat to contact FBI director J. Edgar Hoover to tell him that this was "a family matter" and that his uncle was mentally ill. Hoover told subordinates to follow the case but take no action. After further negotiations, Blanche and Russell agreed to his terms and arrangements were made to dismiss the proceedings, cancel the commitment request, and have him go to Ochsner. All the while Earl maintained that he was not "crazy."[30]

Bob Mann, in his authorized biography of Russell Long, said that the family, in deciding to take him to Galveston, had concluded that if Earl would not get rest, "then we ought to just grab him" and place him in a mental hospital outside the state so that he would be unable to exercise his powers as governor. The decision to do that was a difficult and traumatic one for Russell. In notes that Russell made at the time, he wrote "if we are right, then we are his best friends. If we are wrong, then we are indeed stupid, ignorant, and unworthy of the positions in life which the people and our friends have accorded us. If we proved to be wrong, then we have forcibly seized a Governor from his state, elected by the people to hold the highest and greatest power which can be entrusted by a free people into a single man. If we are wrong, then we have made the Governor of a sovereign state a prisoner in his own mansion, flown him against his will into a neighboring state where his powers do not exist, [and] imprisoned him in a hospital room against his wishes."[31]

Earl later sued *Time* magazine for libel over its article in the June 15, 1959, issue, which said that at John Sealy Hospital he had "drifted aimlessly around" and "strolled up and down the corridor, babbling endlessly to himself." It claimed that he had been headed for a "crack up" all his life and now "the fact was clear: Earl Long had just gone plain crazy." The suit was withdrawn after his death as suits for libel and slander cannot be prosecuted after the death of the alleged victim.[32]

Dr. Harris said he concluded that Long's behavior "resulted basically from some deep-seated organic deficiency." Mrs. Long, in 1967, authorized Dr. Harris to respond to an inquiry from Richard McCaughan, author of *Socks on a Rooster: Louisiana's Earl K. Long,* for a medical analysis of his condition. Dr. Harris wrote

> it was our feeling that Governor Long had suffered a series of light strokes. His physical examination here definitely showed evidence of this and it was probably the primary factor that led to his ultimately being brought here. Governor Long became a very cooperative and fine patient. He had never had sufficient understanding of the nature of his condition to realize that he needed a longer period of hospitalization. He was very much improved at the time he left here. His physical condition was such that he could not stand the terrific pace he set for himself, and, as I have said, he did not have sufficient insight to permit him to appreciate his need for rest and further treatment. It is very conceivable that the numerous small strokes which Governor Long apparently did suffer could have brought about a change in personality accounting for the symptoms which he had.[33]

Earl left Galveston on his National Guard plane; he barely spoke with Blanche and several others on the flight. Accompanying him were Wilma Lockhart, his secretary; Margaret Dixon; Dr. Martin O. Miller; and two doctors and friends from Baton Rouge, Roy W. Wright and William H. Cook. Long perked up when asked by Dixon if he would take over his powers of office once he was back in Louisiana. "Yes, I will do that," he said quietly. Lieutenant Governor Frazar, asked what the situation would be, said that "as far as I am concerned, as soon as Governor Earl Long crosses the state line into Louisiana he is Governor."[34]

The doctors on the plane, who knew him well, said that "his heart muscle needs a rest. He stood the trip very well but had a shortness of breath due to the acute virus he has had. The mental exhaustion from which he was suffering is much improved." What he needed most, they said, was rest. He arrived at Ochsner in the evening and underwent several tests before going to bed.

Blanche claimed that Earl had promised to stay at Ochsner for "two weeks, or longer if necessary," but he said he had made no such agreement. The next morning, he told her that he was leaving for the Pea Patch to recuperate there. He would have to go through Baton Rouge, and she feared that he would go to the capitol and punish those responsible for his hospitalization as well as allies who had failed to come to his side. She called East Baton Rouge Parish coroner Dr. Chester Williams and asked him to draw up commitment papers. She left before Earl did to sign the documents.[35]

Blanche's Petition for Interdiction, submitted to the Nineteenth Judicial District Court, represented that "Earl K. Long is afflicted with insanity, and is a person of destitute means and should be interdicted and conveyed to an asylum for the treatment of insane persons, as provided by law." It requested that a warrant be issued to the sheriff of East Baton Rouge Parish directing him to bring Long before the court and that "an Order issue to the Coroner of this Parish and to another licensed physician directing them, together with a Judge of the Court, to constitute a Commission to determine if the said person be insane and a suitable subject to be committed to a hospital for the care and treatment of insane persons."[36]

Blanche's application required completion of an accompanying form for personal information about the patient, but she filled in only part of it, leaving blank information regarding the economic condition of the patient and value of his property. This was intended to determine whether the patient or a relative was able to pay for his maintenance.

Judge Fred S. LeBlanc issued a warrant for the sheriff and coroner to have "Earl K. Long, an alleged insane person, brought before this court to determine his sanity and the duty of the Court in the premises." He issued an order for the coroner and Dr. Sparkman Wyatt, a psychiatrist selected by Williams, to constitute, with him, a commission "to inquire and determine if Earl K. Long is a person of unsound mind and is a suitable subject to be confined in a State Hospital for the care and treatment of insane persons."[37]

The papers were put together quickly so that the warrant for Long's arrest could be issued. Once that was done, sheriff's deputies, notified they had been executed, pulled the governor's state police car over as soon as it crossed the East Baton Rouge Parish line. They told him they were going to escort him into the city, to the mansion, and Captain Herman Thompson took the wheel of Long's unmarked car from the state police driver. Long chatted pleasantly with Thompson and a deputy until Thompson pulled onto the ramp for the basement entrance to the courthouse. Realizing he had been tricked, he demanded, "What's going on?" Thompson told him that Blanche had applied for his commitment. "Goddamn, Goddamn you all! You all are doing it again," he shouted. "Goddamn, I'll get all of you."[38]

Dr. Williams and Dr. Wyatt were waiting to examine him. Reporters, photographers, and television cameramen had been tipped off and had already gathered there, as did bystanders who came to see what was happening. Long refused to get out of the car and the doctors sat on the curb talking to him through the window. Dr. Williams questioned him about statements he made at the committee hearing and joint session and was particularly interested in the story about the uncle who climbed into bed with a Negro woman. Why would he say such a thing, Williams wondered. "Why, because it was true," Long said. "Negroes just want their womenfolk left alone." Williams asked him about other statements on both occasions, and it developed that he had gone to watch Long at the legislature and had gone to Galveston for the hearing there. Williams, said to be an anti-Long, was fascinated with the governor's actions and went to observe Long in the expectation that he, in his capacity as coroner, might have an opportunity to deal with the governor. He said that he wanted to be prepared should he have to play such a role.[39]

After fifty minutes of back-and-forth conversation in this practice of curbstone psychiatry, Williams and Wyatt conferred in the courthouse while Long sat in the car guarded by deputies. His state police driver, Lieutenant Russell Willie, contacted Superintendent John Nick Brown about the situation with the governor. Brown told him that with a court proceeding underway, they could not interfere with it and had to stand down.[40]

The doctors had to meet the legal requirement of a diagnosis of mental illness for him to be committed. The Certificate of Coroner and Physician they signed said "we have observed and examined Earl K. Long," and "in view of our findings during observation and examination, and considering the information provide by Blanche R. Long, wife of the patient, we are of the opinion, and hereby certify, that the above patient is in need of observation, care and treatment for a mental illness and hospital or other care."[41]

Curiously, the form that doctors Williams and Wyatt were required to complete as part of their certificate exists in the court record in two versions. One has only several lines of questions completed from information provided by Mrs. Long, stating that the patient is of average intelligence; is not a congenital idiot; can count to ten; and can read, write, and speak English.

An entire section of thirty-two questions was left blank. It asked if "normally, prior to onset of illness," was the patient depressed, preoccupied, resentful, self-conscious, suspicious, truthful, aggressive, fault-finding, tense, studious, ambitious, adaptable, friendly, elated, alert, meek, energetic, dependable, intelligent, asocial, calm, self-centered, self-condemnatory, quick to learn, honest, and several other characteristics.[42]

Following the questionnaire, the form said, "Describe the patient's appearance, manner, and all abnormal acts or speech of the patient during examination and state fully anything else bearing on the case as indicating mental illness and why in your opinion hospital care for the patient is needed." That section is blank and this copy of the form has the typewritten signatures of the doctors.[43]

The second copy, signed by them, left the questionnaire blank, with not a single symptom noted, but had their findings below it. Dr. Williams said, "I have observed Earl K. Long in the Legislature, at a hearing on a writ of habeas corpus in Galveston, Texas and today 6-18-59 and I am of the opinion that he is a paranoid schizophrenic in need of hospitalization both for mental and physical care." Dr. Wyatt wrote, "In my examination at the court house today with Dr. Chester Williams I formed the opinion that Gov. Long is suffering from delusions of persecution which are 'fixed.' He would fit into the diagnostic category of paranoid schizophrenia with cycles of manic-depressive activity."[44]

With the doctors' statements in hand, District Judge Fred S. LeBlanc ordered Long's commitment. His order said, "I hereby commit Earl K. Long, as being mentally ill, to the So. East Louisiana State Hospital at Mandeville, Louisiana, for observation, care and treatment." Long, who despised LeBlanc, said later, "I've been trying to beat LeBlanc all my life. If it had been reversed, I might have given LeBlanc a break. I've done that lots of times for my enemies." Long said that the order "was the happiest thing that LeBlanc ever signed in his life."[45]

LeBlanc had a lengthy anti-Long record. After serving as district attorney for West Baton Rouge Parish and mayor of Baton Rouge, LeBlanc was elected attorney general in 1944, defeating the candidate backed by the Morgan-Long ticket. He ran for reelection on the Sam Jones ticket in 1948 but was unseated by Earl Long's candidate, Bolivar E. Kemp Jr. In 1952, LeBlanc was again elected attorney general, having run on the Kennon ticket, defeating Joe Arthur Sims, who ran on the Spaht-McKeithen ticket. Sims, from Hammond, had been the district attorney for Tangipahoa Parish. LeBlanc lost to the Long ticket candidate, Jack P. F. Gremillion, in Earl's landslide first primary win in 1956. He was elected judge in the Nineteenth Judicial District in East Baton Rouge Parish in 1958.

LeBlanc was also an outspoken segregationist. When in 1953 the Reverend T. J. Jemison led a test of a Baton Rouge city ordinance that allowed black passengers on municipal buses to take seats from the rear of the bus toward its front so long as front seats were reserved for whites, Jemison sat in a front seat. The bus company suspended the driver for not enforcing the ordinance, drivers called a strike, and LeBlanc as the attorney general declared the ordinance unconstitutional. He ruled that the ordinance violated state segregation laws.

Blacks formed free-ride groups of drivers, boycotted the buses, and filed suit to desegregate them in a program that the Reverend Martin Luther King Jr. studied and used in the Montgomery, Alabama, bus boycott two years later in 1955. Rev. Jemison called off the boycott after the city council enacted a new ordinance that reserved the first two rows of seats for whites and the benches at the back of the buses for blacks. Passengers could sit wherever they wished in between with the stipulation that whites and blacks could not sit next to each other.[46]

Deputies dragged the governor kicking and screaming, shouting for help from bystanders, from his car and shoved him into a sheriff's cruiser. "Hell, I'm not going to get in there," he screamed and swung his fist at them, but they kicked, shoved, tugged, and pushed him into their car and took off at high speed. When he saw the road sign for Mandeville, he said, "Why, that's a mental hospital. I hope you're not taking me there." He was greeted at Southeast Louisiana Hospital by the acting superintendent. "I'm Dr. Belcher," he said. "The hell you are," Long snapped. "You were Dr. Belcher." Long was admitted, and the next day the hospital issued a news bulletin that he "spent a restful night and was getting along well."[47]

Long's old friend and supporter Theo Cangelosi announced that he had met with Long at the hospital, with Bankston sitting in with them, and would secure legal counsel for Long. Long, already devising the strategy that would secure his release, told Cangelosi to draw up separation papers so that Blanche would not have any further authority as next of kin to commit him again. Cangelosi was also close to Blanche, and he was not happy with the prospect of serving as Earl's attorney in a divorce proceeding.[48]

Cangelosi said he went to see Long at the Mandeville hospital and that "he had become really bitter toward his wife" because he held her responsible for committing him twice, and he asked Cangelosi to file suit for divorce. "He wanted me to file suit against her for adultery with about thirty men," Cangelosi said. "He just about named everybody that is prominent in the state. Very frankly, she was not that type of woman. But Earl was so bitter toward her. He gave me a long list of names. I wouldn't even write them down. Some of them were ridiculous—of people he wanted me to charge her with adultery and be the lawyer to file the suit. I said 'No way, Governor, very frankly, both of you have been extremely courteous to me and in the first place I must tell you, very frankly, I disbelieve that.'"[49]

Long dismissed Cangelosi and brought in Joe Arthur Sims. Sims filed a petition for a writ of habeas corpus, and a hearing was set before District Judge Robert D. Jones in Covington on June 26, 1959. In a visit with Sims to map legal strategy, Long taped a message that was given to radio stations in which he assured the people that he was all right and predicted that "I'll be a free man Friday." Sims was acting as chief counsel for Long, but he had the court recognize additional counsel associated with him. They included several legislators; Dupre Litton; and Shreveport attorney J. Bennett Johnston, who later served Louisiana as a US senator for many years.[50]

In the petition, through his counsel, Long maintained that he was being "illegally detained in confinement, imprisoned and deprived of liberty" by the hospital. It decried the "circus-like atmosphere of the coroner's examination" and said Dr. Williams and Dr. Wyatt failed to fill in answers to more than one hundred psychiatric questions on the commitment, which he maintained was not properly drawn.[51]

The petition stated that the Louisiana Constitution provided the sole and exclusive means by which the governor could be removed and debarred from office, by impeachment or recall. Since neither had occurred, the petition continued, he had been removed and debarred from office by the order of commitment, an action that was null and void.[52]

It noted that the statutes required that an application for Orders for Interdiction to commit him state "the reason why institutional care is needed," accompanied by a certificate of the coroner and one other qualified physician stating that they had examined the patient and that he "is in need of observation or care in an institution." The certificate, the petition said, "shall state the facts and sources of information and personal observations upon which opinion is based."[53] But Long argued that the certificate signed by doctors Williams and Wyatt "does not state any facts or circumstances, contain any sources of information, or note any personal observations showing that Petitioner is in need of observation or care by an institution. The only medical information contained in said certificate is that Petitioner is in a 'run down condition' and 'in need of treatment.'" Long's petition stated that there was no showing that he was mentally ill or in need of treatment. This raised the question of whether the certificate was completed afterward, since it existed in two forms.[54]

Long's petition said that the judicial order to commit him was "illegally obtained" and that he "was arrested as he crossed the Parish Line of East Baton Rouge Parish, immediately taken to the Court House, and there superficially examined in a 'circus-like atmosphere' while he was seated in an automobile. Thereafter, predicated upon this purported examination, orders of commitment were signed." The examination, Long maintained in his petition, "in no wise complied with the provisions of law relative to examination prior to commitment."[55]

To cover his bases, the petition stated that he "alleges he is not, and has never been, mentally ill." But, "in the alternative only, if this Court believes that your Petitioner was mentally ill at the time of the commitment in question, which is specifically and emphatically denied, then, in that event, your Petitioner avers that he has completely recovered."[56]

The court ordered that Bankston and Belcher bring Earl K. Long before it on June 26, 1959, to state the reasons why they were keeping him imprisoned and deprived of liberty.[57]

Long had summons issued for over thirty witnesses, including Blanche; Attorney General Gremillion, who was representing the state and its hospitals officials made defendants; Lieutenant Governor Frazar; Theo Cangelosi; a half dozen state troopers; Captain Herman Thompson of the sheriff's office, who was in charge at the courthouse; Doctors Williams and Wyatt; and several physicians who were personal friends.[58]

Jesse Bankston visited Long daily at Mandeville but continued to refuse to release him. He said the psychiatrists there told him that the governor was suffering from hardening of the arteries and was not getting enough oxygen to the brain when he was under stress and became excited. Dr. Belcher said that he needed "rest and quiet and proper meals" and that "on preliminary examination we have not found anything too abnormal."[59]

Long begged Bankston to order his release, but his old friend said he had to defer to medical opinion and further examination. Lieutenant Governor Frazar, senate president William J. Cleveland, speaker of the house Robert Angelle, and Long's secretary, Wilma Lockhart, met with Bankston and asked him to either release the governor or resign, but he refused.[60]

The day before the hearing, Sims filed a petition on Earl's behalf for separation from Blanche. An associate of his said that it was "the first step toward a divorce." Blanche left for Colorado Springs, where Mrs. Huey P. Long and her daughter, Rose Long McFarland, lived and where she and Earl had been married at Estes Park in 1932.[61]

In his petition, Long maintained that that he had "always conducted himself properly, and has given his wife no cause or provocation for ill treatment, but on the contrary, has done all in his power to make their home comfortable and happy." He said that "on or about the latter part of the month of May 1959, your petitioner's said wife did commit excesses, cruel treatment and outrages toward your petitioner of such a nature as to render them further living together insupportable" and that during the last part of May, "and also on June 18, 1959, Blanche Revere Long did publicly defame your petitioner, thus creating grounds for separation from bed and board." The June 18, 1959, defamation was her statement that he was insane in her application to the court for his detention and confinement.[62]

Long stated that on June 23, he was "advised by an unimpeachable source, and now alleges that his wife has fled the confines of the State of Louisiana and will not return for an indeterminate period" and that she had not returned since her abandonment of him, which was "inconsistent with her duty to him and her marriage obligations." He asked the court to appoint an attorney ad hoc to represent her, and on June 26 the Family Court for East Baton Rouge Parish appointed Luther Cole, who later served as a state representative, district judge, and associate justice of the state supreme court.[63]

Acting through Sims, Long called a special meeting of the State Hospitals Board to convene at the temporary courthouse at the Covington Junior High School immediately before the hearing and obtained proxies from members who would not be able to attend. The hearing was limited to determining whether Long was being legally held; it was not a sanity hearing despite what most writers have stated. If Long had presented his case, he would have contended that he was the duly qualified governor, that the state constitution made no provision for removal or suspension from office for mental incompetence or physical disability, and that the only way he could be legally removed was through recall or impeachment. Arguing his case was unnecessary, however, because in a move that the Kingfish would have applauded, he orchestrated the dismissal of the officials responsible for holding him and the appointment of replacements who ordered his release.[64]

Bankston later noted that the State Hospitals Board functions were advisory in nature and that he served at the pleasure of the governor, and therefore Long could have fired him, but Long wanted to cover all bases.[65] An order dismissing Bankston, ratified by the board, was signed by Frazar, Cleveland, and Angelle. Bankston's successor, Hammond merchant and hospitals board chairman Charles Rosenblum, dismissed Dr. Belcher and appointed a new acting superintendent, Dr. Jesse McClendon of Amite. McClendon was an old friend of Long's and said that the governor was sane. "I have been a lifelong acquaintance of Earl Long and have observed him in recent weeks," McClendon wrote. "In my opinion, there is nothing wrong with him. He should be released and I intend to do so." Rosenblum endorsed McClendon's statement, approving Long's release. Sims then filed a motion to discontinue the proceedings, in which Gremillion joined as there was no cause of action remaining.[66]

Dr. McClendon said afterward that "I don't think the Governor is crazy. He looked wornout and tired and exhausted, but he was talking all right. If your wife was on your tail for four weeks and had you locked up without a telephone or television, wouldn't that run you haywire?" McClendon's son said years later that "he released him and that was that. He had a lot of criticism because he was a general practitioner and he wasn't a psychiatrist. A good family doctor back then had to be a country psychiatrist. You were part psychiatrist just from your actual practice."[67]

As Long got into his car, a reporter asked, "What are you going to do now?" He snapped, "I'm going to be Governor."[68]

Bankston went from the courthouse to his office to clean out his personal effects. He issued a statement saying that doctors who had examined Long at the hospital during the past week all agreed that he required more hospitalization. They included Dr. Robert Heath, chairman of the Department of Psychiatry and Neurology at the Tulane University Medical School, and Dr. Charles Watkins, chairman of the LSU Medical School Department of Psychology.[69]

After a brief stop at the Southern Hotel in downtown Covington, Long set up headquarters at the Pine Manor Motel, where state police could oversee access to him. Shortly after arriving, Earl fired the superintendent of state police for failing to protect him and called a panel of doctors to his side so the public could be assured he was all right. They included Dr. Heath; Dr. Watkins; Dr. Victor Lief, a Tulane psychiatrist and professor; and Dr. Paul Pratt, a psychiatrist. Long wanted them to examine him to reassure the public about his health. Besieged by the media, he held a press conference in his motel room. Sitting on the bed, in an undershirt, sheet draped across him and his teeth in a water glass on the bedside table, he said he was doing fine, his mental state was excellent, and he was going to relax for a few days.[70]

"My weakness is that I spout off too much," he said. "But if I ever closed this big mouth, God help Uncle Earl.[71]

Several days later, the doctors held a press conference at the motel. They concluded that Long had suffered a nervous breakdown caused by overwork and a series of strokes "sufficiently small so as to produce no obvious or dramatic effect such as muscular incapacity, but severe enough to precipitate serious physical illness." They said that "in the presence of such physical illness, it is not uncommon to have accompanying emotional symptoms. Frequently, such symptoms appear as an exaggeration of an individual's usual mode of behavior. As in generally known, Governor Long has always tended to be unusually active, and when faced with a stressful situation, he has responded by increasing his activities. Increased stress or over-activity superimposed upon a damaged nervous system which is not completely healed can cause an overloading. This tendency in behavior coupled with even a mild stroke resulted in a marked physical debilitation. Over-compensation in turn tended to make the Governor accelerate his activities to an even greater degree. In lay terminology, eliminating the additional complication of a stroke, this is commonly recognized as a nervous breakdown from overwork."[72]

They said the diagnosis of paranoid schizophrenia was commonly used for commitment and had no bearing on Long's case. "That means they got to have something to put you in, right or wrong," Long, sitting on a sofa by them, interjected. "They just clamp it in for good measure." He said that it "looked like when a man and his wife had a fight, the first one to the courthouse could get the other put away."[73]

The doctors said that Long's recovery from a severe heart attack in 1950 was "indicative of his recuperative powers," but his heart was still weakened and suffering from that event. They observed that "should it fail under a strain, as it has to a degree, there may be transient or temporary increases in mental symptoms due to impaired circulation in the brain. Thus there is an additional need for rest and avoidance of physical and emotional stress which may overburden his heart, thereby aggravating nervous system symptoms." They were in agreement that "at present the Governor is rational with no intellectual impairment." Long snorted, "That means I'm not crazy." The doctors concluded that "there is nothing that would indicate that the Governor cannot make another recovery. We agree with the Governor that he is better mentally than he is physically."[74]

Long said that the doctors who examined him for commitment to the Mandeville hospital "looked like bulls or bears or wildcats. They were looking for some excuse to put me in. My wife must have coached them." Railing at Blanche, he snapped that "putting a man in the crazy house is like killing your husband because you love him." On one occasion, talking about the possibility of reconciliation, he snorted, "If it took that to be elected, I would just as soon be defeated." As for his medical advisers, "I'm going to follow the findings of my doctors, but if I think they're wrong I'm going to campaign anyway." Railing against his family, Earl said, "I don't want a dog, a poor man, or any man—white or black—to be subjected to the abuse I've gone through."[75]

Perhaps the best evidence that he was not "crazy" was the manner in which he had responded to removal from the governor's mansion, commitment in Galveston, arrest in Baton Rouge, and commitment in Mandeville. In each instance, he took command of the situation and engineered his own release from confinement. As Thomas Martin wrote, Long "had been through an ordeal that might have felled a lesser man."[76]

Bill Dodd said that he

> practically lived with Earl during campaigns and I met with him on a daily basis for many years while we served in high government offices. I saw him under fire in campaigns and under the pressure of his Governor's office. And I saw him relaxed and joking with friends at the Mansion, in small country stores, and at his Pea Patch Farm. Never did I see him exhibit any signs of being mentally sick. High-tempered, uninhibited, crude, and at times a little sadistic, but never crazy or even part crazy. I felt that Earl was run down physically and drained mentally, the latter brought on by worry, fatigue, and a lot of drugs and alcohol that were not compatible. The late Dr. Ralph King, probably the medical doctor in Louisiana who was closest to Earl, told me that Earl was not crazy but just old, tired, and full of drugs that were pulling against each other—depressants and pep pills at the same time, plus whiskey and pills that put together were poisonous and very harmful.

He went further and said he believed Earl "was suffering from periodic strokes, not large, paralyzing strokes, but small, hammer-like blows that sort of stunned Earl for a short time and sent him reeling mentally and physically."[77]

Long was visited at the Covington motel by a "mystery woman" the afternoon of his release from confinement. She was brought there by Long's cousin, David Bell, who was director of the State Office of Veterans' Affairs, and Theodore L. "Ted" Jones, a close friend of State Senator Speedy O. Long. When they escorted her from their car they put a big bandana over her head. Newspapers ran photos of the so-called mystery woman, whose identity was soon revealed as a Bourbon Street striptease dancer, Blaze Starr.[78]

In the early 1959 planning for the legislative session, Long had taken to going to New Orleans and visiting clubs on Bourbon Street as a diversion. He met Starr at her club, and in the following months they had dinner together in his suite at the Roosevelt Hotel and visited. Long's intimates said there was no sexual relationship between them; one described it as "father-daughter," but Miss Starr milked the publicity to become a headliner and later wrote *Blaze Starr: My Life As Told to Huey Perry.* In her book and interviews, she placed herself at the center of events in which she had no part, claimed that Long was going to marry her and run for president, and said that she had orchestrated his release from the state hospital and his candidacy for congressman in 1960. A movie was made, titled *Blaze*, with Paul Newman playing Earl. It did not acknowledge that he was married but showed a woman directing detectives to break down the door of a fictional love nest with Blaze, credited Blaze with directing the strategy that gained his release, had him keeping his boots on for a romp in bed with her, and ended with him dying in her arms in a hotel in Winnfield. None of this was true; it may have been good entertainment, but it was bad history.[79]

Iris Kelso, in her *Times-Picayune* political column, wrote that "none of us who remember those days can forget how sad it was to see Earl Long loose on the world, sick and emotionally disturbed, out of control. Nor can we forget the dignity with which Blanche Long conducted herself throughout the long days of trial. For this reason, it is very hard for us to see anything funny in 'Blaze,' which makes a farce of a human and governmental tragedy. It was not funny. It was sad."[80]

Long's intimates said there was nothing to the affair. Ellis "Easy Money" Littleton, who was with Long from 1947 to his death in 1960, said "she was no more than a friend. If there was anything special between them I never recognized it." He said that "she never was at the Pea Patch," as depicted in the film, "because I was with the Governor every time he was there during this time." He said Starr, whom a reporter had called a "second-rate stripper" on Bourbon Street, did not love him and "just used him for the publicity she could get from being with the Governor."[81]

Miss Starr said "he's a good guy and we're just friends," but the media had a field day. One of Long's entourage said that there could not have been a sexual relationship. Miss Starr later suggested that there was such a one. She visited him at the Roosevelt Hotel, he came to see her at a barmaid's home, and she came to the Davis inauguration, standing on the platform near Long, taking pictures, but she soon went back to The Block, the Baltimore striptease district, and was dancing there when he died. Blanche Long, in her only comment, said that it was all nothing but a cheap extramarital affair. "It took place in the last few months he was in office," she said. "It didn't amount to anything. I knew about the affair. I knew about it shortly before the newspapers found out. He was down there on Bourbon Street a lot, but he would be right at home that night. You know how men do that sort of thing, don't you? But I stayed in the Governor's Mansion right there with him." Some observers believed that Long carried on with Blaze Starr to embarrass Blanche, paying her back for committing him.[82]

When the movie was released, Bill Dodd said "a gang of Hollywood's character assassins are at work on Earl Long. Long was not a saint. But unlike many high officials, he did more dodging than chasing. Earl Long treated fast women like he did fast horses. If they were running when he was betting, he put a few bucks on them. But win or lose, he didn't claim any or bet on the same ones again. Earl Long had only one romantic affair. He lived with her all his life and died in her arms. Her name was Politics." Dodd wrote that "the memory of Earl Long deserves a better place in history than a fictitious love affair with a Bourbon Street stripper. A post-death libel of Governor Long's life won't hurt him but it sure aggravates those of us who knew the real Earl Long."[83]

Ron Shelton of *Bull Durham* fame, who wrote and directed *Blaze*, acknowledged that it was "a fable" and "a Southern yarn," but it saddened many that viewers would believe that it was factual. It did not come out until thirty years after Long's death, with Blaze's book now styled "a novel" in the paperback issued to coincide with the film. The truth is that as soon as Blaze got in the way of his politics, Earl dumped her because he was much more interested in holding onto office than holding onto her.[84]

On June 30, Blanche filed an Answer and Re-conventional Demand in response to Earl's petition for separation. She sought an injunction to restrain him from disposing of any community property; claimed she had always been "a faithful and dutiful wife"; and maintained that "his conduct, particularly in recent weeks," made a continuation of their marriage unsupportable. She alleged that "he has been guilty of multiple acts of cruelty," details of which would be furnished if required by the proceedings. "These acts of cruelty have included fits of temper, more intensely during recent weeks," she said, "in which he has repeatedly, without any provocation on her part, maligned, cursed, and abused respondent and held her to public and private shame and humiliation."[85]

Blanche said that in fairness to Earl, "He has been under great continuous stress and strain, charged as he has been with the responsibilities of the office of Governor, under extremely difficult circumstances, and that during recent weeks he has driven himself both physically and mentally, and has literally enslaved himself to the duties and responsibilities of his office, and, for this reason, respondent has dealt with him with greater patience and with concern and anxiety on her part to help him in any way that she possibly could."[86]

She said that despite her desire to help him, he had sought to persecute her and "that on May 28, 1959, in the presence of family and friends, without cause or justification, he had cursed, abused, maligned, and defamed her, causing her intense mental pain and suffering, and that he threatened her life." She was referring to the gathering of family and friends that told him they would not allow him to start a stumping tour that weekend and confined him to the mansion.[87]

On June 30, Mrs. Long was granted a motion to discontinue an inventory of their community property, which he joined in, but the injunction against disposing of any property remained in force. Presumably neither of them wanted an inventory performed that would be filed with the court and made a public record.[88]

A Baton Rouge *State-Times* story on July 2, 1959, was headlined "Mystery Surrounds Long Home" and said that Mrs. Long was apparently at the house she had recently completed but that newsmen were barred from the site. "Mystery continues to surround the new brick mansion built by Gov. and Mrs. Long on 'millionaires row' just across Capitol Lake from the State Capitol building," it said. "It was reported today that federal agents were probing construction of the home, with contractors and subcontractors being questioned on transactions in connection with it."

The residence, at 1465 Ted Dunham Drive had 4,500 square feet of living area, with formal rooms for entertaining. The story listed the property history from public records and said that Mrs. Long took out a building permit on October 1, 1958, which listed "Governor Long as the builder." It speculated that Earl and Blanche had made plans to build the home in 1958, but after saying he would go around the state constitution to run for governor again, the "mansion" would become an embarrassment for him in the eyes of rural constituents. He feared that opponents would distribute circulars about it, so he insisted that Blanche was building it. After the committals and his petition for separation, Blanche moved out of the governor's mansion and into the new home.[89]

Blanche, in her response, denied his allegations and requested $2,500 monthly alimony. Earl ridiculed the idea that he could pay such a sum. "She's got more money than I have, and, besides, she's 12 years younger and can work," he said. Her attorney advised that the demand for alimony was made in error and would be removed.[90]

Long had asked the Internal Revenue Service to defer its investigation of his income until after the coming election, but a news story said that IRS agents had obtained a court order to open the safe deposit box of Mrs. Cora Russell Schley of Alexandria, who worked at a clinic there and said she had been a public relations adviser to Long since 1952. She declined to say how much of Long's money she was holding but said it wasn't much. One unconfirmed report put the figure at $7,000. Mrs. Schley said federal agents were "checking everybody who might have some of his money." Long kept campaign money in safe deposit boxes in Baton Rouge and Alexandria, and a small safe in his mansion bedroom held cash for his horse race betting. He ridiculed stories that he had money buried in various places and said he would be glad to talk about his finances although "I might not have time to talk about all those millions I made and those tin cans hidden away, buried with money. If anyone finds any of those tin cans, they can bring me half and keep the other half."[91]

Governor Long remained in Covington for several days, went on to his office, and then to the farm. At the Pea Patch he held a wide-ranging press conference on the rear porch, sitting on a rocking chair and wearing pajamas with a sheet draped over his legs. He had an audience that included Dr. Pratt; two of his sisters; several other family members;

friends; state troopers; and members of the legislature, including Senator B. B. "Sixty" Rayburn. "My wife has never liked Winnfield," he said, although Huffman and others later said that she accompanied him there on many occasions. He said that soon after they were married in 1932, he built her "a better house than I was able, up there on Possum Neck, and in six months she didn't want to do anything but go back to New Orleans." He sold that place for $15,500, he remarked, and bought the Pea Patch property and its five-room house. Claiming that separation was the best thing for both of them, he said "she's worried me and I've worried her for 25 years. I think it's time we both had a break."[92]

Blanche, he chuckled, loved to hear people say she was a power behind the scenes. When he was recuperating at the farm after his heart attack in 1950, he claimed, she tried to run his office. When he was asked about that then, he said there would be no "petticoat government."

Now he said, "Talk about petticoat government. She had those articles framed where I said we had petticoat government." Displaying his disarming candor, he exclaimed, "Why, she was trying to run the capitol, making more deals that I was."[93]

Speaking wistfully of Winnfield, he said, "I'm going to do all I can for my home town. I don't make much money here at this place, but I have lots of fun." Turning to Rayburn, he told reporters, "I'm going to help fix all the roads around Winnfield that I can, but don't say much about that or old Sixty there will want all his streets paved." He loved to help people, Long noted, by "running an open welfare department of my own. Every time I come to Winnfield there's some poor old folks, blind ones, sick ones—they all come to Uncle Earl, and I help them where I can."[94]

"I was born here, and I expect to die and be buried here in Winnfield," he said, repeating a promise made previously that he was going to "donate the 'old home place' at the corner of Maple and Pineville Streets" as a public park. "I'm going to put benches in it for white and for colored," he announced. "I'll name it for my old mother and daddy, Mrs. Caledonia Tison and Uncle Hugh P. Long."[95]

He made a stumping trip on July 4 and told one audience, "You have no idea of what I have been through. They say I'm crazy. Come see for yourself. Three jails in five weeks. If I'm nuts now, then I've been nuts all my life." He was fond of saying that the best evidence that he was not crazy was his ability to withstand the treatment by his family and two commitments, held against his will for almost a month, and secure release and resume his office. "I don't doubt that I haven't been a little bit off all my life, but I guess everybody else has been off at one time or another," he said.[96]

After resting at the farm, Long left on a western vacation, flying to Dallas and then a short hop to Fort Worth, where he continued on in his official limousine escorted by two state troopers who met him there. He also took one of the psychiatrists, Dr. Paul Pratt, with him as well as his friend and physician Dr. M. O. Miller and State Senator "Sixty" Rayburn. David Bell and Dick Davis accompanied him for parts of the trip. At several points, he had other officials meet him to go over business, including Dupre Litton and Lieutenant Governor Frazar. The excursion went through several states and into Mexico to visit a Juarez nightclub. Some observers thought the trip was an aimless wandering, not realizing that he was making a tour of racetracks. Newspapers said he needed rest and should be accorded privacy but then sent reporters and photographers after him. They camped in the halls outside his hotel room, took tables next to him in restaurants, and popped big flashbulbs in his face.[97]

Annoyed by the photographers and reporters who had followed him onto the plane in Shreveport, before arrival at Fort Worth he had Senator Rayburn cut eye and nose holes in a pillowcase and he put it over his face, with his hat jammed on top. He was angry because they had pestered him with questions and popped flashbulbs in his face. Rayburn led him off the plane and through the terminal, with flashbulbs popping. Long had thought he was outsmarting the photographers by covering his face, but he played right into their hands, and the resulting pictures in newspapers appeared to confirm the stories that he was crazy. Several days later, shaking his head, he said, "I thought that if they couldn't see my face they would stop popping those flashbulbs at me, but instead I gave them exactly what they wanted." He held a press conference and answered questions, but newsmen persisted in dogging his footsteps. "Why can't you leave me alone?," he demanded. "Do you boys know what hot lead is? I've got plenty of it and I know how to use it. You sons of bitches want to see me well but you won't leave me alone." He held another press conference to apologize and said, "I probably got nutty and said some things I shouldn't have. When a man loses his temper, sometimes he loses his equilibrium." Dupre Litton wrote that the media harassment during the trip was beyond all bounds. He said that in Dallas "the hotel was almost taken over by the media. They filled the halls outside Earl's suite, even sitting and lying on the floors day and night."[98]

In an interview during the trip, he assailed the press for making his vacation as miserable as possible. The New Orleans *Times-Picayune* and the Alexandria *Daily Town Talk* would never print anything favorable to him, he said, and he told a story about the editor of the former: "They said the *Picayune* man was drunk and fell in a ditch. And a fellow came along and they had a hog in there, in the slop, and he said you can tell a man by the company he keeps and the hog got up and left."[99]

After a few days, he sent Dr. Pratt home and said that he was "firing" his doctors. "I don't know about all these big words they use," he said. "Some of their medical terms are such big words that I can't spell them or understand them. Maybe I should write some up myself. After all, unlike them, I have the experience of actually having been in the jug." Becoming thoughtful, he said he "dis-hired" them "because I know more about anything wrong with me than they do. You know, psychiatrists is more or less guess work, more or less self-anointed. Sometimes some of them are crazier than the man they are examining, and after they stay in that business it's not unusual that they lose practically all of their equilibrium. They use such large words that you couldn't understand them unless you had a dictionary right there with you and some of those words aren't in it because I tried to look them up. You'd probably need an, what do you call it, an Encyclopedia Britannica to get them." He said that "if I don't dump them, they'll drive me crazy. Their history is that most of them have mental illness."[100]

In between visits to racetracks, he haggled for boots and hats at western wear stores, went to church, called on governors, and even met with Harry Truman at the former president's library in Independence, Missouri. Long said that Truman supported Stuart Symington, former secretary of the air force and US senator from Missouri for the Democratic nomination for president. The governor stated, "I wanted to discuss with him the presidential setup. I think Symington and Kennedy would be a wonderful combination. Kennedy is a fine boy but he looks too much like a boy than he is." Proclaiming himself "very anxious to help the Democrats win," he commented that "I think [Lyndon B.] Johnson is too far south and the heart attack he had, which was worse than mine, would tell on him with four years in the President's chair."[101]

Uncle Earl said that he and Truman reminisced about politics and told each other off-color stories. "He told me some good ones and made out like he hadn't already heard any of mine," Long said. After spending an hour with Truman, he signed the guest book in the lobby on leaving and gave the guard a one-hundred-dollar cash donation to the library. Truman forwarded the money to his board chairman with a note that "Governor Long was here last Saturday and we had quite a conversation. He left in a very good humor because he left $100 with the Guard, which I am sending to you to place in the Educational Fund of the Library."[102] The former president sent Long a letter telling him what he had done with the money. In a handwritten note he wrote, "Enjoyed your visit very much."[103] When Baton Rouge television newsman Brooks Read sent Truman a copy of his recording, *Earl Long: "Last of the Red Hot Papas," The Voice of Earl Long* in 1962, Truman responded with thanks for "the record of some of the things that the late Earl Long had to say about politics and people. I plan to listen to it at the very first opportunity and know that I shall do so with interest."[104]

Asked about the civil rights plank in the Democratic Party platform, Long said the Republicans were the same on the issue. "Look at Eisenhower, he sent troops in at Little Rock," he said. He told reporters that "there's no question that for the time being the best thing for the south is segregation. The only things we've ever gotten in Louisiana was under the Democratic Party. The Republican Party is the party of wealth and greed and selfishness and the Democratic Party is the party of the people."[105]

Long sent postcards to some legislators and mailed crates of cantaloupes to others. With the trip a national and even international news story, he was dogged by reporters and photographers. He returned refreshed and invigorated and called a special session of the legislature to act on bills he wanted passed. One would make it more difficult for family members to commit a person against his will; another reduced the interest rate that small loan companies could charge borrowers; and in response to a plea from an airline stewardess on the flight to Fort Worth who wanted to get married but would lose her job if she did, he proposed to prohibit airlines serving Louisiana from discriminating in employment on the basis of marital status.

Linda Huffman said that during "Mr. Earl's Wild West Trip," he called her father Clem every night and they talked for a long time: "My Dad kept telling him to come back home, relax, rest up, and see Dr. Moseley." She remembered that during the trip "every day I got a card from Mister Earl and most days I got presents, usually clothes or shoes. He always remembered what sizes I wore no matter what else was going on in his life."[106]

Legislators friendly to him tried unsuccessfully to dissuade Long from holding the special session. They were concerned about the coming state election; the segregation controversy; and the incredible events of Long's collapse, confinement, and the western trip. As soon as the house came to order, a Long floor leader, Ben Holt, moved to adjourn the session. The motion passed overwhelmingly, the senate was advised, and it followed suit. For once the members feared their constituents more than they feared Uncle Earl. Striding into the senate chamber as legislators were leaving, he went to the rostrum and told them that he was "not especially mad at anybody" and "nobody has to look for repercussions." When Lieutenant Governor Frazar, fearing another outburst, urged him not to be upset, Long said, "I'm upset proof." He apologized for his performances in May and said "if I was crazy then, I have always been crazy. So you might say now that you have an opportunity to see a crazy Governor."[107]

9. RUNNING FOR LIEUTENANT GOVERNOR: 1959–1960

Long continued to argue that if he resigned and ran for governor and won, he would not violate the one-term limitation because he would be succeeding Lieutenant Governor Lether Frazar rather than himself. In August 1959, he announced a ticket that included Oscar Guidry as his running mate and embarked on an eleven-stop speaking tour over the August 15 and 16 weekend. He distributed cards that said "Earl Long is a candidate for Governor unless the Lord, illness, or the law prevent his running. He is a proven friend of all the people, regardless of race, color or creed."[1] He spoke in the Washington Parish town of Franklinton in a rainstorm, saying "I thought I would let you see how crazy I am. I've got plenty of snap left."[2]

His circulars proclaimed, "Come Out and Hear the Truth! Governor Long Speaks: Governor Long opens campaign for Re-Election. Come out and bring all your friends to hear the truth. Come out and see Governor Long in person. Nothing will be said to offend or hurt anyone." He began on Saturday, August 15, at Dequincy at 9:30 a.m. and ended at the Court House Square in Lake Charles at 7:45 p.m., with stops at Starks, Vinton, and Sulphur in between. On Sunday, August 16, he opened at Elton at 10:00 a.m., followed by Church Point, Opelousas, Lafayette, and New Iberia and finishing in Houma at 7:45 p.m.[3]

His handbills said that he wanted

> to tell my people who have been so faithful to me just how I have been treated. I want you to personally see and hear for yourself the harassments I have been subjected to. I want you to know the truth and not be guided by the rumors which have been spread among the people and which have been printed in the Alexandria *Daily Town Talk*. Not all of the newspapers and reporters are bad. Many of the newspaper reporters are my personal friends. Some are ugly, and are inflicting on their readers a great deal of sordid

> material that is distasteful. Some, but not all of these newspapers and photographers, have been hounding me all day and all night like a pack of hounds after a wounded animal, scenting blood, trying to catch him and pull him down. They won't allow me, a sick man, a little privacy in which to recover from being dragged, without my permission, through three hospitals. I know you will agree with me that they have somewhat kept me from looking after our state business, which I have been doing daily even while I am trying to rest. I can tell you, as my office force well knows, that I attended to the affairs of state by giving of my time from 12 to 15 hours a day while I was out of state. Only when you know the truth can you judge for yourself what the facts are.[4]

Proclaiming "Father, Forgive Them, For They Know Not What They do," Long said, "I do not propose to punish those who had me locked behind ten doors, and had to have a key to turn on the lights. I would not hurt any of them even though they have vilified me and almost wrecked my physical wellbeing. To those who have helped me in so many ways, I want to personally shake your hand and thank you for your prayers, your letters, and all the help you have given me. Were it not for your prayers, I would still be locked up by so-called friends who forbid my true friends from getting to me."[5]

"Wherefore By Their Fruits Ye Shall Know Them," he announced, stating,

> My motto has always been, and will continue to be, that I have never met anyone that did not have some good in him. I know that I will pass through this world but once, and anything that I can do for the good of our State, and all the people—any kindness that I can show every citizen of our state—be he high or low or humble, I want to do it before I pass on, for I know that I shall not pass this way again. As long as I have lived I have been a friend of the less fortunate. I have always worked to improve their lot, and am still working to do so. These small loan lobbyists who bleed the poor must be stopped! It is wrong for them to take advantage of the poor people. And it is wrong to railroad sane persons into insane asylums where they do not belong, just because somebody wants to get rid of them for their own selfish purpose. After being dragged around, I know personally how many of our people are mistreated in those hospitals. And I am going to wage a fight against those who thrive,

> prosper, and live like kings on the misery of the mentally sick in this state. I want to help these poor, unfortunate people.[6]

"Your Help Is Needed," he said, because "after being dragged through three different hospitals, locked up and jailed, in less than 30 days and losing 40 pounds, I am pleased to tell you that I have gained back nine pounds and hope to gain more. I continue to solicit your prayers and assistance in the months ahead. If the good people of Louisiana continue to stand by me as you have in the past, we will by the Grace of God win our battles against those who would take advantage of the poor, the mentally sick, and those of our people in less fortunate circumstances."[7] At every stop, speaking from the bed of a pickup truck, Long said that it was a miracle that he had not been driven crazy by what was done to him.[8]

After his initial stump tour, Long had to acknowledge the overwhelming opposition to his reelection scheme. The Democratic State Central Committee, of which he was a member, met and approved a requirement that for Long to go on the ballot, he would have to resign prior to qualifying to run. Accepting defeat, unwilling to resign eight months before the end of his term, he cast his own ballot for the resolution.[9]

Determined to play a role in the election, he persuaded former Governor James A. Noe to come out of a twenty-year political retirement to head the ticket, with himself for lieutenant governor. Despite their 1940 battle, when Noe's endorsement of Jones in the runoff cost Long victory, they had renewed their friendship, and Long expected the wealthy Noe to finance the campaign.[10]

The candidates for governor included Jimmie Davis, Chep Morrison, Bill Dodd, Jimmy Noe, and Willie Rainach. Bill Dodd, who had been elected state auditor with Long in 1956, told voters that if they loved Earl they should not vote for him because he was not well. Long stumped the state, flailing "Big Bad Bill" Dodd and "Della Soups" Morrison. Davis, he thundered, "loves money more than a hog loves slop." He said Davis spent much of his term "making movies in Hollywood that were so bad they don't even show them on the late, late, late show." As for Rainach, he snarled, "Jimmy Noe and I are reasonable men. We believe in segregation but we don't want to bring on a race war like little Willie Rainach.

All Rainach wants to do is boil all the poor old colored people in oil. Well, I've got news for Willie Rainach. He has no more chance to be governor than I do to become Pope of Rome, and I'm not a Catholic." In a talk at Marthaville, Long thundered, "That Della Soups Morrison is a cute little thing. He wears his little wig and all that sweet-smelling perfume and makeup. Well, you know, 'Powder and paint makes Aunt Lucy look like what she ain't.'"[11]

In Natchitoches on October 1, 1959, he called Rainach "a squint-eyed little squirt running on a one plank platform. He's going to stir up hell in Louisiana. If he'd just shut up and go home we'd all get along better." As for Davis, "Nero fiddled while Rome burned and Jimmie Davis will sing while Louisiana goes to the dogs." To loud applause he shouted, "If I was crazy then, I've been crazy since I was first elected, but," and here he chuckled, "that makes you crazy too, because you voted for me." In another appearance, Long thundered, "I've done more for segregation in the past few years than Willie Ranch will ever do in a lifetime. What can Little Willie do that we can't do? Does he think he's bigger than the Supreme Court, too? Well, put this down. It takes a big man to be governor of this big state, not a man running with only one plank in his platform. Willie Ranch is just too small for the job."[12]

Noe distributed pictures of himself with Huey and gave lengthy speeches about his service in World War I and in state politics while Earl attacked their opponents. "If you're going to vote for me for lieutenant governor, then please vote for Jimmy Noe for governor," he urged. Bill Dodd claimed that if Noe and Long won, Noe would resign so that Earl could succeed him. Noe denied any deal with Earl and put up a $100,000 bond that he would serve out his term. It soon became apparent, however, that the race was between Morrison and Davis. In the last few days of the campaign, Long abandoned the stump, telling several candidates on the ticket that they would not be in a runoff.[13]

Morrison ran first in the December 5 first primary by a large margin, followed by Davis. Noe ran third and Dodd fourth. Long ran third for lieutenant-governor, behind the ticket mates of Morrison and Davis, but he polled sixty thousand votes more than Noe. The election marked the first time since Huey Long's 1928 victory that a Long candidate failed to make the runoff.

Morrison was elated by his seventy-thousand-vote lead over Davis, and he was assured of the endorsement of Dodd, who was paid $25,000 to cover his campaign debt by the Morrison campaign. The wealthy Noe endorsed Morrison without demanding payment. Morrison announced on election night that he would resume the campaign the day after the primary with a rally in his hometown of New Roads in Pointe Coupee Parish.[14]

Morrison's closest confidante and adviser, David R. McGuire Jr., New Orleans's chief administrative officer, urged Morrison to begin his campaign for the January 9, 1960 runoff in New Orleans instead and to make overtures to Long. McGuire said Morrison should make a personal call on Long to talk things over. For several days, in telephone calls, they discussed this. McGuire said that while Long would prefer a Davis administration to a Morrison one, in the expectation that Davis would not be able to anoint a successor while Morrison could, Uncle Earl would not want to antagonize the overwhelming black support Morrison had in anticipation of Long's intention to run for governor in 1963. "Long may see the wisdom of remaining neutral publicly regardless of whether he works behind the scenes for Davis," McGuire told Morrison.

McGuire thought it imperative that Morrison call Long personally and seek a meeting with him. "It will not work to send an emissary, Chep," he said. "You have to go and you have to go hat in hand and you need to eat some humble pie. You need to tell him how important his stand for Negro registration was, and how you and he both receive most of the Negro voters, except when you split it in 1956, and you should be together in this because Davis is going to be a front for the extreme segregationists."

Morrison told McGuire that he had decided not to go see Earl personally but would send Camille Gravel, who was running his campaign in the Eighth Congressional District. "My God, Chep, that's the worst thing you could do," McGuire said. "Camille parted ways with Long in the 1958 congressional election, when he backed McSween, and McSween is working with Camille on your campaign now. If you want to send Earl through the roof, this will do it. You've got to go see Earl yourself."

Morrison rejected McGuire's final plea and sent Gravel as his emissary. It is debatable whether Long would have remained neutral had

Morrison made a personal appeal to him, but failing to come himself, much less sending Gravel, closed the door to any possibility of that.

Long said nothing for three weeks after the primary. Rumors spread that he was working behind the scenes for Davis. Dave McGuire was told by an employee of the State Department of Veterans Affairs that its head, Earl's cousin David Bell, processed a mailing to veterans for the Davis campaign.

Long was probably appalled by Davis's attacks on Morrison as "soft on segregation," using the primary election results to show that there was a black "bloc vote" for the mayor and that this had injected a "sinister element" in the campaign that placed the southern way of life at risk.

Earl did not hold a press conference to endorse Davis. Several days before the January runoff, however, he announced that he and Blanche had driven to Winnfield to cast absentee ballots and that he had voted for Davis.

Blanche and Earl spoke on the telephone frequently and visited several times, but she was unwilling to consider reconciliation unless he gave up politics and retired. He would invariably, after a long conversation, start on her again for committing him. Nonetheless, she had stated publicly that she would vote for him for lieutenant governor. Blanche and her sister rode with him to Winnfield to cast his absentee ballot in the runoff, and he signed the papers for the home she had built on the Capitol Lake. She said, "I am thankful my prayers and the prayers of thousands of people in the state have been answered and Earl has fully recovered his health. I wish him the best of luck. And I am proud to have had a part in the benefits provided by the Long administrations to the people of Louisiana."[15]

If he had expected peace and harmony from another Davis administration, which the new governor campaigned on, Long was sadly mistaken. Davis rewarded Rainach's endorsement by making him chairman of the State Sovereignty Commission to fight integration. Davis tried to take over the New Orleans public schools when they had token integration but was stymied by the federal courts. Davis called five special sessions within four months to pass forty-seven bills to preserve segregation. Every bill of any consequence was struck down by the federal courts, including laws to deny state funding to integrated schools, deny accreditation to all integrated schools, void the diplomas of their graduates, and prohibit academic credit for them to attend state colleges and universities.

Davis's administration was rocked with scandal. This supported the view that Earl Long preferred him to Morrison because he would have a better shot at returning to the mansion after a Davis administration than a Morrison one.

Once Davis was governor-elect, Earl Long became a nonentity, as happens when a new governor is awaiting inauguration. All eyes of the political class turn to the new chief executive with the transition. With both legislators who were reelected and new members anticipating the first session of the new administration waiting on word from Davis as to who they should elect as house speaker and senate president pro tem, as well as with jockeying for choice committee assignments, they had no need to confer with Uncle Earl. Many of his appointees were looking for employment after May, while the new governor weighed the calls and visits he was getting and the resumés submitted by hopefuls.

Long took care of business with his small staff. He spent three- or four-day weekends at the Pea Patch Farm, visited with old friends and supporters who came by his office in the capitol building and the mansion, and played the horses at several racetracks.

At the time, Louisiana governors were inaugurated in May following the January runoff election. Davis was to be sworn in on May 10. An occasion arose that gave Earl the chance to personally inform Morrison of how deeply the mayor had insulted him by sending Gravel to seek his support after the primary.

In April, when President Charles de Gaulle of France went to New Orleans for a twenty-four-hour stop during his state visit to the United States, the citizens' committee that the mayor appointed to make the arrangements for the events there and the mayor himself snubbed Governor Long. He was not invited to participate in the welcoming ceremonies and in a night parade on April 28, the evening of de Gaulle's arrival. Long was invited by the host committee to deliver remarks at the civic luncheon the next day. The mayor and the committee members were clearly trying to limit the governor's participation; in effect, they were sneering at him as a likely embarrassment.

Long read about the welcoming parade in the newspaper the morning of de Gaulle's arrival, and he called Jesse Bankston to come to the mansion. Bankston was a frequent visitor, his refusal to release Long from confinement forgiven. Long had asked him to return as head of the hospitals department, but Bankston found his work as a consultant lucrative and had no interest in giving it up.

Long asked Bankston if he knew Morrison, because he wanted Bankston to call him and protest the failure to invite him. Bankston said that the person to call was David McGuire, whom he did know. Bankston reached McGuire at his home early that morning and explained the situation. While they were not personal friends, Long knew McGuire from his numerous appearances before legislative committees on matters important to the city. On one occasion, Earl was standing in the lobby of the Roosevelt Hotel talking with several people when McGuire walked by. "There goes Morrison's brains," Long quipped.

Long took the phone from Bankston during the call to McGuire and launched into a bitter commentary on Morrison. "I got to read in the paper that the President of France is coming to New Orleans, and I'm not invited to that," he said. "Last time I checked I was the Governor of Louisiana, so he may be coming to little Cheppie's city, but damn it, he's coming to my state. I don't give a goddamn if he doesn't like me and doesn't respect me, but he has to show respect for the office I hold."

McGuire agreed with him, and Long became very reasonable. "Any time the state has something going in New Orleans, that little Mayor is invited," Earl said. "He fought me on that university and I fired my Levee Board so LSU would get the land for the school there, but I still had him on the platform when it opened. That's how I treated little blue boy. Last month we dedicated that multimillion dollar X-ray deal for Charity Hospital and the LSU Medical School, and I saw to it that he was invited and he came there and made a big deal. So I've been fair with him, but he insults me like this. Well, put this down, he can insult and disrespect Old Earl as much as he wants but he ain't gonna insult and disrespect the Governor of Louisiana."

McGuire told Long that the failure to invite the governor had to be "an oversight." "Yeah," Earl said, "some damn oversight!" McGuire told Long how very sorry he was about this, assured him that his participation was wanted, and said that he would call him back shortly.

McGuire called Colonel Karl Smith at Jackson Barracks, the National Guard headquarters in New Orleans, who was in charge of the military parade, and made arrangements for Long to meet Colonel Smith at the assembly point for the parade near the intersection of Canal Street and Claiborne Avenue. He then called Long back and told him that Colonel Smith would expect him there and that he had arranged for Long to participate in all events on President de Gaulle's itinerary from the night parade through the open-air reception in Jackson Square on the second day.

Morrison was at the airport to meet de Gaulle. Expecting the French president to wear his plain military uniform, Morrison wore his own as a major general in the US Army Reserve, adorned with his ribbons. De Gaulle arrived in a business suit, and he and Morrison got in a convertible with security personnel. When they arrived at the parade assembly point, Long was waiting for them there. When Long went to the car, expecting to get in, he was waved off. Morrison later said that French bodyguards and State Department security officials did not want another person in the back seat.

Colonel Smith, with the governor also the commander-in-chief of the Louisiana National Guard, sought to defuse a situation where Long might pull rank on the mayor. Smith adroitly invited the governor to ride at the head of the parade, in the car with the grand marshal, Adjutant General Raymond Hufft. Hufft had assisted the Long family with Long's forced removal from the mansion the previous year and had supervised putting him on the plane to Galveston, but Long had forgiven him.[16]

Long was happy riding with General Hufft, and he waved a bandana to the immense crowds lining Canal Street, on Chartres Street in the French Quarter, to St. Louis Cathedral on Jackson Square. There, the dignitaries left their vehicles to mount the reviewing stand for the parade.

Morrison stayed at de Gaulle's side but did not introduce the governor to him. Long finally introduced himself to Madame de Gaulle and then to the president. Morrison stayed between them and Long, irritating the governor. Long had lit up a cigarette and had it in hand when the national anthems of the two countries were played. He failed to recognize the *Marseilles* and started to say something to Morrison, but the mayor waved him off.

During a break in the proceedings, Long turned to Morrison and berated him for sending Gravel as his emissary. "You should have come yourself, to talk man-to-man," Morrison later quoted Long to McGuire.

"You sent Gravel, and he lorded over me. Oh, he let me know that he had fought me in '58 and had backed you over Noe and me. He lorded it over me, he said that I was lucky to finish third in my race, that that was better than he expected." Morrison said that Long told him he "might" have stayed neutral in in the governor's runoff, but after Gravel's visit "there wasn't a chance in hell of that."

Long was further offended when he went to the civic luncheon. His place was at the head table on one side of de Gaulle, but Morrison moved the governor's place card to the end of the long table, with two journalists. Long left his seat to talk with Morrison, who, he said, told him, "Five minutes, that's all, don't talk for more than five minutes." Long welcomed de Gaulle, got his hat from his seat, and walked out of the room. Afterward he said, "That two-bit Mayor told me five minutes, but I gave him two minutes back." The papers had a field day with stories about Long leaving before de Gaulle spoke, but Long later said they did not know how badly he had been treated and probably wouldn't have cared had they known. He later said that he received a lovely letter of thanks from de Gaulle for his warm welcome remarks.

There was another contretemps before people were seated for the luncheon. A State Department security officer brushed against Long and told Superintendent of Police Joseph I. Giarrusso that he thought Long had a gun in his coat pocket. Giarrusso went to McGuire and said he was concerned that the security details would remove Long from the ballroom. McGuire went over to Long and asked him if he had a pistol in his pocket. "I sure do," Long said. "Huey had all those body guards but I don't need them. I'm my own bodyguard." McGuire said that he assumed Long meant no harm to de Gaulle. Long said of course not, he was a great man and Long admired him. McGuire told Giarrusso to tell the security officer that Long posed no danger to de Gaulle, but to satisfy them, he would assign two plainclothes officers to stay close to the governor.[17]

Written off again as a has-been, his political death proclaimed once again, Earl Long completed his term, biding his time, planning a comeback.[18] In a letter to this writer Long said, "I have been talked about, criticized and slandered more than any other public official of our state by a certain segment of the press. In my present term of office, they have tried to hold me up as being crazy, deranged, a drunkard, a roughneck, and a man whose personal conduct is reprehensible to the clear-thinking men and women of this state. When the history of this state has been written, I believe that in future years it will be obvious that the Long administrations have operated with less waste and more efficiency, and in the interest of more of the people of this state than all of the reformers put together."[19]

10.
"I WOULD RATHER WIN AND DIE THAN LOSE AND LIVE": 1960

By 1960, Earl Long had become a relic in a new age of telegenic politicians with retinues of media advisers. Long was unable to make the transition that his contemporary, former Georgia Governor and then-Senator Herman Talmadge had negotiated. Son of racist orator and Governor Gene Talmadge, Herman Talmadge smoothly made the transition from hot stump speaker to cool television performer. "I use a calm, deliberate, rational, reasonable approach on TV," Talmadge said. "The viewer sitting in the quiet comfort of his home is not subject to the emotional hysteria of the stump."[1]

Long's health was gone, but his determination and backbone were not. He decided not to accept the elder statesman status so many of his family members had been pushing on him for years. Instead, he decided that the best way to recover his political health was by running for Congress in the Eighth Congressional District—the seat that his brother George Long had held until his death two years earlier. As always, Earl was all in. He pulled out all the stops, knowing that the effort could kill him. The campaign for Congress, he said, was the next governor's race in disguise.

Earl would carry his cause to the voters the same way he always had. Standing on a platform or the bed of a pickup truck, he proclaimed that "as long as God gives me health, determination, and backbone, I'm going to carry my fight to the people."

His faults and foibles were as great and sweeping as his very real and lasting accomplishments, and he certainly stood head and shoulders above the race-baiters and charlatans holding governors' chairs in several other southern states during his tenure. Despite all the events of the turbulent days of 1959, when the eyes of the nation, and a large part of the globe, turned to Louisiana as her governor was committed to and won release from two mental hospitals, Earl K. Long was not finished in Louisiana politics. He still, as he liked to say, had some snap in him. "Old Earl just kept going, like the Mississippi River, just on and on and on," he said.

He was a better politician than his brother Huey. He was the best personal contact campaigner Louisiana ever produced, a rousing, rough-and-tumble self-proclaimed Last of the Red-Hot Papas.

He was down, but he was not done.

11.
UNCLE EARL'S LAST HURRAH

There was no way that Governor Earl K. Long was going to retire from politics quietly and gracefully after the tumultuous events of the 1959 legislative session, two commitments to mental institutions, and defeat for lieutenant governor in the 1959 primary. In 1940, following a razor-thin defeat for a full term as governor, he said, "This is a game of survival of the fittest. I'm the fittest and I'll survive." In a stump speech for the candidate he had picked to succeed him as governor in 1951, he roared, "I am going to stay in politics until I am taken from this earth." In 1956, his nephew, US Senator Russell B. Long, Huey's son, tried to talk him out of running for governor again. "I told him, 'Uncle Earl, you can be an elder statesman,'" Russell recalled. "He looked at me and said, 'I'd rather be dead.'" Told to slow down after a physical exam in 1959, he rasped, "I won't quit until I die."[1]

His political downfall in 1959, when he failed to make a second primary for the first time since 1940, began in 1956, when television began reporting the proceedings of the legislature in depth for the first time. Long recognized that television was not a good medium for him, and he avoided it as much as possible in his 1956 election, making only two or three live appearances on programs with his ticket. It was only after his 1956 victory that television's first full-dress coverage of the legislature gave many citizens their first close-up view of Uncle Earl in action. His freewheeling attacks on his enemies, struggling for control of a microphone with Secretary of State Martin, and his ranting performances, while colorful and entertaining on the stump, where a speaker was often judged on the inventiveness of his invective, were not well-received in many living rooms. Too many people saw visual confirmation of what the newspapers had reported about him all along.

His profane presentations, in which he liberally laced his outbursts with damns and hells, and his anger and rage when he did not get his way, were captured by television. Its camera, while honestly objective, seems to emphasize or exaggerate the worst qualities of its subjects, and in that sense Earl Long was surely one of the most dramatic and publicized victims of the television camera's eye. It is ironic that he began his political comeback in 1960 using in his final act as governor the medium that was so unkind to him.

Long spent $4,000 to air a televised "farewell address" shortly before leaving office in May 1960 in which he said that he had passed legislation to provide transition funds for an incoming governor and to allow the new governor to move into the mansion ten days before inauguration. "These things were done because I know of the need for helping the new governor to get a good start," he noted. "This kind treatment may be extended to me in 1964! Who knows? I say this in all modesty and not bragging or threatening. Don't sell Ole Earl short. There is a lot of good reading in old books. A man 80 years old saved Germany; a man 72 years old saved France. Winston Churchill saved England. Syngman Rhee saved Korea. Uncle Earl is only 64 years old. I'm not bragging, but I might be around for a few more years, the Good Lord being willing, whom I hope I'm on good terms with, if I can keep my equilibrium, which is sometimes harder to do than it is to say." He warned, "Uncle Earl may come again. I've often heard, and I think you have, that truth crushed to earth shall rise again. It might do the same thing in 1964."[2]

Referring to Blaze Starr and a woman whom he took for a drive in Hot Springs on his way home from his western trip, Long said

> the *Times-Picayune* bears down when I attempt to befriend a show girl, and when I greeted with courtesy a family of people from Memphis, Tennessee in Hot Springs, Arkansas, and later some false charges were trumped up against me. They would have you believe that Ole Earl is crazy, a drunkard, a roughneck, and one whose personal conduct is reprehensible; that he is uneducated, an ignoramus, an undesirable, unpredictable, and all kinds of other adjectives. They even intimated that I tried to push General de Gaulle and his wife off the platform when I was only trying to be friendly. General de Gaulle didn't complain. Why did they? As a matter of fact, he complimented me in my absence. If I have ever been crazy, I have been so all my life, and am crazy now. I want the good people of this state to know that I have committed no act that I have been ashamed of. I have conducted myself at all times

> as a gentleman and as a friend to the people. I am a humble man who knew and wanted to know the problems of the people. I talked to children; I talked to the aged; the big and powerful as well; to the hoodlums, bums, preachers, deacons, priests and rabbis, and the colored.[3]

"I maintained, and I repeat, that a Governor cannot have too much experience about lumber, timber, farming, religion, Sunday school, show business, whisky-drinking, crap-shooting, politics, and many other things you pick up in a lifetime," he said. "I have walked on both sides of the street."[4]

Long said, "Whether I am Governor, Lieutenant-Governor, Dog-Catcher, or What-Not, I will always be interested in our people and their problems, especially the underprivileged and down-trodden." Addressing stories of corruption, he said "if anyone knew of any graft, shake-down, or wrong-doing, all they had to do was to notify Ole Earl, and I would stop it P. D. Q., and if I did not, I hoped the Good Lord stops my wiggling tongue." He reviewed the accomplishments of his administration department by department and addressed the racial issue:

> I have been the best friend of the poor white and the colored that has ever occupied the Governor's chair. And, as a result, in spite of Rainach, we have had very little trouble between the races in our state until recently when the uncalled for, unfounded, ill-advised demonstrations broke loose. I did not say in my statement that all colored people had to return to Africa. I said all those who are dissatisfied should visit their motherland in Africa, see how they are getting along there, see how backward they are, how they live, and then I am sure they would think more of their own country. If they like it in Africa, stay there. If not, come back over here and behave themselves, instead of listening to a northern, radical, communist-inspired NAACP. The truth is, and the facts are, that no race on the face of the earth has made so much progress in the last hundred years as the colored people have here in Louisiana.

Discussing several of his initiatives, he said, "I was too far ahead of the times, and that was one of the chief reasons I was temporarily overpowered and sent to Galveston and Mandeville. "Whom the Gods wish to destroy, they first make mad," he noted, insisting that he was not crazy.[5]

Concluding his farewell address, Long intoned, "As I now bow my head to the inevitable succession in office, and may be getting closer to another world in life, it is a consoling thought, and I am deeply thankful to know, that I have contributed what I have to mankind. I know I will have the satisfaction of carrying my deeds with me for the judgment of the next world. If I have any rewards, I will gain recognition for what I have done and what I have tried to do for the poor people of this state."[6]

At the moment that he said this, however, Uncle Earl was much more interested in the judgment of this world than the next, particularly the judgment of registered Democrats in the Eighth Congressional District of Louisiana. Two weeks after leaving office, he announced his candidacy against the incumbent, Harold B. McSween. Unwilling to wait for the next state election in four years, he was an old fire horse answering the nearest bell, and he plunged into the final election of a long career in politics that had begun when he first campaigned for his brother Huey P. Long in 1918.[7]

In a 1959 campaign tour, Earl excoriated his enemies and reviewed his record, then pointed dramatically to the sky above, one arm raised on high, index finger an arrow, and thundered, "They keep records up there! And-you-write-them-yourself!" Although running for Congress, Long's sights were clearly set on another run for governor in the December 1963 Democratic primary. He told intimates that the run for Congress was "more or less the next governor's race in disguise," but he also knew that his health was bad and that the strain of a vigorous campaign in the July and August heat would be telling. He acknowledged that he might be "getting closer to another place in life" and that he did not run because he wanted to go to Congress as much as he did for vindication, fighting for his political life, determined that if this was to be the final record, he would write it himself. He had been a candidate for governor or lieutenant governor in every election but one between 1932 and 1959. He ran for governor three times and won twice; he ran for lieutenant governor four times and won once. If this was to be his last hurrah, he was determined to go out a winner. He did so, and the victory gave poetry and symmetry to his life.[8]

Long was living alone, separated from his wife Blanche, as he made plans for the congressional campaign. They had spoken about reconciliation, but she was insistent that he retire from politics. That had been his life, and he was unwilling to give it up. They spoke on the telephone on many occasions, but their conversations always ended with Blanche insisting that he retire and Earl berating her for committing him to two mental hospitals. He felt the loss of Blanche at his side; she had been a strong right hand in his previous campaigns and ran the headquarters operation. Despite their differences, several days before leaving office he appointed her a member of the Board of Review of the Employment Security Division of the State Department of Labor. The appointment was for a four-year term; the members averaged three meetings a week for which they were paid forty dollars for each meeting.[9]

After the Davis inauguration, Long, meeting with reporters at his Pentagon Barracks apartment on the capitol grounds, was asked what his plans were. He said there was "not much an old man can do but rest," but he went to the Pimlico Race Course in Baltimore for the running of the Preakness Stakes. He took with him a sometime aide, Dick Davis, a Lecompte car dealer who drove Long and carried a state police commission. Davis, who had gone on the western trip, told newsmen that he was Long's bodyguard.

They went to the Baltimore striptease district, where Long met Marcia Katz, who disrobed under the name Candy Cane. She said that "he threw money at me during my performance. So afterwards I had a drink with him. He invited me to spend Monday with him in New York. We were going to see a play and I was going right back Monday night." After a night on the town on May 23, she called police early the next morning to claim that $240 had been stolen from her hotel room. Davis said that when the officers who responded spoke with him and saw that he had a revolver in a belt holster, they tried to shake him down for $600 for violation of the strict New York gun laws. He claimed they accepted his explanation that he had a special state commission and returned the gun to him but demanded money. When Davis complained about his treatment, Long telephoned the police commissioner, who initiated an inquiry and turned the incident over to a grand jury. Davis testified before it that "two detectives and a plainclothesman tried to shake me down for $600.00." On May 31, the grand jury cleared the officers and the matter was ended.[10]

Miss Katz told a reporter she had testified that the policemen had not been bribed and described her shopping trip to a furrier with Long. The newspapers had a field day with the story, identifying Candy Cane as "Long's companion." She said that Long bought a mink stole and a silver fox for her and then five more mink stoles. "Listen to this," she said. "A raccoon coat with a mink collar, a sheared beaver coat, seven fox stoles, all for different women in New Orleans. I heard him give addresses." The news story headlined "All was Lovely on Date Here, Until She Was De-Minked, but not Out-Foxed," said "You've got to appreciate Miss Katz's position. She'd started out the day with a mink stole and silver fox. And by evening she'd had her mink snatched by the ex-Governor. What's a poor girl to do? Get out of town while she's still got her fox, right?" The reporter said that Katz called the newspaper soliciting an interview before she boarded a train back to Baltimore. She gave the reporter her measurements but insisted she was not a stripper. "Actually, what I am is an ecdysiast," she explained. "That's what they told me I am. I was making $60 a week in the chorus and they gave me $125 to strip. Then they said I was an ecdysiast. I looked it up once. It's not dirty." The story said the word was not in the dictionary, but *ecdysis*, a zoological term, was. It meant the "act of molting or shedding an outer cuticular layer, as in the case of insects or crustaceans." As applied to Miss Katz, it apparently meant taking off her clothes.

In another interview, the stripper said that when "the Governor took my mink back I figured I'd better get out of town while I still have the fox. The Governor sent me a note saying I was 'still a nice little girl.' I told him as far as I was concerned his New Orleans stripper, Blaze Starr, could have him with a pink ribbon tied around his mouth." Asked why a ribbon, she said "because he rants so. I tell you, he's definitely eccentric. If I'd known it was to be like this, I'd never have come. I thought we'd see some plays, that's all." Enjoying her moment in the spotlight, she asked the reporter, "You don't think I'm a gold digger?"[11]

On May 17, before leaving for Baltimore, Long told newsmen that he was going to New Orleans to meet with three doctors. His physicians were Dr. Martin O. Miller, Dr. Robert Bernhard, and Dr. R. M. Willoughby. Long said he felt very nervous because he was receiving two shots of cortisone a week and other medications for a bad back. Receiving the reporters at his apartment in the Pentagon Barracks, he said that he was going to divide his time between Baton Rouge and his farm in Winnfield.

Long was admitted to Baptist Hospital in New Orleans two weeks later, on May 31, 1960. The hospital administrator declined to discuss his condition but said that following tests and a conference with the doctors, he might undergo surgery the next day and would probably stay in the hospital for ten days.[12]

Long had said that he was going to have "minor surgery" for an undisclosed ailment that had bothered him for a number of years. He did not elaborate, but the hospital said that he was under the care of Dr. Willoughby, a urologist. Long's personal physician, Dr. Bernhard, was an internal medicine specialist. Dr. Miller was an old friend.[13]

On June 1, 1960, the hospital said that he had undergone surgery and that his condition was good. A news story said, "Long was in the operating room for an hour for surgery and two surgical procedures. His attending doctors would not comment on the nature of the surgery." The following day, a hospital spokesman said Long was "cheerful and doing fine."[14]

When qualifying opened on June 1, 1960, for the Democratic primary in Louisiana's Eighth Congressional District, the first two entrants were the incumbent, Harold B. McSween, and former State Representative Ben Holt. State Senator Speedy O. Long of Jena, who had run in 1958, initially declined to count himself either in or out, telling the Alexandria *Daily Town Talk* he had "no commitments to anyone."[15]

From his hospital room on Thursday, June 2, Long announced that he would seek the Eighth District seat in Congress in the July primary and would open his campaign on Saturday, June 4, with a 7:00 a.m. speech in Boyce, followed by appearances at Lecompte at 2:30 p.m., Bunkie at 5:00 p.m., and Marksville at 7:00 p.m. He scheduled stump speeches for Sunday, June 5, in Plaucheville, Cottonport, Bordelonville, and Simmesport.[16]

On Friday morning, June 3, the final day of qualifying, the *Daily Town Talk* reported that "political observers were turning their eye toward New Orleans in anticipation of former Governor Earl Long's next move." The story reported "wide speculation that Long would not make the race but instead would put former State Representative Lloyd Teekell, former State Senator C. H. Downs, or state Board of Education member Estes Cole in the primary." The story was written before its writer became aware of an advertisement Long had placed in the *Daily Town Talk* announcing his weekend speaking schedule.[17]

Working out of his hospital room, Long telephoned Dupre Litton, who had served as his executive counsel, on the last day to qualify. Long wanted to know where he could file qualifying papers. Litton told him they could be filed with the chairman of the Democratic Committee in DeRidder but that it had to be done before 5:00 p.m. that day, by cash or certified check for $210. Litton arranged for the papers to be sent to Long for signature, and later that morning Long called back to say that he had received and signed them in the hospital but had neither $210 in cash with him nor time to obtain a certified check. Litton said that to be sure everything was in order, Long should send the papers to Baton Rouge for Litton to review and notarize, and he would exchange a personal check from Long for $210 in cash. Long's messenger met Litton, he notarized the papers, and they were filed prior to the deadline.[18]

On the afternoon of Friday, June 3, two days after his surgery, Long was discharged from the hospital and said he was going to his farm to rest before opening his campaign the following day. He said that he would file a statement of his net worth with the secretary of state, as required by a 1950 law, before the June 9 deadline. His net worth was about $275,000, compared to $150,000 when he took office in 1956, and he explained that "some property which I considered a loss turned out to be a gain."[19]

The Eighth District seat had been held by Long's brother, Dr. George Shannon Long, known as Shan or Doc throughout the area. Born in 1883, he was ten years older than Huey and twelve years older than Earl. Trained as a dentist, he moved to Tulsa, where he became involved in Oklahoma politics and served two terms in the state legislature. He came home after Huey's death and established himself in Pineville. George supported Earl in his 1948 campaign for governor and was appointed superintendent of the Pineville State Colony & Training School. He quarreled with its business manager, who accused him of requiring that foodstuffs be bought from one of his friends at higher prices than were available from competitors. George fired the man for insubordination, but when he appealed to the governor, Earl reinstated him and fired George. George ran for Congress three times against incumbent A. Leonard Allen, a younger brother of Governor O. K. Allen, who served eight terms. Earl had not supported George in those races, but when Allen announced his retirement in 1952, George won the seat with Earl's support.[20]

Long's entry was a surprise to many, including the incumbent, Harold McSween. McSween explained years later that, in the wake of Earl's tumultuous 1959, he did not believe Long could mount a credible campaign. He also had reason to believe that Long could not survive an arduous campaign in the heat of summer.[21] McSween had graduated from Bolton High School in Alexandria and obtained his law degree from LSU. He served in the Merchant Marine and Naval Reserve and was in private practice when elected to the Rapides Parish School Board in 1954. Politically active, he was a volunteer in Russell Long's first election to the Senate in 1948 and was a district leader for the gubernatorial campaigns of Hale Boggs in 1952 and Chep Morrison in 1956.[22]

In Earl's final term as governor, he and McSween engaged in two pitched political battles in central Louisiana. In 1956, McSween defeated Long's sister, Clara Long Knott of Many, for the Eighth District seat on the State Board of Education at the same time that George Long was reelected to Congress.[23] The governor supported both siblings but was particularly upset by his sister's loss. He had not campaigned for George, who had token opposition, beyond saying "I will vote for him," but he campaigned actively for Mrs. Knott. In an election-day broadcast, Long said that McSween had supported him for governor at the outset of the 1956 campaign, but when he was not made district campaign manager had abandoned him to back Morrison. He assailed McSween as "a little squirt." In his victory statement, McSween called Long an "unmitigated and deliberate liar" and said that Alexandria attorney Camille F. Gravel Jr., Democratic national committeeman and one of Long's closest advisers, would confirm that he had no involvement with the Long campaign.[24] Earl had also gotten heavily involved in the 1958 Eighth District congressional race after George Long died, supporting State Representative Lloyd Teekel against McSween and Speedy O. Long.

When Long opened his campaign on Saturday, June 4, he had little support. Many political leaders in the eight-parish district had deserted him after the events of 1959. The political establishment had written him off, but once he took to the stump in the largely rural area, voters came out to see his show, and many of them admired the old trouper's courage in mounting an aggressive and punishing campaign. A number probably supported him because they sympathized with what he had gone through, and as they saw the toll on his health, wanted to see him go out a winner if this turned out to be his last hurrah.

Long's speaking tour that weekend followed the schedule he had announced from his hospital room on Thursday. On Saturday, June 4, he started at Boyce in Rapides Parish, then headed south to LeCompte. From there, he continued into the Avoyelles Parish towns of Bunkie and Marksville. On Sunday, Earl campaigned the entire day in Avoyelles Parish, visiting Plaucheville, Cottonport, Bordelonville, and Simmesport. His advertisements and circulars announced that "nothing will be said to offend anyone. People of all walks of life are invited. None of my opponents' names will be mentioned on this campaign until after they have started on me."

A crowd of three hundred turned out in Boyce for his first appearance. He said that he was "feeling a little weak" and had been told by his doctors to stay in the hospital for several days to rest, but he had made these engagements to speak and he was not going to let his listeners down. He said in a telephone interview that there were three hundred whites and fifty Negroes in the crowd and they were "very enthusiastic." Promising to conduct a clean campaign based on the needs of the district, he claimed more experience and familiarity with it than either of his opponents, the incumbent Congressman McSween and former State Representative Ben Holt. Long promised not to start calling any names unless they did so first.[25] Holt had been a floor leader for Long in the 1956 and 1958 legislative sessions but broke with him after the events of 1959 and led the move to adjourn the special session in 1960. He did not seek reelection to the House in 1959.[26]

At Lecompte, Long proclaimed that he was "one million per cent for segregation" and addressed a group of Negroes directly: "I'm for you. What I done for all people has helped you people. But I also tell you Earl Long is for segregation one million per cent, and don't ever make a mistake about that." Described as "perspiring through his silk suit in 90-degree heat" and still wearing a hospital identification tag on his wrist, Long said that segregation was not unique to the races, but to classes as well: "White people sometimes segregate white people. The Boston Club in New Orleans, you might say, segregates Earl Long." Long said his platform planks were for flood control, forest service, federal land, and better forest fire protection. He said that the federal government should sell the front two acres of all of its lands facing highways to people for home sites, and he called for a flood control levee system for the entire Red River, a return of Fort Polk to active service, and the retention of England Air Force Base at Alexandria.[27] Long distributed a card with his picture on one side and a message on the other: "Earl K. Long. Candidate for Congress. 8th District. First Primary—July 23, 1960. Get out and get your friends to register who are not qualified to vote. Those who voted in the governor's election can still vote. I expect to conduct a clean campaign. I will not mention any of my opponents' names unless they start working on me. Thank you very kindly for reading this."[28] At one of his speeches, Earl repeated his pledge that he would "not start slinging mud until mud is slung at me."[29]

In his speeches, Long indicated that he would hold the seat only until the next round of state elections in 1963. He said that if he won election, in his first term he would "give two of the best years of representation during the four years I'm in Congress." Described by a reporter as "noticeably weak" and "still wearing his hospital identification armband, Long tired easily on the speakers stand and made brief speeches to all gatherings." He told the crowd at Cottonport that he "broke out of that hospital" and was supposed to go back in two days, explaining that he misunderstood his doctor when he scheduled the stumping tour. "I thought he said I'd be in the hospital two or three days, but I guess he said I'd be in bed two or three days. He wanted me to rest eight or ten days."[30]

Again pledging that he would not attack his opponents, Earl proceeded to denounce the big newspapers and McSween. McSween, Earl said, "was born with a silver spoon in his mouth. Some of us wish we had, too, but I'm proud I was born poor." Chuckling, he said, "They say I'm a stripteaser. They say I'm a horse bettor. They say I'm a whiskey drinker. I might have done some of all of them. I know forestry. I know farming. I know a little about stripteasing. I even know a little about the church."[31]

With the primary set for July 23, McSween remained in Washington while Long stumped on June 4 and 5. McSween's own campaign was shortened by his decision to stay in the nation's capital until Congress adjourned, and he did not hurry home once Long began campaigning. Despite the rural nature of much of the district, he planned to focus on national rather than local issues, citing his opposition to civil rights and foreign aid.[32]

At the outset of the campaign, Speedy Long said that he was going fishing and would be neutral in the race. He had planned to run again, but Earl's entry forestalled that. Speedy believed that if Earl had supported him in 1958, he would have captured the seat then. Earl initially planned to support Speedy and had spoken with his longtime sound truck drivers Ray and Jack Ellington about painting several station wagons with Speedy's name on them. Ray Ellington said that "Mr. Earl then decided to run himself, and told us a few days later to repaint the signs to read "Elect Earl K. Long for Congress."[33]

A news story said that Uncle Earl had "retreated to his one-time political stronghold to make a last-ditch fight to stay alive in state politics." Observers speculated that the race would be a prelude to a campaign for governor in the next state election.[34]

After his initial stumping foray, Long spent time organizing his campaign, painting several station wagons left over from the state election and two new ones, dealing with posters, circulars, and the speaking schedule, and raising money. He was in New Orleans on business on Tuesday, June 14, when he was issued two traffic tickets and booked on three municipal charges in connection with a minor traffic accident at 8:20 p.m. on Gentilly Boulevard. Driving alone, he struck the rear of another car, knocked it into a parked car, and then hit the parked car. No one was injured, and damage was minor, but when police came to the scene and asked for his driver's license, he could not produce it. The officers said they would have to take him to jail to book him for driving without a license. According to their report, he became abusive when they tried to explain that a city ordinance required them to book a driver involved in an accident who had no license; otherwise, he could have surrendered his license, received a citation, and been released at the scene. The policemen called the night supervisor, Major Dominick Palmisano, to the scene. He tried to explain the situation but when Long continued to curse the officers, Palmisano ordered them to take him to the precinct station and book him. When Long refused to get out of their car at the station, they had to grab him by the arms and pull him out.[35]

Long was booked with disturbing the peace by using obscene language, resisting arrest, reviling police, reckless driving causing damage, and having no operator's license. At the station, he contacted Municipal Court Judge Andrew Bucaro, who paroled him until he could appear in court.

Later that night, contacted at the Roosevelt Hotel by a reporter whom police had tipped off, he said, "I'm going to fight this thing in the courts. I wasn't intoxicated. I wasn't speeding and I wasn't endangering anyone's life." He appeared in court the next morning and asked for a continuance so that he could fulfill speaking engagements, which was granted.[36]

The accident was probably due to a lack of concentration and how little driving Long had done. He had a state police driver while governor and usually had someone driving him when out of office. At the Pea Patch he often drove a pickup truck in his long johns into Winnfield to pick up the Sunday newspaper, but he had not done much driving on highways or in New Orleans. On another occasion, Long had a minor incident on a narrow street in the French Quarter when he ran up on a curb but did not cause damage. The police officer who came to investigate asked him for a license, which Long went through his wallet and retrieved. The policeman looked at it and said "Governor, this is not a driver's license, it's a hunting license." Long quickly responded, "What do you think I'm doing in the French Quarter?" The policeman let him go.[37]

With the campaign set, Long was ready for his typical caravan of speakers, entertainment, and handouts. While many elected officials in the district kept their distance, he had at his side men who had been with him for years, and they knew enough about stumping to help him with the speaking schedule and arrangements.

In a column later that year, Baton Rouge *State-Times* reporter F. E. Shepherd wrote that

> there is a saying among political writers in the state to the effect that a newsman "hasn't lived" unless he accompanied Long on a political campaign. It was a real experience not likely to be forgotten for a long time. His campaign junkets were always fast-paced and never dull. He never followed the script, instead using happenstance situations to the best advantage. Many opponents learned to stay out of sight until Earl had finished haranguing his own audience, lest they become embroiled in a public name-calling contest in which the former governor was most likely to come out on top. Earl loved night meetings while campaigning, often just "visiting" during the day, inviting all to a big gathering, which more often than not featured hillbilly bands, free hams, and lots of old-fashioned shouting and name-calling. Newsmen never could fathom Earl's ability to single out people in the audience, calling them

> by name; asking about a hound dog; the five children, by name; and the house that was being built when they last saw each other three years before.
>
> There is little doubt his uncanny ability to remember names, places, and assorted data was responsible for much of his success in politics. The rural Louisiana voters prided themselves on the fact that "Ole Earl" knew them personally, and did not mind stopping by to sit a spell and talk about the plowing conditions and the hogs, while gulping down a glass of cold buttermilk or a couple of cups of black coffee. Earl's ability to campaign long hours each day and still remain fresh and seemingly tireless perplexed many an opponent, but newsmen long ago learned his secret. Between campaign stops he was the picture of relaxation, sitting in the front seat with his driver or turning around to talk with a traveling companion about anything except the campaign.
>
> He had a habit of stopping at a small country store for meals, ordering crackers, cheese, the Vienna sausage he loved so much, and assorted other tidbits, then sitting down on a box or step to leisurely stow it away. Of course, this common touch stood him in good stead with the rural voters. It was not unusual for him to drive up to a town for a speaking engagement in a sound truck and be mingling with the crowd before anyone was aware he was around.[38]

When one of his sidemen asked why Long wanted to stop for gas when they had half a tank, Long told him to stop at a station every time the gauge was down a quarter. Many of the rural stations had one or two pumps with a mechanic bay, and some had small stores where people met for coffee and conversation. Long said these stops gave him the opportunity to buy gas from the owner, chat, and politic with whomever was there. Likely as not, he explained, the owner would boast that Governor Long had stopped by.[39]

Earl did not have the finely tuned political machine that Huey did at the height of his power. Civil Service had eliminated most of the patronage, and contributions by employees as deductions from their salaries were now illegal. Huey's organization had been built in large part on jobs, and his machine was self-sustaining financially, fueled by contributions from state employees called "deducts," contractors, and companies and individuals doing business with the state. Like Huey, Earl did not believe in grooming a successor. When the Kingfish died, five of his lieutenants each claimed that he had privately anointed them as his candidate for governor in 1936, and they had to negotiate a compromise ticket that included Earl. Earl was not going to let one of his gang supplant him. Edgar Coco, an old political ally from Avoyelles Parish, said "he'd rule by confusion. He wanted to make damn sure no one else called the shots."[40] There was going to be only one top dog, and he was going to be Uncle Earl. According to one study, "Earl was always careful to see that no other Long adherent got into a position which might endanger his primacy; consequently he tended to quarrel and then make up with politicians in and out of the Long faction."[41]

"He had no permanent precinct captains or district leaders," Stan Opotowsky wrote in *The Longs of Louisiana.* "Instead he had an organization built upon the patronage and rewards of the moment. One man fell out and another stepped in." Many of his political arrangements were for one election only. "There was no attempt to make the Earl Long organization permanent. There were some men, of course, who habitually fell in line for campaign after campaign, and these, in a sense, could be called Long district leaders. But except for the New Orleans Choctaw Club, a city political machine in the classic sense, there was never any attempt to make these relationships any more formal than they were permanent."[42]

Long said that the workings of his organization were all in his head and before each election he pulled his personal following together in what amounted to a coalition of interests rather than a political machine. He had a remarkable memory and could sit by a telephone dialing one number after another, calling people throughout the state. His mind was his Rolodex.

Earl Long had never stopped politicking, from Huey's first race in 1918 until his own death in 1960. When out of office, he attended the legislative sessions and traveled the state, mending fences and maintaining relationships. Over the years he built a loose network of friends and supporters and gathered additional strength through the prevailing ticket system, in which candidates for governor ran with a full slate for all state offices and frequently endorsed candidates for the legislature and some parish offices. Many officials, particularly in the rural parishes, were longtime incumbents as sheriff, tax assessor, and clerk of court with whom Earl had personal relationships dating back many years, and these courthouse gangs were usually receptive to him. Most sheriffs backed him in gubernatorial elections because the keystone of his Home Rule policy of noninterference with local affairs was that state police operations would be restricted to highway patrol and traffic enforcement and cooperation with local authorities on serious criminal matters where troopers could help. Those matters did not include gambling, and state police would not be sent on raids. This allowed those sheriffs, particularly in South Louisiana, who permitted gambling to regulate it and levy their own "taxes" on it. When a ministerial group called on him to shut down gambling, and the New Orleans *Times-Picayune* called on him to do his duty, he sent troopers to crack down but denounced the newspaper for publishing racing cards and results at the same time that it crusaded against gambling. "The *Picayune's* running two pages daily on horse race results and news," he said. "It's like handing a drink to an alcoholic."[43]

Long liked to say that "all you got to do is know where a man itches. Then, when you scratch him, you've got him." One of his minions said "that's the kind of thing Earl's good at—knowing every local politician in the state and remembering where he itches."[44] "Earl is not an expensive campaigner," Opotowsky wrote. "One of his opponents has said 'he can do more with $1,000 than most candidates can do with $10,000 because he knows where to go and who to talk to and how to spend it."[45] Huey said, "You give Earl a few thousand dollars and turn him loose on the road and he will make more contacts and better contacts than any ten men with a barrel of money."[46]

Bill Dodd probably put it best when he said that Earl enjoyed support from many local officials, but, unlike Huey, he did not control them. A man who was with him in one election might be against him in another. "It was kind of like the old feudal system," Dodd said. "Earl Long was the top lord and he had the ability of bringing all the lesser lords into his camp, but they remained independent in their own areas."[47]

Dupre Litton said of Earl that "he never stopped politicking. He was in Baton Rouge every day of every legislative session. Nary a day passed that he was not contacting people throughout every area of the state. He often told me that he could politic eighteen hours every day and that 'I'm politicking when my opponents are sleeping.'"[48]

As he girded for battle in the congressional campaign, Earl Long labored under several handicaps. In the races for governor he had jobs, board appointments, and contracts to dispense, and raising money was not a problem. In the congressional race, many former contributors failed to respond. He also lacked the base of support from courthouse officials in the eight parishes that he received for many of his statewide races. Other supporters thought that this race was a forlorn hope and either sat it out or backed one of his opponents; some indicated that they had wanted Speedy to run with Earl's support. They thought that the old war horse was on his last legs—tired, worn-out, and in bad health—and that he should have retired, something that he was just not capable of doing.

He lamented that politicians whom he had befriended and in some cases whose careers he had sponsored failed to come to his aid. One of those was Public Service Commissioner John J. McKeithen, who was a freshman house member in 1948 when Long made him one of his floor leaders. In 1952, Long put McKeithen on the Spaht ticket for lieutenant governor; unsuccessful there, he was elected to the Public Service Commission with Long's support. McKeithen, a few years after Long died, said that he had not helped because Long had "run me off" after taking office in 1956. He claimed that Long had become impossible to deal with and had driven many friends away. State Representative W. K. Brown said that was not true. "He had no ill feelings toward anyone," Brown said. "Oh, he'd get mad at you and say things to you, but he'd call you up a few days later and apologize."[49]

For his road show, Long had at his side loyal men who had stood by him in prior campaigns and were not going to desert him now. They had other jobs or businesses, hauling gravel and taking care of farms, cattle, and properties for themselves and others, but when called on they responded. The sound truck drivers, from the Alexandria area, were the Ellington brothers, Ray and Jack, and Jimmie "Red" Harkins. Ray Ellington said at a 1998 symposium on Long's career that "I never told this story to anyone. He said, 'Ray, I'm going to run for that congressional seat and I'm going to beat that fella. I don't care if I die the next day I'm going to beat him.' He had the strangest look in his eye when he said that—when he said 'I don't care if I die the next day.'"[50]

Edgar Coco, former mayor of Marksville, and C. J. "Bobby" Dugas were part of the campaign show. Dugas was an outstanding athlete at LSU and owned and edited a weekly newspaper in Donaldsonville. He held appointive positions in both of Long's four-year administrations and was the Noe-Long candidate for state comptroller in 1959. A popular man with a rich fund of stories, he was a warm-up speaker at many of the meetings.[51]

Coco told Cajun stories to the stump crowd while they waited for Long to arrive from the prior stop. He played the harmonica and when Long got there played "In the Garden" and "The Old Rugged Cross" while Long sang along. Coco, whom Long appointed chairman of the Insurance Rating Commission, owned an insurance agency and real estate business in Marksville in addition to serving as mayor of the town.[52]

J. W. Thompson and his Country-Cousin Band provided entertainment for the primary and runoff campaigns. Long hired it for the duration because it was popular in the area, with a television show on the Alexandria station and many engagements for functions in the district. Their guitar player was Kenny Gill, who later played with Jimmie Davis and went on to country music fame.[53]

The Thompson band played country and gospel music, and Long hired Jay Chevalier to play guitar and sing rockabilly. Chevalier, a country singer living near Alexandria, wrote and sang "The Ballad of Earl K. Long" when the governor was released from Southeast Louisiana Hospital and embarked on his vacation trip. One verse went "Clap yo' hands, sing yo' song, Just a little story 'bout Earl K. Long. He's drivin' aroun' in a big limousine, And everywhere he goes there's a great big scene." Chevalier, age twenty-three, said one hundred thousand 45 rpm records were pressed, and he had visions of fame. Determining that "I had to get close to the Governor some kind of way" when Long began campaigning for lieutenant governor with Noe, Chevalier caught up with him at a stump speech in Bossier City.

Chevalier was on the platform, singing his ballad, when Long drove up, listened for a while, and called him over. Chevalier played at seven stump talks that day, and when they finished, Long told Edgar Coco to negotiate a salary for Chevalier to travel with them. When Coco told Long that the singer wanted $500 a week, Long snorted that "the son of a bitch thinks he's Elvis." Long gave him two tickets to an LSU football game and an overnight stay at the mansion and ended up paying him $200 a week and all he could eat.[54]

Chevalier had been seeking gigs out of state when he decided to come home. He said that he had crossed the state line when he heard a news broadcast on his car radio. "It said Earl K. Long has announced for Congress in the Eighth District," he recalled. "I said 'Thank you Lord, I'm going to get me a job campaigning with Uncle Earl again.'"[55]

Long's traveling companions had rich funds of stories about him, some of which were highlights of a 1998 symposium titled The Life and Political Career of Earl K. Long by the People Who Knew Him at Louisiana College in Pineville. Chevalier told of going to Leesville when Long told his driver to stop at a house along a rural road. The lady there served them coffee and Long asked about a chicken and its chicks in the yard, telling her that he had been looking for a hen just like that for the Pea Patch. The woman's husband told him to take the hen and chicks as a gift, but Long insisted on paying seven dollars for them. A few miles down the road, Long said to stop again, and the woman there brought out coffee. Long then showed her the hen and chicks in the trunk of his car and said that he had brought them from the Pea Patch as a gift to her. "He had 150 votes right there for $7.00," Chevalier said, because "the family he bought the chicken from would tell everyone in their family, and the family he brought the chicken to would do the same thing."[56]

"Earl's campaign was like a sideshow coming to town, with music, sound trucks, speakers, free gifts," a participant said.[57] On this campaign swing, Long had other speakers with him, including Bill Dodd, Joe Arthur Sims, and State Representative W. K. Brown. With five, six, and even eight stump speeches over one day, he used a "team approach" for the outing. Robert Gentry wrote that the campaign was "the end of one era and the beginning of another in the way that political campaigns were being conducted. Politicians reached the people by going from town to town and speaking. This was accomplished by the use of sound trucks. They were station wagons with two big speaker horns mounted on the roof and an amplifier with a turntable inside the vehicle. Uncle Earl had two or three sound trucks. One would come into town and go throughout it announcing that Earl Long was going to be speaking. When the sound truck driver got finished drumming up a crowd, he would go to the appointed place, plug his system into somebody's electricity, and start playing a record on the sound system. He would also find somebody's old pickup for Uncle Earl to use as a podium, set up the microphone, and get ready to start the program."

Gentry recalled, "There was a band to get the program off. They would perform about 15–20 minutes. Then the speakers would start. Uncle Earl carried from one to six or seven different speakers. It was their job to tell the crowd what a good guy Uncle Earl was and get them warmed up for the main event. But without question, Uncle Earl was the main attraction. He knew it and everybody else did. Many times he was late for the meetings, but the crowd normally always waited for him. As all this was happening, the second sound truck was in another town getting all set up for the next stop. It was like a traveling road show and there was never any want for excitement and things that were entertaining."[58] In his statewide campaigns, Long bought the station wagons new from dealers, painted them for the campaign, and after the election repainted them and sold them back to the dealers or to other buyers.[59]

Once Long arrived at a meeting and took the microphone, the other speakers would move on to the next stop. Long would arrive when the advance team of speakers was winding up, and they would move on while he spoke. He would stay for a few minutes afterward, shaking hands, handing out cakes to ladies and giving coins to kids, and at the bigger meetings, holding drawings for hams, slabs of bacon, sacks of flour, buckets of lard, and boxes of groceries. There were usually soft drinks, candies for children, and combs for women that were imprinted "Gift for Ladies 8th District from Uncle Earl."[60]

A member of the campaign caravan said Earl's campaign stops featured lots of giveaways. "He'd give away buckets of lard, loaves of bread, and hams. He'd have peppermint sticks for the kids. He always had a pocket full of quarters and loved to see the kids gather around him as he threw a handful out and watched the kids scramble for them. But the way we had done things was all changing. Television was taking over as a way to campaign. And unfortunately, Uncle Earl looked terrible on TV and came across even worse. It was the days just prior to the political consultants taking over."[61]

Easy Money Littleton said that Long would tell him to stop at a bank and give him two or three one hundred dollar bills to buy rolls of quarters. Long would unwrap them in the car and dump them in a wooden water bucket. When they got to a meeting, he would take a big handful of quarters out of the bucket and fill his pants pocket with them. If necessary, he would send Littleton back for more. On other occasions, he would fill the bucket with nickels, dimes, and quarters and an occasional half-dollar. Littleton said that at the bigger meetings, "After he spoke he'd look at me and say, 'Get the bucket.' He would take his hands like this, like you were feeding chickens," and throw the coins to kids.[62]

Joe Arthur Sims, Long's attorney, introduced him at most meetings. Sims had represented Long when he orchestrated his release from confinement at Southeast Louisiana Hospital. He was born in Shreveport in 1914 but the family moved to Hammond, where his father served as principal of Hammond High School and worked to establish the Hammond Junior College that later became Southeastern Louisiana University. Sims was a law partner of Congressman James H. "Jimmy" Morrison of the Sixth District. He served as district attorney for the Twenty-First Judicial District from 1948 to 1952 and was the unsuccessful candidate for attorney general on the Long ticket headed by Carlos Spaht in 1952. A big, impressive man, he was an old-style stump speaker, close to being Earl's equal in flailing political enemies.[63]

Robert Gentry, a student at Northwestern State College in Natchitoches, became Long's p.r. man in the campaign, writing press releases and filing stories that weeklies published under his byline. He was working part-time for the Natchitoches *Enterprise*. Each weekend he would hitchhike home to Marthaville and back to Natchitoches. One weekend, he went with his father to hear Uncle Earl speak at Spanish Lake on a Sunday afternoon. Long drove up in a "beautiful new white Buick" with only a driver. When Gentry saw that the next stump speech in Cloutierville would take him through Natchitoches, he told his father that it would be a big help if he could catch a ride with Long to Natchitoches. His father asked Dick Davis, who said they would be happy to have the boy ride with them. With Uncle Earl and Davis in the front seat, Gentry rode in the back. He said they were very cordial in asking questions about him and his plans in life.[64]

Long was always telling his drivers to go faster and to pass cars regardless of the road conditions. Davis was driving them from Olla to Winnfield when Long complained about how bad the road was. "Earl, you shouldn't complain," Davis said, "you built it."[65]

Long was hungry when they got to Natchitoches and told Davis to stop at Grappe's Grocery, on Washington Street. He sent Davis in for sardines, Vienna Sausages, cheese, crackers, an onion, and Cokes. Dick brought him the food and went back in to use the restroom. Long spread a newspaper on his lap, took out his pocket knife, and prepared to eat. He turned to Gentry and said, "Let's go." Gentry slid behind the wheel and asked where, and Long said to the next speech, at Cloutierville. When Gentry asked about Davis, "Uncle Earl responded with some 'F' word that I had never heard before."[66]

As Gentry drove Long along historic Front Street in Natchitoches, "by then, Uncle Earl had sliced up the onion, opened the cheese and crackers, emptied the sardines out onto the newspaper in his lap, and tossed the empty can out the car window. He reached under the front seat, fumbled around a minute, and pulled out an old glass, opened his Coke and poured it into the glass." They got on Highway 1, behind a slow-moving car, and Long bellowed, "Pass him." There was another car coming toward them, and Gentry said he could not pass. "If you can't pass 'em on the left, pass 'em on the right," Long instructed. "In those days," Gentry recalled, "if there were any shoulders on the highways they were narrow and were not hard-surfaced. It had been a dry spring that year, so in a cloud of red dirt and flying gravel, I followed Uncle Earl's directions as I passed on the right. I glanced briefly in the rearview mirror and we looked like a West Texas dust storm coming down the road. As I passed the other car, I looked over at the driver and could see an utter look of disbelief and fear on her face. I often wonder if she voted for Uncle Earl in that election."[67]

After the talk in Cloutierville, they headed for Campti. A state trooper soon pulled them over, and an outraged Dick Davis got out of the police car. He ordered Gentry into the back seat, and as they pulled off, "he and Uncle Earl then engaged in a rather heated discussion, or as we called it in the country around Marthaville, a 'cuss fight.' But when each had their say, everything was okay between them." They went back through Natchitoches to Campti, and on Front Street, again, Gentry saw Long bend over doing something in the front seat. Gentry raised up to get a view and saw that "he had reached under the seat, gotten his glass, and was relieving himself into it," after which he poured the contents of the glass out the window.[68]

Long apparently had to urinate frequently after his prostate surgery, and he did so in the car and behind buildings at their stops if a restroom was not immediately available. Gentry said that after a speech in Marthaville, he relieved himself in a telephone booth in front of the Rains Store. On another occasion, they stopped at the Asseff Store in Pleasant Hill to buy some things. Dick Davis told Asseff to unlock the back door so Long could pee, but Asseff was busy selling. All at once Long started unzipping his pants. "Don't pee on my floor," Asseff cried as he headed to the back to open up, with Long behind him, "wetting all over the floor." Davis told Asseff, "It's too late to get it open. You were too busy trying to make a dollar and I tried to tell you."[69]

Gentry said that the trips between speakings were always interesting. Uncle Earl bought watermelons and peas at roadside stands, gave them away at the next stops, and put a bunch of peaches in an ice chest of Cokes in the back seat to chill them. "He loved to stop on the side of the road and buy peaches," Gentry recalled. He knew many of the people at farm houses and stopped to visit and give them gifts. On a Saturday morning in Marthaville, they stopped at Lawrence Crumps's farm. They drove up to the chicken houses, blew the horn to scare the chickens, and grabbed a bunch of them. Long paid for the chickens, tied their feet, and put them in the trunk. He stopped to give them away further along the road.[70]

Gentry said that Long often took naps between stops. If he was hungry and the cookies, fresh peaches, and watermelons in the car were not enough, they would stop at small cafes for country cooking and the buttermilk Long loved. Gentry said "he had a habit of grunting. It was usually three short grunts in succession, over and over and over." He also "wore false teeth and would often take them out and put them in his back pants pockets after he finished speaking. If he got food under them, he would sometimes take them out of his mouth wherever he was and lick the excess food off with his tongue. Sometimes he would take his big red bandana and wipe the food off. Campaigning in the heat, he wore loose-fitting dress pants, a short-sleeve white shirt, a tie, suspenders, and a straw hat."[71]

After a heavy rain on a late Saturday afternoon, Long told Gentry to stop when he saw a dog by the side of the road. The dog was wet and smelly, but Long recognized it as a Catahoula Cur, the breed he loved, and wanted it. He put the dog in the backseat, saying it was "one of the finest dogs I've ever seen."[72] On another occasion, on the way to Mansura, they stopped at a rural bar to play pool. Robert Gentry said that running late was no problem because "people always waited on him no matter how late he might be."[73]

In Campti, Red Harkins, one of the sound truck drivers, was having problems with the sound system when Long climbed onto the back of the pickup truck to speak: "It made Uncle Earl mad and he again started cussing. Just as he started into his rage, Red got the sound system going as Uncle Earl's words floated to the ears of the crowd of 200 and into the dark of night." Long regained his composure and made his speech. Dick Davis told him afterward, "Earl, you really showed your ass here tonight and you know we have that newspaperman here" with us, referring to Gentry. "He's probably gonna write bad things about you. What are you gonna do about it?" Without hesitation, Long called for Gentry, telling him, "I need somebody to be my press man during this campaign. I can't pay you a lot but I want you to work for me. I'll pay you a hundred dollars a week. Will you take the job?"[74]

Recalling the scene many years later, Gentry said that he was thrilled by the offer of "$100 for a part time job while I was working my way through college. It was a God send. But the greatest thing was the wonderful and exciting journey I knew I was embarking on. Shoot, I really would have worked for nothing. And thus began my days with Uncle Earl."[75]

Gentry recalled what Long did after speaking in front of Law's Drug Store in Marthaville. He "sat on the sidewalk, pulled his Barlow knife from his pants pocket, took off his brand new shoes, and cut some slits in them because they were hurting his feet."[76]

Working for Long was an adventure, Gentry recalled. He said that they got to Winnfield late on a Saturday night in July,

> We got to bed about midnight and I had hopes of sleeping late on Sunday morning since the first speaking was not until noon in Avoyelles Parish. And I had hopes of avoiding him. About 7:00 a.m. Sunday I was busy sleeping when I was abruptly awakened by one of the hired hands at the Pea Patch. "Wake up, Mr. Earl wants you," he excitedly told me. Hastily I got up, put on my clothes, and hurried to find him. I found Uncle Earl in the back yard, clad in an undershirt, boxer shorts, and rubber boots, no false teeth, and holding a Lucky Strike between his fingers, with a water hose, washing his pickup truck. He was a sight to behold. I spent the rest of the morning washing his

> truck, collecting rotten water melons from his big patch to feed to his hogs, and separating young calves from their mamas. By noon I was near the point of collapse and the day's campaigning had not yet started. Uncle Earl enjoyed every minute of it and was ready to go on to the next adventure. His energy seemed boundless. But he was burning the candle at both ends.[77]

Earl's car served as the campaign's headquarters. Easy Money Littleton said that the back seat of the Buick usually had cheese, crackers, and cans of Vienna sausages, and sometimes candy bars, "although Mr. Earl was not big on sweets." Littleton said that he loved fresh fruit, especially the sweet peaches grown in Ruston. "We had a washtub on the floorboards," Littleton reminisced, "and I iced down in it Cokes and the Red Pop that Mr. Earl liked. We kept a bottle of whiskey in it, and when he wanted a drink I would fix it for him. Sometimes he took a small drink, no more than maybe one ounce, straight, to clear his throat, but on other times I would take a bottle of Coke, drink it half-down, fill it with Bourbon or whatever we had, and then Mr. Earl could step out of the car with it in hand and no one would see that he was having a drink." Littleton said that happened only at one or two of the meetings, when they were holding six or seven daily, and Long took a drink only "for a little pick-me-up." Littleton said that in the summer heat, Long would wind up drenched with sweat at the stump talks. He said that in between stops they ran the auto air conditioner at full blast, and he worried that Long would get a bad cold.[78]

"I remember that it was very hot that summer," Robert Gentry said. "In the beginning, Uncle Earl only spoke to Saturdays and Sundays. Sometimes he spoke at as many as seven different places a day and into the night. As the election got closer, he started speaking on Thursday and Friday nights. It was a grueling pace for an old man who was in terrible health. After his heart attack in 1950 he quit smoking but started again when he had so many problems in 1959. He smoked Lucky Strikes, and it seemed he always had one in his hand. I always heard about Uncle Earl drinking, but during the time I was with him I only saw him take one drink of whiskey."[79]

"Uncle Earl liked to call himself 'The Last of the Red-Hot Papas,'" Gentry reminisced, "and he would add, 'When I'm gone there won't be any more.' And he was right. He was one of a kind. If he wasn't the most colorful figure in Louisiana politics, he ranked near the head of the class. He was legendary. He was flamboyant."[80]

Gentry said that Long loved music, particularly popular songs of the day like "Bill Bailey Won't You Please Come Home" and "Kansas City." "He loved ragtime piano music and I bought him the latest album issued that summer by Del Wood, titled 'Hot, Happy, and Honkey,' and the sound truck man played it at every stop. But Uncle Earl loved Gospel music most. His favorite hymn was 'In the Garden.' We had a version by Tennessee Ernie Ford which was played at every stop. Folks in the rural areas loved gospel singing and we always gave them a good dose of it. I can remember at a speaking in Natchitoches on a hot Saturday afternoon. Uncle Earl ambled up to the microphone unannounced while J. W. Thompson and his band were performing, and in his gravelly voice he belted out a few songs with them. He was in his prime and the audience loved it, even though Uncle Earl could not sing very well. For his part of the singing, Uncle Earl asked the boys to close out with 'In the Garden' and he sang along."[81]

While Long discussed the issues and flailed his opponents, he also told some of his stories to the country people. One of his favorites was about an old Baptist woman who had prayed for years that her wayward son would be saved. Finally her prayers paid off and he *was* saved. She was happy when his baptizing day came. The preacher led him out into the pond and immersed him, to the delight of his dear old mother. Out from his pocket came floating the 10 of diamonds, then the Jack of diamonds. His mother cried, "He's lost, he's lost!" Then out came the Queen of diamonds. His mother cried again, "He's lost, he's lost!" Then the King of diamonds floated out, followed by the Ace of diamonds. His mother raised her eyes toward heaven, tears streaming, and sobbed again, "He's lost, he's lost!" The preacher man looked at that Royal Flush floating down the creek and said, "Sister Smith, he ain't lost. If he can't win with a hand like that, he can't win at all."[82]

Robert Gentry said that Long gave away quarters to kids, pails of Cudahy's Lard from Shreveport, and Holsum Bread from the Cotton Baking Company in Alexandria, as well held drawings for hams, sides of bacon, and watermelons. He said that at their stops, after he spoke and mixed with the crowd, they always backed the car up to where he was, whether by the platform or across the street visiting a store owner, "so he could get in and we could immediately leave. He never liked to wait."[83]

Returning to the stump on Friday, June 17, Long spoke in Pollock, in Grant Parish, at 4:30 p.m.; Tullos, in LaSalle Parish, at 6:15 p.m.; Georgetown, in Grant Parish, at 7:15 p.m.; and Olla, in LaSalle Parish, at 8:10 p.m. On Saturday, June 18, his schedule was Jena, in LaSalle Parish, at 10:00 a.m.; Colfax, in Grant Parish, at 11:30 a.m.; Natchitoches, in Natchitoches Parish, at 1:30 p.m.; Zwolle, in Sabine Parish, at 3:45 p.m.; Converse, in Sabine Parish, at 5:15 p.m.; and Clarence, in Natchitoches Parish, at 7:30 p.m. On Sunday, June 19, the meeting was for 7:30 p.m. at Marksville, in Avoyelles Parish.

Handbills announcing the events said that speakers with Long would be Joe Arthur Sims; the former state senator and former president of Northwestern State College, A. A. Fredericks; F. E. Cole, former senator and current member of the State Board of Education for the Eighth District; and Representative Willard Rambo of Grant Parish. The announcement said, "Everyone invited. Nothing said to offend anyone. You owe it to yourself, your state and your community to be informed as to who is the best qualified man to fill all offices. We're making a vigorous campaign. We especially invite ladies and young people." Long announced that at Clarence, "free drinks, candy, souvenirs, hams, groceries and bacon will be given away at this meeting only, furnished by friends of the Clarence community."[84]

In his talk before a crowd of two hundred at Zwolle on June 18, Long said that he knew more about the district than Holt or McSween. "I love these hills," he roared, "and I love these forests." He proposed that some of the five hundred thousand acres of Kisatchie National Forest be opened for homesteading. "Let the people own their own homes, have children and be happy," he said. "Then we won't have to worry too much about Communism." Noting the large turnout, he said, "This shows intelligence and an interest on your part. There are a lot of good Spanish, hillbillies, Baptists, and so on here. You all understand each other and get along good together."[85]

The Natchitoches *Enterprise* said Long was "subdued" when he spoke there on June 18. Joe Arthur Sims, leading off, "painted a picture of Long confined in a cell-like room with barred windows, without furniture except for one straight chair, deprived of radio, TV, newspapers or cold water, afraid to eat for fear of being drugged, finally being forcibly drugged." Sims claimed that "this was done because of the theory of government that Earl K. Long has—he helped the poor." He said that "big corporate interests" and newspapers like the *Times-Picayune* and the *Daily Town Talk* were behind Long's confinement. Sims said there was not a word of truth in what they printed about Long's western trip, "that he was half the time drunk and the other half with strippers."[86]

Sims assailed Holt as a turncoat who had betrayed Long. He said Long "elected that boy representative in 1956, and got him five attorney fees any one of which would support him and his family. Governor Long fed that boy and his family for four years."[87]

Long spoke from the bed of a pickup truck under a landmark live oak tree on Second Street. The news story said that as a trio of musicians played, he arrived "with Marthaville journalist Robert Gentry in the back seat." Long "remained seated in the car for some moments, his appearance indicating the truth of a Sims statement that he had left a New Orleans hospital after recent surgery about a week or ten days too soon. He moved uncomfortably as if bothered by abdominal pain and his breathing was short and hard. However, his face was tanned and unmarked by fatigue, and after the speaking was over, while he was still sitting in the truck bed in a chair borrowed from New Drug, he looked approvingly at the milling crowd in the hot sunshine, sighed contentedly and murmured 'This is fun, isn't it?'"[88]

He told one crowd, "If they ever stop that big mouth of mine, I'd be in a fix, because you know the newspapers won't say anything good about me."[89] He told another, "They say I'm worn out, but I've got some snap left, and some in my garters, too."[90]

Long denounced "Catfish mouth McSween," saying he represented the "wealthy people" and voted in Congress with Republicans more than Democrats. Proclaiming himself "a jillion per cent for segregation," up from a million at one stop and a billion at another, he said, "Let them have their good churches, their good schools, let them have their women." He assailed "that damn Rainach" for trying to set the races against each other, belittled "storytelling, baldheaded Morrison" in New Orleans, accused Ben Holt of stabbing him in the back, and discussed his platform with the reporter afterward. Long said that the old age pensions he provided made the difference between life and death for some small towns and stopped people from having to move to the city: "They can live in their own home, have a few trees around them, a dog and a cat, a few chickens. That's a better life than living in a city out of a tin can. It's healthier. It's healthier for the country, too. They don't want cities now of over half a million. With the atom bomb, too much damage can be done when a really big city is hit."[91]

In another speech, he proclaimed, "I'm one million per cent for segregation, but I want the colored people to be happy. But that don't mean we have to shack up with 'em."[92] He told audiences, "I want the nigger vote and I don't make any secret about it. I tell 'em I want it. And I get it, because them colored people know I've tried to help 'em."[93]

In Marthaville on Sunday night, June 19, the Earl Long campaign set up shop at the courthouse square with Joe Arthur Sims bellowing an introduction, sound truck drivers distributing raffle tickets for hams and boxes of groceries, and a band playing country music. Sims thundered that "Earl Long never took a crooked dollar" and ridiculed Holt's stories about stripteasers. "If a stripteaser came down here now, I'd leave the microphone and take a look at her," Sims said. After Long spoke, Dick Davis presided over drawings for groceries, bacon, hams, and buckets of lard.[94]

Scheduled to speak at Colfax at 11:45 a.m., Long did not get there until 1:45 p.m. By that time, the crowd that had gathered had melted away. He went into a crowded cafe, shook hands all around, enjoyed a meal of gumbo, buttermilk, and beer, and on leaving paid the checks of all the patrons.[95]

Another four-day stumping tour began on Thursday, June 23, and ended on Sunday, June 26. He spoke in Calvin, Dodson, Sikes, and Urania on Thursday; Flatwoods, Simpson, and Bentley on Friday; Florien, Leesville, and Pitkin on Saturday; and Ajax, Powhatan, Campti, and Flora on Sunday.[96] Many of the places where he spoke were just crossroads with a store or gas station and villages of as few as one or two hundred people, but people came from the surrounding area, and their cars and trucks lined the roads.

Going after the incumbent McSween, Long sneered, "If ever there was a full-fledged faker and anointed jackass it is Harold McSween, and if you'll help me we'll put him back on the 23rd of July where the little sapsucker belongs." Sims said that McSween was "the only man who can talk out of both sides of his mouth, whistle, smoke a cigar, and hold his hand out the back door for a payoff at the same time."[97]

In his Natchitoches Parish meetings at Powhatan, Campti, and Flora, Long thundered, "I know you and you know me. Do you know of anything I've ever done to hurt you? I'd rather have the warmth of your hearts than all the money in the world, because if I go where I want to go I won't need any money." He said he knew what it was like to be both poor and hardworking: "I drove a bakery wagon for two bits a day. I stacked staves for fifty cents a day. I scaled logs in a sawmill from six to six. I got my law degree by working in the day and going to school at night."[98]

On Thursday, June 30, Long spoke at Goldonna at 6:45 p.m. and Ashland at 7:50 p.m. His ads for the rallies proclaimed "Uncle Earl's The Man" and featured a photograph of him at a microphone, arm outstretched: "Earl Long is loaded with free groceries at Ashland and important information about the race for Congress. Free public drawing for baskets of groceries, lard, hams donated by local well-wishers . . . candy for the children."[99]

Robert Gentry filed a story with the Natchitoches *Enterprise* that said "Earl K. Long's free hams, sides of bacon, buckets of lard, boxes of groceries, and a hillbilly band brought an estimated 200 people" to the rally. Long said he had always fought the "big shots" and thought a congressman should have a little bit of knowledge about everything, including "strip teasers, crap shooting, whiskey drinking, horse trading, timber growing, and flood control. You've heard that Ole Earl is a whiskey head. Nothing could be further from the truth. I despise whiskey. I haven't had enough whiskey to make me stagger since I was 19 years old. No one can truthfully say that they ever saw me drunk."[100]

Long pledged support for the Rural Electrification Administration, saying the "REA has done more to end drudgery and bring light to the poor people than anything else in the country." He said that the very first vote McSween cast as a congressman was against the REA, "yet he had the nerve to speak at the annual meeting of the REA in Natchitoches last Saturday." He also assailed McSween for voting against the $1.15 minimum wage bill.[101] He denounced the congressman as "a genuine, number one, 18-carat smart aleck." McSween may tell voters that Uncle Earl was "crazy," he chuckled, but "being crazy is a matter of opinion. I'm not crazy enough to hand out government checks" from his office that Long claimed went to "deadheads."[102]

With J. W. Thompson and his Country-Cousin Band preceding him, Long spoke in Lena, Flatwoods, Glenmora, and Pineville on Friday, July 8; Zwolle, Pleasant Hill, Provencal, Campti, Tullos, Jena, and Simms on Saturday, July 9; and Cottonport, Plaucheville, Simmesport, and Mansura on Sunday, July 10.[103]

In Provencal, Long charged that McSween had voted against the REA because "he is on the payroll of the Electric Bond and Share Company. He's not your kind. He was born with a silver spoon in his mouth and you couldn't twist it out with a crowbar or a corkscrew." In Campti he railed, "They say I'm a scoundrel, a turncoat, and a rascal. They can't prove it. I can look everyone in the eye and say that I am guilty of no wrongdoing. When the great score is written I don't think they will write whether you won or lost but how you played the game."[104]

He made four stops in Rapides Parish on Friday, July 1: at Gardner at 5:15 p.m., Hot Wells at 6:00, Wardville at 7:15, and Deville at 8:00. There were seven stops on Saturday, July 2, at Verda, Dry Prong, Pollock, Boyce, Lecompte, Montgomery, and Winnfield. Sunday, July 3, was spent in Avoyelles Parish, with rallies at Dupont, Plaucheville, Moreauville, Hamburg, Moncla, and Bordelonville.[105]

While Earl Long was burning up the roads during June, McSween did not issue his formal statement of candidacy until the end of that month. He promised "not to deal in personalities" and said he was running on his record of opposition to foreign aid, extravagant federal programs, and "vicious anti-South" civil rights proposals that he had testified against before the House and Senate Judiciary Committees. He criticized "recent mob demonstrations by racial agitators."[106] Starting his campaign late, McSween kicked off with ten stump speeches, in Pitkin, Leesville, Many, Zwolle, Converse, Pleasant Hill, Marthaville, Robeline, Provencal, and Cloutierville.[107]

Ben Holt issued his formal statement of candidacy after McSween, citing the need for stronger representation to develop the district's potential.[108] Campaigning on the slogan "Win with Ben," Holt said that he was "running my campaign for Congress on the merits of my ability, not the demerits of either of my opponents." He invited people to come for a "political meeting-Speaking-Hand Shaking" at Goldonna, Campti,

Robeline, and Provencal on July 1 and at Natchez, Natchitoches, Powhatan, Cypress, Melrose, and Gorum on July 2.[109]

Long took off on July 6 to visit the legislature, strolling into the house chamber while it was in recess, talking to reporters and chatting with Negro janitors as they cleaned up. He said that he had just visited with Governor Davis, who, he said, "told me he could tell my health is better just by looking at me. But, then," Long said, "you don't tell a dead man he's looking bad, do you?"[110]

Long distributed a circular at rallies and also did mail outs. In one datelined at Winnfield, July 8, 1960, from "EARL K. LONG: Farmer—Stock Raiser—Timber Grower—Former Traveling Salesman—Attorney—Former Lt. Governor—Former Governor," he reviewed his qualifications and outlined his platform. "Surely you know, I am more or less the father of the old age pension, the free tablets, pencils and free buses, the free school lunch program, schools for spastics, the fine school at Chambers, the new bridge at Alexandria, better pay for teachers, improvements in our state hospitals, a helper and a continuous builder of the charity hospital system." He wrote that

> I wish to thank you for the privilege of serving you so long, and the opportunity to do the things that I thought fair, just, right and proper. As I now bow, and have bowed out of the Governor's Office, and am fast drawing to the inevitable, it is a consoling thought to know that with the help of Almighty God and you, I have had the chance to help my fellow human beings. I have made mistakes, I readily admit, and I say to you, humbly, I think I have helped to accomplish much to make the lives of many people more pleasant and more livable. Therefore, as I have said before, this is the consoling thought which I can take to the Great Beyond, with me—I would rather have the respect of all the people, especially the fine Christian women, rich or poor, white or colored, than to be the richest man in Louisiana.[111]

Addressing the "good women of this state" in a postscript, he said,

> I have appointed more women and given more recognition to what women can do in public life that all the other governors put together. For instance: I appointed Mrs. Mary Evelyn Parker as Welfare Director; Mrs. Wilma Lockhart as my Secretary, then transferred her as a member of the Tax

> Commission; Miss Esther Walder as my Secretary, and countless other fine women to just about every commission and department of state, too numerous to name. I have shown my confidence in them in public life and am happy to report that they have made good in every instance. I further want the ladies to know that I have never been drunk, regardless of what they hear. I drink very little whiskey and I have been and will continue to be honorable, honest and straightforward so that our good women need never have to apologize that they supported a great rascal when they helped Uncle Earl. Thanks.[112]

Back on the stump on Saturday, July 9, Long spoke in Zwolle, Pleasant Hill, Provencal, Campti, Tullos, Jena, and Simms. On Sunday, July 10, he addressed gatherings at Cottonport, Plaucheville, Simmesport, and Mansura.[113]

The *Daily Town Talk* reported that Long "kept his audience waiting 60 minutes in Glenmora but promises of good old hams, sides of bacon and greens, held the crowd until the ex-Governor was through speaking. Long, obviously weak, spoke only five minutes and then called for a chair so he could sit while shaking hands. When Long finished a seven-minute speech in Pineville, he invited 'rich, poor, colored or what not come up here and let me shake your hand.'"[114]

Ben Holt scheduled rallies at Ajax, Clarence, and Bermuda, with "special music and entertainment by Al Ferrier and The Vamps" on Sunday, July 17, and a parishwide rally at the Natchitoches Parish Fair Grounds on the evening of Tuesday, July 19, featuring "Free Bar-B-Que and Cold Drinks." His local supporters made the mistake of holding the barbecue at the same time as a Baptist revival on the riverbank, and when Holt's function started there were only 144 people in the stands "plus a small handful of colored in the opposite stands." When he finished speaking, there were only 171, although a reporter said more were waiting for the food to materialize. A police officer said there were 750 attendees and a Holt supporter said they served 900 sandwiches.[115]

Holt said he was running on his own merits and not the demerits of his two opponents, but he proceeded to say that Long was "a sick man who couldn't do anything for the people of the Eighth District no matter how much he wanted to." He said he told Long two days before he led adjournment of the special session that legislators were against it but Long "wouldn't listen because he was a sick man and didn't know what he was doing"[116] and Long responded that Holt "took a run-out on me while I was sick."[117] Holt also said McSween was an ineffective congressman, during whose tenure "not fifty cents has been spent on Red River toward correcting your problems and not a single project started of any benefit" to the district.[118]

Holt's speaking schedule was no match for Long's. His ads and handbills said that "some of the finest music and singing in the state will be heard at these meetings on Friday, Saturday, and Sunday. If you appreciate good music and good speaking, too, be sure to attend our meetings where you will hear intelligent discussion of the issues."[119]

Earl Long's next campaign swing started on Thursday, July 14, with afternoon and evening rallies at Cheneyville, Fairview-Alpha, and Mitchell. His schedule on Friday, July 15, began at 2:40 p.m. at Montgomery in Grant Parish and ended at 7:30 at Pitkin in Vernon Parish, with stops in between at Marthaville in Natchitoches, Rosepine and Anacoco in Vernon, and Gum in Rapides. "Best Musicians, Hillbilly Band, Good Singing, Piano Playing" and speeches were promised for Saturday, July 16, at Leesville, Many, Natchitoches, Evergreen, Bunkie, and Alexandria. Sunday's schedule began at 10:10 a.m. in Cloutierville and ended at 7:45 p.m. in Marksville, with stops at Echo, Dupont, Goudeau, Cottonport, and Moreauville." There were prizes, hams, bacon, and in Marksville "music, entertainment, street dancing, candy, cold drinks, hams and bacon."[120] Long's schedule for Thursday, July 17, through Sunday, July 20, had twenty-two stops over those four days. Promotional materials promised "some of the finest music and singing in the state."[121]

A news story described Long "hitting the back roads and small towns in an attempt to gain his usual rural vote in the district. Long lost weight and was panting at times under the hot sun during his crossroads tour." It said that unlike McSween, he did not use television heavily, and with political broadcasts being done live, "he failed to show up for at least two television engagements and one of the stations substituted an old western movie, showing Long as the sponsor of the show."[122]

Dupre Litton said he did not believe "that any candidate for any office worked as hard and as long as did Earl did in this race." Long said he emptied his bank accounts and called on old friends and supporters for help. He had great difficulty getting contributions and told Litton, "Raising money is tough these days. The ones who used to give a thousand give a hundred, the ones who used to give a hundred give ten, and the ones who used to give ten I can't even find."[123] When former State Senator Alvin Stumpf of Gretna, in Jefferson Parish, sent him a contribution, Long responded, "I appreciate very much the assistance you sent me by mail. It will do a lot of good and if it were not for friends like you I don't know how I would have gotten through this campaign."[124]

Long contacted an old friend, George W. Woodard of the Capitol House Hotel in Baton Rouge, soliciting his help raising campaign funds. His note, intended to be read by people Woodard asked for help, said "this will introduce to you Mr. George Woodard & possibly Joe Arthur Sims, who are authorized to solicit contributions for my Eight [*sic*] District for Congress Campaign. You may rest assured any money or checks given them will reach me. I hate to ask my friends, some of them the second time. This is the most expensive small campaign I have been in. 75% of the total used up to date came from friends and me. This is more or less the 1964 Governor's race in disguise. Whether you are to contribute or not we will still be friends. Give what you think you are able to give and no more. Thanks. EARL K. LONG." On the envelope addressed to Woodard he added, "You may ask anyone else you think of. E.K.L."[125]

Long also asked Jesse Bankston—the man he'd had fired as head of the state Hospitals Department in order to win his release from Southeast Louisiana Hospital in Mandeville—for help. Bankston recalled that "he asked me to contact a list of persons he named and ask them to bring him a 'few dollars' for his campaign. He said that they would give me around a thousand dollars. I contacted each person he named and collected $1,600.00 and took it to Alexandria hoping to give the money to him but he was out campaigning." Bankston said he hated to leave the money at Long's headquarters rather than deliver it to him personally. Experience in the 1956 governor's race had taught Bankston that money left for the governor—even with family members—did not always make it to him. "One time I picked up a $100 contribution and brought it to his Baton Rouge apartment. Mr. Long was not there and I gave it to Mrs. Blanche Long. When I came in later with a contribution he asked me what I did with the last $100 contribution. I told him that I gave it to Mrs. Blanche. 'She says she did not get it,' he said. From that day I was sure to give the contributions to Mr. Long and to no one else. One morning I called and said I had a few contributions and asked if he would be there. When I got to his apartment I was told that he was dressing, but I could go in. I found him on the toilet. I told him that I wanted to give money only to him and I would do so even if it meant interrupting his morning exercise."[126]

Long went to see other former friends, including Camille Gravel. He told Gravel that he did not expect his help but hoped that for old times' sake Gravel would not do anything to injure him. Gravel had planned on supporting McSween but said he would be neutral.[127]

In full-page newspaper advertisements on July 15, Long went after McSween, demanding that he explain what his district office employees did for their paychecks. The ad reproduced a February 24, 1960, *Daily Town Talk* article listing staff salaries of the state's congressmen. Long asked, "Did you have Mr. Jack McBride drive a sound truck for $25.00 a week during your campaign for Congress (in 1958) with the understanding that if you won, he would be put on your Congressional payroll for $100 a month for part-time employment for 2 years during which time he would finish college? From a clipping reproduced at left we note that Mr. McBride is now on your Congressional payroll for $548.00 per month." The ad reproduced a check for one hundred dollars, dated October 23, 1959, payable to Jack McBride on the Noe-Long campaign account, signed by Long's secretary Esther Walder, for one week's expenses. Long said there were seven other checks to McBride for his weekly salary at his headquarters. Long asked, "Mr. McSween: Did you know that that while Mr. McBride was on your Congressional payroll and a student at Northwestern State College last fall, he also drove a sound truck for Earl K. Long during the gubernatorial campaign?" The ad claimed that three other McSween staffers, paid hundreds of dollars each month, "are not even residents of Louisiana much less the Eighth Congressional District: Is this correct or just rumor?"[128]

Another ad aimed at McSween demanded that he explain checks for $281.10 from the clerk of the US House of Representatives to Mary Helen Foster for her monthly salary as a member of his office staff. The ad reproduced an affidavit by Mrs. Foster dated April 4, 1960, stating that she was a resident of Pineville and that

> on or about July 10, 1959, she was advised by a representative of Congressman Harold B. McSween that she was being put on his payroll at a monthly

> salary of $281.10; that she was not to perform any services for Congressman McSween but was to turn over each month the proceeds of her check to the Congressman's representative; that since the first day of August, 1959, she has received a check and on each occasion endorsed these checks and turned them over to Congressman McSween's representative; that she has never performed any services whatsoever for Congressman McSween, his office, or his representative and that she has never retained any money whatsoever from the checks sent to her by Congressman McSween; that she is a housewife, the mother of six children, and has never had any experience whatsoever in clerical, stenographic, or other related work and is not qualified to perform any.[129]

Another Long advertisement, headed "Here is the truth about Congressman McSween," reproduced a letter from Tom Street, vice president of Central Louisiana Electric Company to McSween dated June 9, 1959. Street informed McSween that he had "made arrangements with Mr. Joe Mooney to bring the amount you asked for to Washington with him. . . . Here is a list of the men I contacted with respective amounts: Mr. Robert Scott, V-P, Southwestern Electric Power Company, Shreveport, 50; Mr. L. P. Smith, Gulf States Utilities, Baton Rouge, 50; Cleco, 50; Mr. J. M. Mooney and Mr. W. O. Turner, Chairman of the Board, Louisiana Power and Light Company, 100. Total 250. If you write to thank be sure to mark letter personal and confidential and just thank them for their assistance." In a further note, Street said that he had seen McSween's wife and "she looks fine." Street wrote McSween while Long was confined in Galveston and said, "Have just returned today from Legislature. Don't know what the real story is on Uncle Earl & don't think anyone else does either." Long's ad said that McSween's relationship with the power companies explained why he voted against the Rural Electrification Administration.[130]

In handbills distributed at meetings and mailed to voters, Long said that with the primary campaign closing and issues clearly defined, "Instead of running for office some of our honorable opponents will be running from the law." He said he wanted the people to know the truth about McSween's "bogus checks," which he said "I expect to give to the best of my ability." Defending himself, he averred that "throughout the years that I have held public office not one iota of graft or crookedness has ever been proven against me, yet some of our opponents would try and make you believe that I am a corrupt man."[131]

Speaking on the banks of Cane River in Natchitoches on July 16, Long predicted that he would win in the first primary, with over 50 percent of the vote in Natchitoches, Vernon, Grant, Winn, and Sabine Parishes, a lead in LaSalle and Avoyelles, and "neck and neck with them in Rapides." He said if he was elected in the primary, he would campaign across the country to elect a Democrat as president because that was the only way to get Fort Polk, which had been closed, reopened.[132]

The 200,000-acre army base, located in Vernon Parish, ten miles east of Leesville, began as a base for the Louisiana Maneuvers of 1940–1941, when 350,000 soldiers and some fifty thousand vehicles participated in a sham battle to prepare the US Army for what many people believed would be our inevitable entry into World War II. There was already a small facility at Camp Evangeline that spanned 23,000 acres adjacent to the 604,000-acre Kisatchie National Forest. Army chief of staff George C. Marshall secured state approval to expand the training area across parts of Winn, Grant, Natchitoches, Vernon, Rapides, Claiborne, and Webster parishes. The army also secured sparsely populated areas in East Texas. Author Mark Perry wrote in *Military History* magazine that "the 3,400 square miles combined maneuver area was also laced with rivers—the Sabine and Calcasieu to the west and the Red to the north—natural barriers that would present valuable training obstacles for the engineer units obliged to bridge them."

There were two major training events in 1940 and two in 1941, with the final one in September being the longest. Marshall said the 1941 war games were "a combat college for troop leading" and a laboratory to test the "new armored antitank and air forces that had come of age since 1918." On September 15, 1941, the Red vs. Blue army conflict brought to the fore young officers including Lieutenant Colonel Dwight Eisenhower and Colonel George S. Patton Jr. while Marshall's deputies reviewed lists of senior officers, "culling those who had failed the test of the Louisiana Maneuvers." Those who survived the process were marked for combat commands, "and history records the achievements of Patton, Clark, Bradley and Eisenhower, who replicated in Europe what they first practiced in central Louisiana."[133]

Fort Polk opened and closed sporadically in connection with the presence or absence of large-scale US military needs after World War II. It was ordered closed in 1959 during McSween's first term in Congress.

In the campaign, Long berated McSween for failing to keep Fort Polk open and said that he would work to reopen it and that electing John F. Kennedy president would help him do that. The post usually held over ten thousand soldiers with hundreds of support employees and had enormous financial impact over a large area.[134]

Earl Long shouted to his Natchitoches audience that he would stand by the common people. "When it comes to making a decision between masses and classes," he said, "I'll stand by the people."[135]

The hams and slabs of bacon on his sound trucks were usually drawn for, with the sound truck drivers distributing two-part tickets, with the buyer holding one part while the other went into a container from which the winning number was drawn. Other grocery items were given to all comers. There were angel food cakes and layer cakes for all the ladies at a number of meetings. Easy Money Littleton said that he went to Cotton's Bakery in Alexandria to buy all the "day-olds" to hand out.[136]

At a rally in Bunkie before a largely black audience, Long shouted, "Hey! I want the blackest and ugliest nigger in the crowd to come up and get this last ham." Dupre Litton wrote that "no one moved and a sudden hush came over the gathering. Long pointed to an elderly black man near the truck and hollered in his hoarse, raspy voice, 'You there, old man. You're the blackest and ugliest. Come on up here and git this ham.' The elderly man came up and took the ham and the crowd roared with laughter. That scene could not have been repeated by any other politician here or elsewhere. The blacks knew that regardless of his words, Earl Long was their friend."[137]

The night before the primary, Long gave two tremendous watermelon parties in Alexandria, one for the whites, one for the blacks. The ad for the parties said they were at "Earl Long Headquarters, Main Street, for White Only; Maude Mae's Cafe, Lee St. between the railroad and 16th Street for Colored Only! These are watermelons raised on Governor Long's farm at Winnfield."[138] The Natchitoches *Enterprise* political reporter wrote that "when the Old Master finally took the microphone, he was in much better form than on his recent visit here several weeks ago, and had back again that occasional rasping falsetto that will curl every hair in the House of Representatives if he ever gets to use it there."[139]

Assailing McSween for putting "deadheads and kickbackers" on his office payroll, Long said "McSween is goin' where they've been trying to put Uncle Earl for thirty years. He thinks the Alexandria Bladder and the Shreveport Times will answer for him. He wasn't interested in Camp Polk or anything else except his own miserable hide."[140]

Strangely, speaking at Boyce on July 15, Ben Holt told his audience that Rapides Parish was better treated under Earl Long's administration than any in the past. He blamed McSween for faltering economic conditions, although what appeared to be praise for Long was intended to highlight his own role as the governor's floor leader. Holt told listeners, "You have gotten more for Rapides Parish the past four years than ever in the past and you probably got 30 times more than you will get in the next four years." Holt said that he and Long had worked together in the past but were no longer connected. "Long has been sick since 1959," Holt declared. "He couldn't do anything if you picked him up and carried him to Washington."[141]

Holt and McSween both took their campaigns to Long's hometown of Winnfield on July 16. Speaking on the courthouse square in the morning to what a reporter called "only a sprinkling of people," Holt repeated his mantra that Long was "a sick man" and that the district was in worse shape economically than at any time due to McSween's poor representation. Long, Holt said, "got sick in 1959. He's been sick ever since and he's not able to represent you in Congress no matter how much he may want to. I've heard people say they thought they would vote for Earl Long because of things he's done in the past, but you can't live in the past."[142]

That afternoon, McSween attacked Long's "smear tactics" but said that this was nothing new with him because "he even put out a fake handbill on Huey in 1932." McSween, ridiculing Long, said "he says a congressman should know a little about whiskey, a little about women, and a little bit about a lot of things. If that's the case, he should be qualified" and added, "I never pulled a pillow case over my head, or bought a carload of watermelons or 24 horse collars."[143]

A Holt ad conceded that the former governor "has a long record in Louisiana politics and in the past accomplished many things of benefit for the state and its citizens. However, he is now ill and unable to serve as congressman. Too, he does not actually desire to actually serve in this capacity and has already announced that his main purpose is to again try for the governorship in 1963."[144]

Earl's campaign appeared to be gaining momentum. On July 17, he held a massive night rally at City Hall Square in Alexandria with a crowd of 1,500. He passed out hams, bacon, baskets of groceries, and buckets of lard to his audience, asking it to elect him in the first primary on July 23.[145] A July 20 night rally in the village of Georgetown in Grant Parish drew five hundred people and snarled traffic all along US Highway 65.[146]

In advertisements that ran in newspapers the day before the primary as "A Message to the People of the Eighth District," Long asked for the votes of everyone: "White, Colored, Protestant, Catholic, Jew, rich or poor. I'm 1000% for segregation. I think this is the best for everyone concerned. And still I am the best friend the colored man, poor white man, businessman, rich or poor, who wants a square deal for all ever had in the governor's office of this state."

He said, "Mr. McSween should now be preparing his defense against the bogus check charges which he must face instead of telling the people that Earl Long is drunk and crazy. No man or woman ever saw Earl Long drunk. Crazy is a matter of opinion. One thing is certain, he was not crazy enough that he dished out government checks like hot cakes to people who did no work whatsoever for the federal government to earn them."

"The fact is, I have never been crazy," Long wrote. "I do admit that I was tired and worn to a frazzle and that I needed rest like Governor Davis needed the other day when he went to the Baptist Hospital in Alexandria for a rest and check-up after his first session of the legislature. I hope no one calls Governor Davis crazy because he is sick and exhausted just like I was. Being Governor of this state, if you take your work seriously, is a hard job—almost too much for one individual."[147]

The final Long rally before the primary was held in Chestnut, in Natchitoches Parish. It was a general meeting for the Chestnut, Readheimer, Ashland, Goldonna, Creston, and Black Lake communities.[148]

Long listened to the returns on July 23 in a rural store while eating cheese and crackers. He did not lead, but went into a runoff with McSween, who was ahead by about 3,800 votes, with Holt far behind. The official results from the 316 precincts were McSween 29,747, Long

26,010, and Holt 10,221. McSween led by over 4,000 in Rapides. McSween and Long each carried four parishes. A news story said that "Long, with the remainder of his battered political career hanging in the balance, carried Winn, with 2,289 to 1,705 for McSween and 320 for Holt."

McSween said, "I think Mr. Long has polled his full strength," but Long responded that in the August 27 runoff he would win every parish. "I ran his shirt-tail off in this" primary, he said, justifiably because after all of Long's tribulations, he had forced the incumbent into a runoff. Long continued to appeal for Negro votes, although their registration was only 15 percent of the district total, while McSween blasted the civil rights platform plank adopted at the Democratic National Convention.[149]

12.

THE RUNOFF CAMPAIGN: ALL IN

The runoff campaign kicked off the following week. Long returned to the stump on Saturday, July 30, with rallies beginning in Jena at 9:30 a.m. and ending in Rosepine at 7:45 p.m., with stops in between at Pollock, Colfax, St. Maurice, Provencal, and Hornbeck.[1] On Sunday, July 31, he spoke at Mora, Natchez, Flora, Campti, and Ajax.[2] He told an audience of 150 at Campti that he was "not exactly pleased" with the primary results, but on the other hand not too disappointed. He said he did not run first "because about 30,000 country people didn't get out and vote." Holt, he laughed, "says I'm too old. I still have some snap. I got it in my suspenders and socks too. I had enough snap to beat him three to one."[3]

On August 1, in Alexandria, Ben Holt endorsed McSween, and Long immediately denounced him for "selling out." Holt announced his support of McSween in a live television program on KALB-TV and was followed on the air by Long. Holt cited Long's confinement in two mental institutions, his western trip and its escapades, his attempt to hold the special session of the legislature that Holt helped kill, and what Holt claimed was his arrest in New Orleans on a drunk driving charge, which was not true. "Since leaving the governor's office," Holt said, "Mr. Long has continued to embarrass and humiliate his friends, the people, and the state of Louisiana by his escapades in Baltimore, New York City, and New Orleans. This conduct does not recommend him to any office, particularly one in which he would represent us in our nation's capital. This conduct, unfortunately, shows that his condition has not improved." Holt said that after conferring with supporters and friends and taking into account the best interests of the district, "This was the only possible course for me to take on this vital matter." Holt concluded that "this is no longer a matter of just politics. It is a matter of decency and principle and we have every right to expect our public officials to conduct their offices in decency."[4]

Long, outraged by Holt's attack on him, said that he was at his Hot Wells resort motel room shortly after the primary when Holt came to see him and "began talking about $30,000. I told him I didn't have it, and he came to $20,000. I told him I didn't have that either." Long said Holt told him "I spent a lot of money and I want my money back." Long said he told Holt there was a state law prohibiting defeated candidates from selling out in a second primary, and "I said Little Ben, you got the wrong man."[5]

Holt angrily denied a sellout to McSween. He said Long telephoned him twice to talk about an endorsement, but "I told him on both occasions that if he wanted to talk to me that I would be glad to see him at my office during business hours, but that I could not endorse him. There was never any talk about money and it was never mentioned." Holt said that "several friends of the Governor from outside of the Eighth District who did call me in his behalf and tried to talk to me about endorsing the Governor did try to talk about money." Holt said he would not be surprised by any "irresponsible statements" from Long "because he is a sick man and is not responsible" for his actions.[6]

Long responded that Holt had led the adjournment of the special session because "I was going to cut the interest rate on small loans from three and a half per cent to two and a half per cent per month and he was in the loan business." He added that "Ben Holt came to me and asked me to cut all the district attorneys off the fee basis but to leave Rapides Parish alone because he was going to run for D.A. He said the D.A. up here now had made $23,000 in one year and that the one before him had made $30,000 but that he could run it up to $50,000."[7]

In newspaper advertisements thanking voters for their support, Holt said, "I do not wish to tell anyone how to vote in the second primary. As an eliminated candidate I do not have that right," but he then attacked Long in the same vein and endorsed McSween. Holt said that in Long's "present physical and mental condition he is unable to discharge the arduous responsibilities of a member of the U.S. House of Representatives."[8]

Holt lambasted Long for bringing in out-of-district speakers to campaign with him. He charged that Sims was being paid $500 a day to campaign for Long. "We don't need people outside this district to tell us how to vote," he said.[9]

On August 3, Holt blasted Long's "ham campaign" and claimed that he spent over $100,000 on groceries in the primary. Long, in New Orleans for a follow-up on his recent surgery, denied that he had suffered a stroke on August 2 and said he was returning to the stump to give "both Holt and McSween a stroke."[10] Back on the stump, Long said he spent only $8,000 and told newsmen they were free to check with the two firms from which he bought "90 per cent of the provisions." The Alexandria *Daily Town Talk* did so but was disappointed to have to report that "one of the firms, Rapides Packing Co., said the governor's first primary grocery bill was $8,800. The other, Cotton Bros. Bakery, said it had records of $190.25 in Long purchases and that the entire amount bought there would not reach $1,000."[11]

Long held meetings at Bellwood, Belmont, and Converse on Thursday, August 4.[12] He told a reporter, "I want the nigger vote and I don't make any secret about it. I tell 'em I want it. And I get it because them colored people know I've tried to help 'em."[13] On Saturday, August 6, he went to Red River Landing, Moncla, Plaucheville, Moreauville, and Bordelonville, all in Avoyelles Parish, and on Sunday, August 7, he gave speeches in Florien, Fisher, Zwolle, Marthaville, Powhatan, and Tioga, covering Sabine, Natchitoches, and Rapides Parishes. His ads and circulars asked people to "come out and hear the real issues discussed, especially the young folks and ladies, because we would like to get them interested in public affairs. Nothing will be said to offend anyone. Free stick-candy for all the children and free cold drinks for everyone, favors for the ladies, first class music, Popular and Religious."[14]

With Jay Chevalier playing the guitar and singing rockabilly songs and Edgar Coco playing his harmonica, Long led his confederates in singing his campaign song while Coco played the mouth organ. Sung to the tune of "I'm Looking Over a Four-Leaf Clover," it went,

All of the voters
In the Eighth District
Are votin' for Uncle Earl.
Some may retract,
And vote for Harold Mac,

The voters will deman'
That Uncle Earl's the man.

All the old agers
And welfare people,
And those in business, too,
Know that in electin' him
They'll be gettin'
The best man for me and you.[15]

In a televised address on August 5, McSween said he was fed up with Long's attacks against him: "I took his vilification and abuse in the first primary without drawing my sword," he said. "But it was no holds barred from now on." He charged that Long was a "trickster" who put out fake sample ballots in his 1932 race for lieutenant governor. "Huey had to denounce his own brother," McSween said. "Huey called him 'Earl Kangaroo Long.'" McSween said that a man who had been in and out of mental institutions was not fit for Congress.[16]

McSween made eleven stump appearances on Saturday, August 6, from eight in the morning until eight in the evening. He spoke at Pitkin, Leesville, Florien, Many, Zwolle, Converse, Pleasant Hill, Marthaville, Robeline, Provencal, and Cloutierville.[17]

McSween and Long clashed with each other at Florien on August 6 in what went down in political lore as the Battle of Florien. Long was speaking from a platform when McSween arrived for his own meeting and Long shouted at him to "come on up here and tell 'em about them checks." When McSween took the stand, he followed up on the hard-hitting attacks on Long he had launched in a television address on Friday, August 5. In it he assailed his opponent as "Earl Kangaroo Long" and said that he had spent the last two years of his term embarrassing the state and its people. He said Long's middle initial stood for Kangaroo rather than Kemp, and that the name Kangaroo was given to him by Huey after Earl betrayed him.[18] McSween, fighting back against Long's attacks on him, said that "if being locked up in the nuthouse and running stripteasers are qualifications for Congress, then Governor Long is well-qualified."[19]

Shaking a fist at Long, McSween roared, "You say Ben Holt adjourned the legislature on you. You say he stabbed you in the back. Well, I guess I would have been unhappy too if I hadn't got his endorsement."[20]

He berated Long for bringing in speakers from outside the district and pointed at Joe Arthur Sims, who had introduced Long, crying "shame on you for slandering somebody you don't know anything about. What are you doing up here in the Eighth District telling people how to vote. Look at him sitting over there in his black Cadillac." McSween told the crowd, "Maybe Earl Long can tell you what he's doing up here. I understand Long's going to come back up here and make another speech and make a rebuttal" to his own talk, McSween said. He also attacked Long for bringing State Senator A. O. Rappelet of Lafourche Parish into the district to speak for him and lashed at Long for turning on Holt.

Glaring at Long, McSween cried, "I didn't make Holt your floor leader."

"He sold out to you, didn't he?" Long rejoined.

McSween said that when Long ran for lieutenant governor against Huey's ticket in 1932, he put out a fake sample ballot that implied his brother supported him. Long, who had stepped down from the platform, was walking into a store near the speakers' stand when McSween shouted at him, "Why did you testify against Huey?" in the Overton hearing. Long came to within six feet of McSween and they both shook fingers in each other's faces as McSween roared, "Shame on you for testifying against your brother, Earl Long." Long raised his right hand, as if taking an oath, and shouted "I didn't do it. And shame on you for stealing them checks." McSween snapped, "I didn't do that, either," but Long shouted, "You damn sure did." As Long walked back into the store, McSween attacked him for accumulating $125,000 in additional net worth while he was governor. He lashed out at Long for running around the West "embarrassing the state of Louisiana."[21]

The two combatants crossed paths again in Zwolle, taunting each other there. At Mathaville, Long told a crowd of 150 that they had squared off in Florien and Zwolle and said "if he wants rock 'em sock 'em politics, well he's met his match. I can give it and I can take it." Lambasting McSween, he said, "I'm the man who invented rock 'em, sock 'em politics."[22]

State Representative W. K. Brown of Grant Parish joined Long on the stump on Thursday, August 11. They made appearances together in Belmont, Anacoco, and Evans.[23]

Taking the gloves off, the McSween campaign paid for newspaper advertisements assaulting Long by the Committee to Save Louisiana from National Embarrassment. Roy "Peanut" Conn of Pineville signed the ads as chairman, but there was no information on just who had formed the group and who the committee members were.

The first full-page ad featured a large photograph of Long with his hat on a pillowcase over his head. Escorted by three deputy sheriffs, only his nose was visible in a hole cut in the pillowcase, and one smiling deputy had him by the arm to guide him. Headed "Pillowcase Contest," the ad asked, "Who Is This Man?" A box said "Clue No. 1. This picture was taken in July 1959 in Fort Worth, Texas. Westward Ho!" It asked, "Is this to be our next Congressman from the 8th Congressional District?" and said there would be more clues the following week.[24]

Another large ad repeated the photo and exhorted, "Do Not Reward Such Conduct—Vote McSween, No. 3, On August 27, 1960." It reproduced the news story about Dick Davis's claim that policemen in New York City tried to shake him down because he was carrying a gun and featured a photo of exotic dancer Candy Cane, identified as "Long's Companion."[25]

Other photos showed Long pulling open the breathing hole in the pillowcase, with one eye showing, and trying on a hat in Taos, New Mexico. Blaze Starr was shown taking photographs at the Davis inauguration while Earl leaned over a platform rail to greet someone. Another showed Long after his minor auto accident in New Orleans and was captioned, "Earl Long has busy night. Former Gov. Long is shown to friends and a waiting car by policemen after his parole from a police station. As the result of a minor accident in which no one was injured, Long was booked for resisting arrest, reviling police, driving with no operator's license, reckless driving, and disturbing the peace. Long, now running for Congress, reportedly used salty language to the police in discussing the accident." A final picture, "Mystery Guest Walks from Gov. Long's Motel," showed a woman, actually Blaze Starr, with a large handkerchief draped over her head, who "spent a half-hour inside the motel" with him. The ad proclaimed, "He Must Not Be Our Next Representative."[26]

Long issued a circular dated August 12, 1960, that was mailed out and distributed at rallies in which he said "we are in a hot campaign and my honorable opponent has seen fit in his hour of desperation to bring forth some of the most ridiculous stuff that I've ever heard of in my life. He's sending out pictures of me with a pillow slip over my head. I did this to stop newspapers from taking my picture after they had harassed me when I was ill and asked to be left alone." Criticizing "embarrassment and harassment" by the newspapers, he continued, "I was supposed to be on a rest and recuperation trip and so-called vacation. If you knew the facts about these newspaper lies and harassment you would sympathize with me even though politically you were against me." Denouncing McSween for calling him a drunkard and crazy and using politicians from outside the district to campaign for him, Long said that McSween could not get a single colleague from Louisiana to support him, and the only other congressman he could get "was a Republican from Michigan who introduced him on radio and TV in the first primary."[27]

Criticizing McSween's voting record, Long wrote, "I started out to conduct this campaign on a high plane. If you heard Mr. McSween on radio and TV the night of the first primary he sounded like a typical roughneck looking for a fist fight." Responding to McSween's attacks on him, Long said, "I guess I am one of the most investigated men that ever lived in Louisiana, and not one act of crookedness nor rascality has ever been proved against me."[28]

In another circular addressed to the ladies, he attacked McSween for putting deadheads on his office payroll and said that "the way I've been investigated, if this could ever have been established against me, my address would be Angola or Leavenworth." McSween, he said, was calling him crazy because he had "a temporary let-down and sickness in May of 1959." As for McSween's charges that he was chasing strip-teasers, Long said, "This is absurd. What would a man of my age do if he stumbled up on one? I have recently gone through some operations. If I could tell you about them, it would be further proof as to the absurdity of these allegations. There's not a man in Louisiana that has any more respect for lady folks than I do. I had one of the best mothers that ever lived and five wonderful sisters who were all school teachers. I would not do anything to bring discredit on them or the women of the Eighth District."[29]

Many years later, Dr. Paul Pratt, one of the psychiatrists who examined Long at the Pine Manor Motel in Covington following his release from Southeast Louisiana Hospital, told Jay Chevalier that Long could not have had a sexual relationship with Blaze Starr. Pratt, who accompanied Long on the western trip, said that "Blaze's only mission in life was to raise the dead," because Long was impotent. Long, he said, could not obtain an erection. "He confessed this to me one day and said it was about to drive him crazy. He wasn't crazy, just sexually frustrated that he'd lost his manhood."[30]

As for Ben Holt saying that he was too old, Long reminded audiences that his brother George was fifteen years older than he was and was elected to Congress three times. "I beat Mr. Holt three to one, moustache, Cadillac and all," he wrote. "Maybe he has a little more respect for his elders than he once had. We all know there is a lot of good reading in old books. That's how books become classics, because they've proved themselves over the years. I maintain that there's certain things that you gain by maturity than you can't get any other way." Urging people to vote, he concluded, "Really and truly I think I have an excellent chance of winning if the people will turn out and vote."[31]

In Echo on August 14, Long laughed: "They talk about me running after stripteasers. What would I do if I caught one? Sixty-four years of age! They say I'm a whiskeyhead. The man don't live that ever saw me drunk. Says I'm crazy. You better look out, I might bite you!" McSween, Long sneered, "never worked a day in his life. He don't know what sweat is. He wears a high hat and a high collar. He has to get on a stump to spit he's such a big shot. You put one of those monkey suits on me that he wears, it'd look like socks on a rooster, it wouldn't go on."[32]

"Send Uncle Earl to Washington," he implored the crowd. "You sent my brother, Huey! You sent my brother, George! You sent my nephew, Russell! Please give Uncle Earl the same shot. Send me to Washington and I'll be Johnny-on-the-Spot for you. Please give me the chance. Vote for me! I need you! I don't care if you've been for me or against me, if you're a Longite or a socialite. Come on in! I need you! Please Vote! Vote for me! But even if you don't, please go vote. Don't sell your vote. Sell butter and eggs and chickens and cows. Sell timber and the products of the sweat of your brow. But don't sell your vote to no sapsucker. It's the most precious thing you have. You've given it to me many times before.

Please give it to me now. Uncle Earl needs you like I've never needed you before. Please win this one for me!"[33]

On Saturday, August 13, McSween's schedule began at Pollock at 8:00 a.m. and concluded at Powhatan at 8:00 p.m. He spoke in Jena, Tullos, Olla, Sikes, Dodson, Winnfield, Calvin, Goldonna, and Campti in between. He held only one meeting on Thursday, August 18, on the bank of the Cane River in Natchitoches, and one on Sunday, August 21, in Cloutierville.[34] In Winnfield, McSween and Holt attacked Long, with Holt now claiming that he could have gotten $100,000 from Long for his endorsement. McSween said he had conducted a "Sunday School" campaign in the primary, "but now I'm fighting back. Nobody ever poured it on Earl before and it's making him squirm."[35] In Simmesport, he said that "Earl Long has caused more embarrassment, humiliation and disgrace than any ten men in the history of Louisiana, and we've had some beauts."[36]

McSween was intrigued by two strange notes he received that he believed were from Julius Long, Huey and Earl's older brother. McSween told this writer many years later that several people who were well acquainted with Julius recognized his prose style and typing. The clerk of court and chief deputy "compared the typewriter impressions with those in some of the lawsuits that Julius had filed here in workers' compensation cases. They were identical."[37]

The notes referred to Earl as "Kangaroo." McSween said that the name got attached to Earl during the Overton hearings because "Huey called the proceedings a kangaroo court" and somehow the "K" for Kemp in Long's middle name became Kangaroo because he testified against Huey.

One letter, postmarked from Shreveport on August 16, 1960, had typed on the envelope, "Evil forces are making a last ditch fight to retain a foot hold in Louisiana." The letter said

> some guess that Kangaroo Long will get Gerald [L. K.] Smith, as he did in 1940 race for governor, to stump for Kangaroo soon. If what Bill Dodd has said about Earl Long repeatedly heretofore is true, then Kangaroo is not fit for any office. The undisputable fakery of Kangaroo constantly of E. K. Long in the past thirty years shows him the worst man ever to run for high office in the State of Louisiana. He advertises he is a graduate of Louisiana Tech and the L.S.U. on his political literature, whereas he was expelled from the Tech in Oct. 1913 and never returned, and attended L.S.U. without advancing from

> 1914 until he had to quit in 1915 because he was a bonehead. He never tried a law suit, but received a few big fees by political power. He has really lived about forty years on fakery and double crossing. He will be 65 years old Aug. 26, 1960. How much longer will he fake?[38]

A second letter, dated August 22, 1960, said that "Kangaroo by cute or baby like acts, such as the pillow slip on his head, puts on shows that has heretofore got him votes. He has been at such all his life. He has never worked much except at clowning. He expects his family to come running when he wants them but to expect nothing in return. He will be a real tramp at 65 if defeated this time. Evidently Speedy expects to inherit all that gets votes in Earl Long. Speedy does not need any aid in double-crossing. We doubt there will ever be another politician in Louisiana who will plainly try to buy votes by chunking meat for the people to grab. Possibly Kangaroo will find it did not work well."[39]

With former State Senator Albert A. Fredericks and State Representative Curtis Boozman supporting Earl and campaigning with him, McSween turned his fire on them, reminding people of their past differences with Long. Fredericks served three terms in the state senate and was Long's executive secretary in his first full administration. He was also president of Louisiana State Normal School. Long, after winning a first primary victory for governor in 1956, broke with them both when Boozman sought reelection to the house and Mrs. Fredericks sought a house seat, both from Natchitoches Parish, in second primaries. In a February 15, 1956, mailing piece to Natchitoches Parish voters, Long enclosed sample ballots for his candidates and said, "Never in my life have I been as disappointed in a man elected to public office as I have been in Mr. Curtis Boozman. He is a turncoat of the worst type who brags about playing both sides against the middle and is ignorant enough to actually think he is cute." Long said the Fredericks family had been treated well by the people. Damning them with faint praise, he wrote that

> Mr. Fredericks represents the railroads and receives a large salary as well as an expense account. He is also drawing one of the largest teacher retirement checks in the state, and owns thousands of acres of fine land in Natchitoches and draws a salary from the Abraham Land Company. He is on the State Board of Education, an honor which I gave him, and takes long trips all over

> the United States at state expense and his wife goes with him. He has a fine son-in-law, originally from Texas, whom he brought to Louisiana recently and gave a good job at a trade school as a result of his being a member of the State Board of Education. His brother-in-law, Earl Morris, who is a friend of mine, is presently your Sheriff, and I think a capable one, and his good wife was, and probably still is, one of his Deputies. She is a fine lady, and I am sure earns her salary. I don't particularly object to all of this, but believe the Fredericks family has just about gotten enough from your parish." Long wrote that "this fine lady, Mrs. Fredericks, has been giving people the impression that I am supporting her. Nothing could be further from the truth, and she and her husband both know it, especially Mr. Fredericks."[40]

McSween's ad, reproducing Long's letter, was headed "Just Four Years Ago—Remember This!" It asked, "What Strange Force Now Brings Together Boozman, Fredericks, and Long?"[41]

Fredericks responded to the McSween attack. In an advertisement that praised Long, Fredericks listed public works Earl had sponsored for Natchitoches Parish and urged people to give him a "thank you" at the polls.[42]

Bill Dodd stumped with Long on August 13 in Natchitoches Parish. They had been on-and-off allies since 1940, and Dodd generously responded to Long's call for help in the congressional race. Dodd said that "ever since the time of Christ, every person who has talked about helping the needy has been criticized." He said that such statesmen as George Washington and Abraham Lincoln were called crazy for some of their ideas and predicted that "Earl Long is going to go down in history as one of the greatest, if not the greatest, government officials in the state. Judge Earl by what he has already done for you in government," he said. Dodd was a marvelous stump speaker who loved to "skin a cat." A big, heavy man, balding, usually wearing a cowboy hat, with a booming voice, he did a masterful job for his old mentor. On one occasion, for a rally on the riverbank in Natchitoches, below the bridge, Dodd and the rest of the entourage were already there, and Big Bad Bill was in full throat when Long's car came onto the bridge. Long had Easy Money Littleton pull over, high above the riverbank platform and crowd. Easy Money asked him if he wanted to drive on down to the speaking. Long took a drink of bourbon from a bottle in the bucket on the floorboard of the car and said, "Hell no, Bill's doing so well now I'm just enjoying hearing him skin McSween. I don't want to interrupt that."[43]

Dodd attributed both of his defeats for governor to Earl Long's failure to support him. While Earl said he did not support Dodd in 1951 because Dodd "tried to take over" in 1950 when Long was recovering at the Pea Patch Farm from a heart attack, Dodd believed that Long did not want to be succeeded by a strong member of his faction. "Earl wanted a weak anti-Long or an impractical reformer during the four years he had to wait until he could run for governor again," Dodd said. "That way he could cuss and harass him so effectively that the voters would almost draft Earl to run and bring back the good old days."[44]

In Robeline, Long urged people to vote, rasping that "your most precious heritage is your right to vote. Sell your chickens, hogs, cattle, and horses, but don't sell your right to vote." McSween, he said, was "a smart aleck and a spoiled brat. He was born with a silver spoon in his mouth and you couldn't twist it out with a monkey wrench. He talks to his father like you would talk to a bootblack. He's just a natural born smart aleck." Dodd urged people to judge Long by his record and said everyone in the state had benefited from the Long program.[45] Many years later, Ben Bennett confirmed to this writer that Long had reason to be worried about vote buying. He said that much of what happened in the election, "including vote buying and other questionable activities, is not pretty."[46]

In stumping over the August 13–14 weekend, Long endorsed the standard-bearers of the Democratic Party. In Mansura he roared, "I am for the Kennedy-Johnson Ticket one million per cent" and chastised McSween for associating with Republicans.[47] This author and two friends followed the Long campaign August 12–14, 1960, and played a tape of Long's speeches for the author's father, David R. McGuire Jr., who was the chief administrative officer of the New Orleans city government for Mayor Chep Morrison. They were supporting Kennedy, and McGuire said Long's endorsement was a very important factor. He called a close friend, Walter G. Cowan, who was the night editor of the *States-Item*, and suggested to him that Long's statement was newsworthy. This author went to the newspaper office and played the tape to Cowan, who wrote the story headlined "Will Campaign for Kennedy, Long Pledges."

In an evening speech in the little town of Echo, Earl thundered, "Now, about this man McSwine. He's a high flyer. Born with a silver spoon in his mouth and you couldn't get it out with a crowbar. He talks to his fine old father about like you'd talk to a colored bootblack. He is an accomplished liar. He can talk, whistle, lie, sing, and spit out of his big old mouth all at the same time, and all the while he's chewing gum and eating candy. He's a flim-flam man." He called McSween "Catfish Mouth," described him as "a hothouse plant," and claimed that "the only time he ever bent over was to pick up a golf ball." McSween, Long thundered, "has a mouth like a catfish. He can talk out of both sides of his mouth, smoke a cigarette, whistle a tune, and lie, all at the same time. Oh, yeah! He's a big shot. He's Catfish Mouth McSween."[48]

McSween's Committee to Save Louisiana from National Embarrassment unleashed another barrage on August 18 with newspaper ads showing Long with the pillowcase over his head and the "mystery woman" visiting him at the Covington motel after his release from Southeast Louisiana Hospital. The ad was titled "He Must Not Be Our Next Representative From The 8th Congressional District" and boxes featured newspaper clippings: "El Paso, Tex., July 20, 1959. Yesterday morning, twitching his hands nervously, Long heard Dr. W. Herschel Ford thunder 'You can't live with the Devil six days and live with the Lord on Sunday' as he attended services at the First Baptist Church. After the services Long said, 'That's good preaching. It was only 35 minutes long. In the country they used to preach an hour and a half. That's too long for an old man to sleep.' Long, affable and joking, fidgeted through the sermon, spit on the floor and nearly lit a cigarette."[49]

Another clipping read, "Long Thinly-Clad to Greet Minister. Fort Worth, Tex., July 14, 1959. Gov. Earl K. Long of Louisiana conferred with the president of the General Ministers Assn. of Fort Worth today for two hours in his undershorts and a sport shirt. The president of the association, the Rev. G. W. French, said that part of the time Long had a towel draped over his bare legs."[50]

"Baton Rouge, June, 1959" said that "state police cars whisked a French Quarter jazz band and entertainers to Gov. Earl K. Long's party at the Mansion." Another bulletin quoted Long saying that "a governor cannot have too much experience about lumber, timber, farming, religion,

Sunday School, show business, whiskey-drinking, crap-shooting, politics, and many other things you pick up in a lifetime." An August 27, 1959, story said the East Baton Rouge Parish Grand Jury might hear a report "on an alleged $5,000 bribe paid Gov. Long to influence legislation in 1958." Another report said the air force was investigating Long's use of National Guard planes. It said, "The Governor has pressed National Guard planes into personal use on numerous occasions." A May 4, 1960, clipping said Long had taken over a meeting of the State Pardon Board to commute the death sentence of a murderer to life imprisonment" and grant clemency to six applicants. Describing the July 14, 1960, auto accident, a story reported "Long Booked After Crash, Salty Words. Former Gov. Long indulged his penchant for salty language with the wrong people and ended up in a New Orleans police station."[51]

"Long Visits Home of Barmaid," a September 3, 1959, story, was headlined. "Blaze Starr Calls Governor on Arrival." It reported that "Gov. Earl K. Long whiled away a couple of hours in the home of a French Quarter barmaid, a friend of stripteaser Blaze Starr. A few minutes after Long departed, Miss Starr emerged from the house, carrying the baby of a neighborhood woman in her arms. She got into a car with three other women, paid a short visit at the Sho-Bar, 228 Bourbon, and left by plane to return to Miami." The bulletin continued that Long had gone to the Roosevelt Hotel and telephoned the *Times-Picayune* from there, "mad as a hornet." He blasted newsmen for "harassing that poor woman." Long said that any meeting or conversation he may have had with her was none of the newspaper's business. "I know a lot of people she knows, that's all." he said. "You people are determined if you can't find where I stole or grafted you are going to any (expletive) length you can to hurt me. There's no limit to what you'll do. You'll make a mountain out of a mole hill." He said that when the media harassed him like that "they're helping my campaign." Miss Starr, contacted in Miami, had no hesitation in confirming their meeting. "He's such a nice guy," she said. "He's entitled to a little happiness." She said they had only a friendly visit with "at least fifteen people present, my friends and state policemen." The final story, from Denver during his 1959 western trip, recounted his visits to a racetrack "before he shuffled back to his hotel room."[52]

McSween spoke in Natchitoches to what the political reporter for the Natchitoches *Enterprise* described as an "intimate" gathering of about forty people on top of the riverbank, five on the river bridge, and twenty-nine cars, including the candidate's car and sound truck, near the live oak where the speaking was done. Ben Holt got a big hand when he shouted that "if he could be bought he would be out speaking for Earl." McSween thanked people for his first primary vote and said he understood that he was the first candidate to ever carry Natchitoches Parish against Earl Long. He criticized the members of Long's entourage who had come from outside the district and said the state would suffer national embarrassment if Long was elected. Claiming that Long would run for governor again, he urged voters not to lose their "investment" in his seniority.[53]

As for Long, McSween said, "I have the questionable distinction of being that man's Representative. He lives in Winn Parish, he is one of my constituents. During the events of last year important men in both the Senate and the House came to me and asked me what was going on in Louisiana. I was almost laughed off the floor of the House. It was pretty hard to take."[54]

On Friday, August 19, breaking his silence, State Senator Speedy O. Long, whose district included Winn, Grant, LaSalle, and Caldwell Parishes, joined the Earl K. Long caravan for appearances in Gardner and Pitkin. "Vote for Uncle Earl, No. 2 on the voting machine," Long's ads for August 20 said. "Be a good alert citizen. It is your duty to vote." Former State Senator Estes Cole, from Sabine Parish, the Eighth District member on the State Board of Education; Joe Arthur Sims; Representative W. K. Brown of Grant Parish; former Grant Parish representative Willard Rambo; and Edgar Coco all got licks in on McSween in a tour that took them to Leesville, Many, Natchitoches, Montgomery, and Colfax, with a windup rally at City Hall Square in Alexandria. Sims charged that "McSween is the only congressman in the history of the state who has sought re-election and cannot get one single fellow congressman or senator from Louisiana to appear with him on TV, on the radio, or on the stump. Why, he can't even get one letter of recommendation from any of the other seven representatives or two senators from Louisiana." McSween responded that any attorney "who hires out as a hatchet-man for Earl Long does not deserve the respect of his fellow lawyers and fellow citizens."[55]

McSween charged that the race for Congress was only a warm-up for the next governor's election for Long and that he would not hold the seat beyond that, causing the district to lose seniority in its member. He said Long would hold the seat for only two years and then turn it over to Estes Cole. At a rally in Many, introducing Long, Cole said that McSween's claim was "a lie."[56]

Long spoke on the riverbank in Natchitoches on Saturday, August 20. He said it was "the best crowd I ever had in Natchitoches Parish" and claimed 2,500 listeners. The newspaper there reported "Johnny Makar guessed there were at least 500 present while Norman Fletcher plumped for 800." The story said that it had rained when McSween had spoken earlier, but "the skies lowered for Uncle Earl; the downpour politely waited to fall until just after he had finished speaking. Long's appearance, in vivid contrast to the sedate McSween speaking, was one of those grandiloquent political hullabaloos that only the Longs have a gift for. 'If we could just put it all on television every week, we'd be rich,' Norman Fletcher sighed afterward. Just by way of example, when we got down to the riverbank, the former Mayor of Marksville was happily sitting in the back of the pickup-podium playing a mouth organ, and believe us, it isn't just everybody who can get a former Mayor and a guy very much enjoyed by all who know him to turn out and give with music for his campaign."

Speedy Long shouted that "Earl's enemies are trying to destroy Longism" and "the issue is whether you're for those who have or those who have not." He told "the predominantly colored audience that crowded around the truck" that when vote-buying time came around, you should "take their money, put food on your table and clothes on the backs that need them, but Saturday when you go to vote, vote Earl K. Long, No. 2."[58]

Political observers said that "vote hauling" was a common practice for obtaining the Negro vote. Negro campaign workers would drive a carload of registrants to the polls, giving each one five dollars. The drivers were paid fifty dollars for the day and made multiple trips. While no one would talk publicly about it, Ben Bennett said that Long "had me hire drivers for him in the first primary," but "I didn't hear from him in the second primary." Bennett said that a candidate he was supporting for a post in the judicial district lost in the primary and "Sookie Roy won and his supporters hired the transfers for Long in the second primary."[59]

The political reporter for the Natchitoches *Enterprise* wrote that "Bill Dodd, the next batter up, would very possibly have been elected governor on both tries had he spoken as well on behalf of Dodd as he is speaking for Earl Long in this campaign." Dodd said, "They asked me if I was going to talk about homestead exemptions and welfare and hot school lunches and I said yes, my preacher uses the same Bible this year as he used last year, he don't change, and I'm not going to change either. I'm going to talk about the record." Dodd told several stories and importuned, "Let's don't send a Shetland pony to do a horse's job." He lashed at McSween for calling him an "outsider" and said "I lived in the Eighth District before that young man was born."[60]

Long may have been "a little more subdued in Natchitoches than he is in the rural areas," the reporter said, but he still "came out swinging," calling McSween "a young man with a rich father who had a sugar tit in his mouth all his life. There never was a sapsucker needed beating worse than him." Long accused McSween of being "on the power trust payroll" and collecting big fees as a member of a prominent Alexandria law firm, and he said "the Bible says you can't serve two masters. Seven out of seven will tell you he's a smart aleck." Long ended the rally by sitting on a chair in the back of the pickup truck, greeting all comers and handing out coins to kids.[61]

At another stop, Long said that McSween "hasn't cast one vote to help the common people." Shouting, "He's got a rich papa and he's got a rich mama, and he's never sweated a day in his life," Long said, "On the other hand, I went to night school and worked in the daytime to get my education. I know what it is to suffer. I know your problems. The Bible says, 'By his deeds ye shall know him.' I believe that. I'm willing to be judged on my deeds." As for Holt, campaigning with McSween, "He's a slicker. He made more money in the Legislature in four years than any three other representatives. But I'm gonna unslicker him."[62] Bill Dodd roared that Holt was still "drawing $750 a month that Old Uncle Earl got for him" in attorney fees. Long jumped in, deliberately mangling McSween's name, saying "he oughta split with me, 'cause I'm unemployed now. He oughta split with me like McShane [McSween] splits with Foster and McBride."[63]

At the rally on August 20 at Alexandria, Camille Gravel shook hands and chatted with Long at the edge of the speakers' platform while Bill Dodd was talking. Asked by a reporter if there was any significance to this, Gravel said that he was neutral in the race. He acknowledged that he had supported McSween against Teekell in 1958, but "I am definitely not involved in the campaign in any way."[64] In the 1958 race, Long was at the microphone at Teekell's final rally in Alexandria. He spotted Gravel in the crowd and they exchanged barbs for several minutes. Long said that Louisiana did not have many crazy people because of its balmy climate. "On account of that it's possible for people we might otherwise have to lock up to be out and about, and that's why Camille Gravel is allowed to run loose," he laughed. This time Gravel left the rally just as Long took the stand. Afterward he told newsmen, "I went to the meeting only to hear what would be said. I try to go to all of the meetings here."[65] Thirty years later, Gravel told an interviewer that his failure to support McSween in 1960 "was nothing personal, he had just been too conservative for me." Despite his claims of neutrality in the runoff, in 1989 he acknowledged that Long "called me one day after he learned I would not support McSween. He asked me to meet with him at Hot Wells, and I supported him in the election against McSween."[66] In a 1990 interview on "Law Talk with Lester Gauthier" on Acadiana Open Channel, Gravel said that "when he ran for Congress just before he died all of our differences had been resolved. I thought he would make a very good congressman. I supported Earl actively and aggressively and I was really active in his campaign. I visited him right before he died in his hospital room. We were back together in those days."[67]

Long's speakers for the three-hour rally at Alexandria included Mrs. Jewell Long, George's widow. The rally finally broke up at 11:00 p.m. after a truckload of watermelons had been given away, but a news story said "Long stayed around about a half hour longer, conferring with his lieutenants and tapping his foot to the hillbilly music being played."[68]

McSween made nine talks on Saturday, August 20, flailing Long for embarrassing the state with his western trip antics and turning up at a Baltimore race track "all dressed up in a silk suit and a silk tie with a diamond stickpin in it, but he didn't have any socks on! Isn't that something?" He berated Long for the New York incident with Candy Cane and claimed "he was throwing away $100 bills there like he throws quarters to the kids here. He likes to show off." McSween asked, "What would happen if this man was turned loose in Washington? Do you think he would spit on the floor like he did in a Baptist church in Fort Worth? He just might. He has caused more embarrassment to Louisiana than any 10 other men in the history of the state, and he hasn't even apologized. He doesn't think he's done anything wrong."[69]

On Saturday, August 20, one week before the election, Richard A. "Dick" Davis, who had sometimes acted as a driver and aide since Long's release from Southeast Louisiana Hospital, announced that he had broken with him. In a sworn statement released at his mother's home in Lake Providence, Davis said he was "through" with Long because his mother had begged him to break relations and Long had asked him to sign "a false affidavit." Davis told his press conference, "I am sick and exhausted. I am through. My mother, who is a good Christian woman, pleaded with me to change my way of living and said a good place to begin would be to break off my association with Earl Long. This is one of the major factors in my decision to disassociate myself with Governor Long and make this statement."[70]

Davis said that following Long's release from the hospital, he pleaded with Earl to "take care of himself," but Long would not follow his advice. He also said that Long had persuaded him to get the affidavit from Mrs. Mary Helen Foster stating that McSween gave her monthly paychecks for work that she did not perform and which were endorsed over to a McSween representative. Davis said that Mrs. Foster had executed another affidavit stating that the first one was false and that she had signed it without knowing what it said.[71]

McSween displayed Mrs. Foster's counteraffidavit in a television broadcast. In it she said that Dick Davis had brought the first affidavit to her. She claimed that she actually gave the checks to Davis to pay a debt of her husband's and that she did not perform any personal services for McSween while on his office payroll. McSween's case was injured when she said no work was involved, but he wanted to show that her first affidavit was false. He responded to the charge that Jack McBride, his sound truck driver, had been drawing over $500 monthly from the office payroll by displaying a statement from the House clerk that he drew only $97.85 monthly while working part time in 1959. Long responded that "he is a beat duck and he knows it."[72]

Davis executed an affidavit saying that Long had told him to draw up the false affidavit for Mrs. Foster to sign. He said that Long paid him to get it, but Long denied that and said Davis "got the affidavit up" on his own initiative. He said Davis was never his bodyguard and claimed "the affidavit was worked up in April by Dick Davis and Mr. Foster, who is now chauffeuring Mr. McSween."[73]

A news story reported that on Sunday, August 21, "former Governor Earl K. Long, plagued by bad weather and total inability to live up to his awesome speaking schedule, sloshed from one end of the Eighth District to the other, making a last-ditch stand with his political life at stake." With Speedy Long by his side, they both lambasted Uncle Earl's enemies. Speedy implored, "Send Earl Long up there to Congress and if he don't do any better than McSween in two more years we'll send somebody else." The newsman wrote that "and thus Speedy Long discarded once and for all the reputation he had gained as an 'anti-Long Long.' An unsuccessful candidate for Congress himself two years ago, Speedy had resisted Earl's efforts to bring him onto the stump until this weekend."[74] Long now had Speedy Long, Jewell Long, and his sister Clara Long Knott of Many campaigning for him. Mrs. Knott and a friend drove to many of the meetings. On one occasion, Robert Gentry said, they roared past Long's car to get ahead of him for the next stop. He said that Mr. Earl got mad when Mrs. Knott tried to give him political advice and tell him what to do, and "toward the end I believe he told them to stay in Many."[75]

"Long's murderous schedule began in a downpour of rain in Cloutierville at 10:10 a.m. and ended exactly twelve hours later under threatening skies in Marksville," Bill Bailey wrote in the *Daily Town Talk*. "During those 12 hours the governor made at least five speeches in communities some of which were 100 miles apart. While Long wasted crowds in Belledeau, Hamburg, Spanish Lake, and Goudeau by either failing to appear or arriving more than an hour late, he did manage to throw a block in the path of McSween in two communities. He held McSween up for more than an hour in Cloutierville, where Long was scheduled to speak at 10:10 a.m. and McSween at 10:30. And he accomplished the same thing in Belledeau as his speakers and band appeared without Long himself.[76]

There was a frantic nature to Long's efforts as he picked up his stump schedule. He spoke from school steps, makeshift platforms, and in courthouse squares and stood on benches and pickup truck beds as he summoned all of his strength and pulled out all the stops in his quest for victory. "I don't know if I talked a week I could tell you good people more than you already know about me," he said. "Please go vote. Vote for me! You won't be sorry. I'll do everything I can to make you glad you voted for me. And I won't get the swell head. I been Governor and I been Lieutenant Governor. I been a salesman and I been a lawyer. I been a farmer and I been a stock-raiser. I been up and I been down. I been a little of everything, and I got the same size head, I wear the same size hat now that I always wore. And when my little ol' head gets to swelling to where I think I'm better than you fine people that made me, I hope she pops. I-hope-she-pops!"[77]

A news report said that

> Long did not personally take the stump in Cloutierville until 10:55 a.m. and he spoke until 11:25 a.m. He was due in Spanish Lake at 11:45, but his advance guard, including speakers and a three-piece band, had left by 1 p.m. and the former governor had not made an appearance. As Long made late appearances in Avoyelles Parish, he claimed the car in which he and his attorney were riding got stuck en route to Spanish Lake and that this was the reason for the delay. But a reporter who made the trip from Cloutierville to Spanish Lake observed that roads were paved all the way between the two communities. The Long and McSween paths crossed only at Cloutierville as the ex-governor strayed so far from his schedule that McSween had spoken and left before Long arrived at the other points on the Sunday itinerary.[78]

Long responded to Dick Davis's claim that he had paid him to get Mrs. Foster to make a false affidavit. He said the affidavit was true and that Davis had stabbed him in the back. He renewed his charge that Holt had "sold out" to McSween. "Do you know why Holt is for McSween?," he asked the Goudeau audience. He then shook his pocket, saying "that's why." He made the same charge against Dick Davis at other stops. "Money will do a lot," Long thundered.[79]

At Cloutierville, Long said he had heard that A. J. Foster, Mrs. Foster's husband, had said he would "whip" Long for calling his wife's name. "Mr. Foster ain't gonna whip nobody," Long said. "You know, Smith and Wesson made all people equal and when he jumps on Uncle Earl he's gonna get entertained." Told what Long had said, Foster responded, "You can tell Earl Long that Smith and Wesson didn't stop when they made one gun."[80]

Long had good reason to be suspicious of Davis's loyalty and to feel betrayed by him. McSween told this writer many years later that in the runoff, until he left the Long campaign, Davis reported to him nightly on what Long had been doing, who he was seeing, who was giving him campaign money, and other details of Long's activities. McSween said Davis had thrown out the idea that he would head McSween's congressional office in Alexandria, but no commitments were made.[81]

Long continued to say that he was "one million per cent" for the Kennedy-Johnson ticket in his Natchitoches Parish appearances, but "he changed his approach somewhat in staunchly Catholic Avoyelles Parish. He told his audience in Goudeau, 'You got some narrow-minded people up in the northern part of the district who might vote against Kennedy because of religion, but I won't.'"[82]

McSween had to wait one hour in Cloutierville until Long finished, and in Belledeau he "worked a crossword puzzle while viewers dodged rain drops and listened to speakers for Long." In Goudeau, Mansura, and Marksville, McSween was able to follow his own speaking schedule. He claimed that members of Long's group who had previously fought with him had rejoined him for this campaign because "a doctor went to them with a little black bag and administered a little of that green medicine." He denounced Long, shouting "Shame on you Earl Long! Shame on you Earl Kangaroo Long!" McSween said the district had only two congressmen who served long enough to bring benefits to it and that "under Earl Long's proposition you would have three Congressmen in six years."[83]

Long took time off from the stump on Tuesday, August 23, to go to Winnfield to sign papers donating the old family "homeplace" to the city for a park. He had previously promised the property to the city at a July 4 celebration, but in a stump speech in Winnfield on August 13, McSween claimed Long had repeatedly promised the land to the city, but he doubted the city would ever get it. "If you do," McSween joked, "I think I should get credit for prompting Ole Earl along." Long said that his sister Clara Long Knott had bought an adjacent tract that had been part of the original family property and that it was included in the donation, which he valued at $30,000. He used a deep freeze on the back porch of his farmhouse as a desk and after signing the deed said he had done so "to keep his self respect. Any man would have done it after what McShane said," again intentionally mangling McSween's name. A news story said that after the brief signing ceremony with Winnfield officials, Long took "a short nap before resuming the final lap of the blazing stump schedule that has carried him into practically every hamlet and crossroads in the district."[84]

Robert Gentry said Long was fond of the "old homeplace" site, and "we drove by it almost every time we left out from the Pea Patch." Gentry recalled that "he would have me slow down and he would look, without saying anything. He would just look. But you could tell he was deep in thought. Thoughts about what had been and thoughts about what was soon to come."[85]

The only condition Long put on the donation was that the property be maintained and that a forty-by-one-hundred-foot plot be reserved for burial of members of his family. The donation papers were drawn up by District Attorney Sam Wells of Colfax, whose Eighth Judicial District included Winn and Grant Parishes. Wells and a Winnfield *Enterprise* reporter witnessed the document, after which Long took a short nap before returning to the stump.[86]

Long announced a schedule of talks that would keep him on the road stumping through Election Day, Saturday, August 27, with a speech on Wednesday, August 24, at Bentley at 6:45 p.m., followed by a television program with Speedy O. Long and Mrs. George Long. On Thursday, August 25, he had rallies scheduled at Evergreen, Bunkie, Lecompte, and Glenmora.

Friday, August 26, called for stops at Effie at 4:30 p.m., Pineville at 6:00, and Joyce at 7:45. He said that he would speak on Election Day at Belledeau at 8:00 a.m., Bordelonville at 9:00, Cypress Bayou at 9:45, and Bunkie at 11:00. Long said he had been so busy campaigning that he had neglected to cast an absentee ballot, so he would go from the final rally on Election Day to Winnfield to vote and would then return to his headquarters on Second Street in Alexandria, across from the Bentley Hotel.[87]

In a telephone interview with the Baton Rouge *Morning Advocate* on August 23, which described him as "in high spirits," Long said that he had conducted a "hard, intensive campaign," and had spoken at "places where I hadn't talked for a long time." He observed that he had done everything he possibly could to win by appealing directly to the people because "everything in the Alexandria *Daily Town Talk* is slanted. All I get is what I pay for." Long said Bill Dodd would make radio broadcasts for him Thursday and Friday. Denouncing Dick Davis, Long said,

"Everything he says is the reverse of the truth. He demanded a ridiculously large sum of money from me and when I refused to be shaken down further he started popping off. I never told him to get me any affidavits about McSween. In fact, it was all his own idea and he once told me he was willing to go to jail if he would take McSween with him." Claiming that Davis wanted to secure more affidavits against McSween, Long said, "I told him I didn't need them. It looks like some of those people will vote for McSween no matter what he does. If people made charges against me like they do against him, they'd send me to Africa to campaign. I'd say getting rid of Davis has helped me and not hurt me."[88]

Long, returning to the stump, predicted victory, while McSween abandoned the campaign trail to make a series of telecasts beginning on Tuesday, August 23. Falling back on race to attack his opponent, he charged that Long was the only southern governor who failed to testify against civil rights for Negroes at hearings before Congress in 1959. McSween said he supported the Kennedy-Johnson ticket, calling the nominees "my good friends," but he said he was opposed to the party platform plank on civil rights and legislation that he characterized as "vicious and anti-South." Long, reiterating his "one million per cent" support for the national ticket, said he failed to understand how McSween could be for the candidates but against the platform they had pledged to support and were running on.[89]

On Wednesday, August 24, in a speech at Bentley, Long charged that McSween had a "Republican stripteaser" on his staff and predicted that the incumbent was "on his way to the federal jug" for taking payroll "kickbacks." Speedy Long, noting that McSween had called Earl Long crazy, said "they also called Huey Long crazy." Long workers distributed circulars accusing McSween of voting against legislation that would have reopened and improved Esler Field at Alexandria. McSween, in an appearance later in the day, said that he had voted against one bill for the airport project because it involved "twice the budget called for" but maintained that he voted for a second bill that brought costs with budget limits. He said he didn't know anything about "having a GOP stripper on the payroll" and denied he had called Long "a drunkard," although "I realize he's sensitive about this and I hope he'll be able to stop this bad habit."[90] McSween said Long had polled his full strength in the first primary and would gain no additional support in the runoff.[91]

Long appeared on a live television program with Senator Speedy O. Long and Mrs. George Long while Bill Dodd made radio talks for him Thursday and Friday.[92] Uncle Earl reiterated his opposition to integration, declaring "I'm for segregation but I'm not the Willie Rainach type of segregationist where he wants to boil the colored in oil."[93]

The Baton Rouge *Morning Advocate* on Thursday, August 25, noted

> former Governor Earl Kemp Long, fighting to stay in the political spotlight after months of successive defeats, Wednesday night went into the homestretch of his race for Congress. Long, who will be 65 years old Friday, will try to unseat Rep. Harold McSween, 34, in Saturday's Democratic runoff primary.
>
> In campaigning for the House of Representatives from his native Eighth District, Long has portrayed himself as the champion of the common man while depicting McSween as a pawn of big business. He said "McSween is a better Republican than Eisenhower." Long has stumped over the eight-parish district through the hot August days and nights emphasizing his record while governor. Speaking a half dozen times on a single day to bunches of voters scattered over 100 miles, Long has told them how he sponsored old age pensions, charity hospitals, trade schools, free lunches for school children, the State School for Spastic Children and the State Colony and Training School.[94]

Adras Laborde, the managing editor of the *Daily Town Talk*, wrote in his Talk of the Town column on August 25 that "an upset victory by Mr. Long—something that is doubted by even his friends, many of whom see a close contest but with the ex-governor on the short end—would have to be considered a remarkable comeback."[95]

The Committee to Save Louisiana from National Embarrassment ran a full page ad in the Natchitoches *Times* on August 25 titled "As Others See Us—Louisiana's 'Goodwill' Ambassador," with pictures of strippers Candy Cane and Blaze Starr, Long with the pillowcase over his head, and the message, "Do Not Reward Such Conduct—Vote McSween, No. 3, on Aug. 27."[96] McSween, relying on television, accused Long of "mud-slinging" and said he was using "a band of hatchet men, most of them outsiders, imported into the district as mercenaries." He charged that

Long was trying to "borrow" the seat to remain in the public eye until he could run for governor again."[97]

Long's closing ads asked, "Can a man serve two masters? The Bible says no. Who are Mr. McSween's masters? Here are a few of the Giant Corporations who hire his services: Central Louisiana Electric Co., Alexandria Daily Town Talk, Texas Oil Company, Standard Oil Company." He said there was not much demand for McSween's legal services before he was elected to Congress, but a few days afterward he and his father were asked to join the LeDoux Provosty firm, one of the largest corporate law firms in the state.[98]

"I have worked hard and tried to conduct a clean campaign," Long said. "If you will really think and think hard you will know that Dick Davis brought the affidavit up that they talk about. This affidavit was worked up in April by Dick Davis and Mr. Foster, who is now chauffeuring Mr. McSween. This man never was my bodyguard and never will be. Neither will he have charge of my office in Alexandria. When he approached me with the affidavit he told me that he was willing to do anything to defeat or hurt Mr. McSween. I told him that would help McSween more than hurt him. He said he did not think so."[99]

Long said he was "speaking and doing everything my health and funds will permit. I think I've convinced Mr. Ben Holt I'm not as old as he pretended to think I was. There is lots of good reading in old books; also there are valuable abilities, assets and experience which you can get only through age and maturity. I sincerely believe that at this critical time common sense is badly needed in Washington. A good beating will do little Harold more good than anything else. Here's hoping we give it to him on August 27th. I think I've said enough and appreciate your reading this. I also appreciate your consideration of the issues in this campaign. Go to the polls Saturday. Be a good citizen and vote Earl K. Long—No. 2. Don't forget 'Uncle Earl.'"[100]

Long set a full schedule for the end of the campaign, with stump speeches on Thursday, August 25, at Fairview-Alpha at 5:00 p.m., Chandler's Camp at 6:00 p.m., and Campti at 7:00 p.m. Friday, August 26, the day before the election and his sixty-fifth birthday, called for Vowell's Mill at 5:00 p.m., Provencal at 6:00 p.m., and West Natchitoches at 7:00 p.m. Ads headed "Uncle Earl's the Man" said that Bill Dodd and Speedy Long would be among the speakers. Another ad revised the schedule, adding stops at Evergreen, Bunkie, and Glenmora on Thursday and at Effie, Pineville, and Joyce on Friday in the frantic, last-minute push.[101] Long's schedule for Election Day, Saturday, August 27, listed speeches at Beldeaux, Bordelonville, Cypress Bayou, and Bunkie, after which he would go to Winnfield to vote and return to his headquarters in Alexandria.[102]

Ed Wingate, a cousin, tried to dissuade Long from stumping on Thursday and Friday, telling him he should spend his birthday resting. Long refused, saying he had last-minute campaigning to attend to and was not going to stop when every vote he could get was important. "Ed, I've got a long time to rest," he said. "If I could beat him, I'd die happy."[103]

After several stops on Thursday, with Easy Money Littleton driving, Long headed for Glenmora, where Littleton backed the car up in front of City Hall. They arrived as W. K. Brown was delivering a stem-winding introduction for him. Long motioned to Littleton for a drink, and Easy Money poured him an ounce of Seagram's Seven Crown from a bottle in the wooden bucket of ice, whiskey, and mixers. Long downed it, got out of the car, and began talking at 5:00 p.m. Littleton later remembered that Long was standing in the back of a pickup truck when he grabbed his chest: "He turned to me and asked me to fix him a drink. His chest was hurting. He told the crowd his throat was kinda dry and that he'd have to cut it short. I mixed him a drink of whiskey and 7-Up, which looked like water to the audience, and he sipped it down. I didn't know whether it was a heart attack, but I knew he was sick, seriously sick."[104]

Brown said it was apparent that Long was sick when he cut the talk at Glenmora short. As Long got in his car, he told Brown to continue on with the other speakers the next day. "I tried to get him to go to the hospital and he told me he wasn't going to the hospital," Brown recalled in a letter to this writer. "He told me if he went to the hospital the press and the newspapers would build it up and spread it so bad that he would lose the election. He said he would stay in his room at Hotel Bentley and 'die right here' before he would go to the hospital."[105]

Long and Littleton headed for the hotel, but on the way there they made a brief stop in Lecompte at a furniture store. Long told Easy Money to blow the horn; Littleton said a short man came out and they talked. He may have received a contribution from the man, and despite how he felt, he did not want to pass it up. Littleton said, "I thought he needed to see a doctor, but he was afraid for anybody to know that he was sick so close to election day. If he had let me take him to the hospital right then, he would have lived for several more years; I am convinced of that. But he wouldn't see a doctor. He knew nobody would vote for somebody who might be dying."

Littleton said that when they got to the hotel, reporters were swarming. But "they didn't know he'd had a heart attack," and he walked quickly to the elevator to go to his suite.[106]

Dr. R. U. Parrott, the husband of Earl's niece, came to Long's bedroom at 6:00 p.m. His "Personal History" notes on his patient's hospital chart said Long told him that he developed a severe pain in the left chest about noon and it persisted, which accounted for breaking off the speech in Glenmora. "This pain persisted until about 6:00 at which time I first saw him, complaining about severe pain in the chest running out down to the left arm," Parrott wrote. "The pain was excruciating in character. He was found to have no pulse and no blood pressure; he was cold and clammy and had an involuntary bowel movement. He was only semi-conscious at that time and was complaining of severe pain and rolling and tossing in the bed at that time. He was advised to be admitted to the hospital but would not do so at that time."[107]

"If I go to the hospital now I'll lose a lot of votes from people who figure I'll die," Long said. "I'd rather stay in this hotel room, win the election, and then die, than go to the hospital, lose the election, and live."[108]

Littleton said that Dr. Parrott wanted to have oxygen equipment in the room, and he had the bell captain, Joe Spiro, bring it to the room in pieces. Parrott told Littleton, "Easy, let him keep it on five minutes and take it off for 15. I did that all night long."[109]

After a fitful night, Long gathered his strength to receive newsmen on Friday morning, August 26. Long wore undershorts, an undershirt, and an unbuttoned white dress shirt, and one reporter wrote that "he appeared rested but said he has been getting only four or five hours of sleep nightly during the runoff campaign."

Predicting victory, he said, "I'm not a braggart but I think I am going to win. People are churned up over this election. There's a tide, a current running in my favor. Politics is like that. Right now the current is running in my favor." Congratulated on his sixty-fifth birthday, he laughed, "I'm going to stop having birthdays. Man my age doesn't need to count them anymore. Fact is, more and more men are cutting their ages down just like women who say they're 'over 21.' Some say I'm too old for this job, but my brother [George] was older than I am." Stung by the attacks on him in the ads run by the Committee to Save Louisiana from National Embarrassment, he said "the committee is a lot of bums and non-workers. The front man is McSween. Everything in the ads is written by McSween."[110]

Long put his pajamas back on and returned to bed after the newsmen left. Later in the day, when newsmen asked Littleton, Brown, and others about his failure to appear at scheduled speakings, at which surrogates were representing him, he had them put out the story that he had eaten some "overripe pork" in a sandwich from a roadside stand and had ptomaine poisoning. Newsmen were told that he had a badly upset stomach and nausea.

On Saturday, August 27, Election Day, an Associated Press story said "two physicians gave Long a sedative and put him to bed" on Friday, but "Long awakened at his usual early hour today and sought to complete his speaking engagements but his sister, Mrs. Lucille Hunt, persuaded him to return to bed for another lengthy nap." Mrs. Hunt and Jay Chevalier both denied rumors that he had suffered a heart attack.[111]

With the oxygen tent set up, Long remained in bed Friday and Saturday. Laboring for breath, he refused to take another sedative because he wanted to remain alert, receive reports on turnout, and make telephone calls. Dr. Parrott slipped a tranquilizer into his coffee and implored him to go to Baptist Hospital a few blocks away. The medication made him groggy, but he refused to leave. "Only death will get me out," he said.[112] To dispel concerns about his health, Long received reporters in his pajamas on Saturday morning. Described as "calmly lying in bed," he said that when he stopped at a drive-in for a sandwich, he had asked for barbecue beef but was given pork instead. He said he was going to take a nap and when he woke up he would make telephone calls to raise campaign money "because I've got an overdraft now. I feel fine, he added. The doctors told me I had a touch of ptomaine," Long averred. "I'll take it easy today and I won't visit the polls."[113]

Joe Spiro sat with Long in the bedroom when Littleton ran errands, going to the campaign headquarters where his wife Bertie worked to check on telephone calls and messages there. Easy Money said Long's breathing was very heavy but "he never did say what was wrong with him," although Littleton believed he had suffered a heart attack in Glenmora.[114]

With reporters and photographers camped in the hallway outside his suite, on Saturday evening, before the polls closed, Long admitted them to his bedroom, where he was resting in his pajamas. An Associated Press photograph showed him sitting up in bed, holding a telegram from a well-wisher. Maintaining the food poisoning story, he grumbled, "I'd ordered beef but somehow I got pork." He predicted that he would carry seven of the eight parishes, losing only in Rapides, and there by less than three thousand votes. McSween had predicted that he would win by eight thousand or nine thousand votes. Neither thought Long's illness would have any effect on the outcome. Joe Arthur Sims said it was "not serious and I don't think it had any effect at all." McSween agreed, saying, "I don't think it will mean anything. I hope it is nothing serious."[115]

The early returns were suspenseful, with McSween and Long swapping the lead five times, but after half the precincts were in, Long led and never fell behind. He won by 4,590 votes. W. K. Brown was in the sitting room of the suite when Long called him into the bedroom. He asked Brown to take Mrs. Hunt and Mrs. Jewell Long to the television station to make an acceptance speech for him.

McSween conceded at 10:15, saying "I hope Mr. Long gets along all right and there is nothing seriously wrong with him." Surprised by the outcome, he acknowledged "I thought I was going to win. I just can't see what happened." Reporters in the hallway outside Long's room wanted a statement, and he let them in. "Uncle Earl, half asleep, said 'I really thought my lead would have been six or eight thousand votes. A lot of things were brought out in the campaign that were very unpleasant, about me being crazy. I don't think that helped McSween. I think it hurt him.'" The story noted that Long was resisting pleas by his doctors to go to the hospital. "I may go to the hospital later tonight for a medical checkup, but I don't think anything's wrong," he said.[116]

W. K. Brown returned to report that Long's sister and sister-in-law had made gracious victory statements for him. "He thanked me and I told him it was all over and time for him to go to the hospital and he agreed," Brown recalled. Dr. Parrott called for an ambulance and when it got there the attendants brought a gurney to the room. Brown said that "at this time there was a hall full of photographers and reporters. I asked to please not take any pictures of him on the stretcher and as far as I know they didn't take any."[117]

Littleton said that as they left the hotel at 11:05 p.m., "We were swarmed by reporters, just like a bunch of bees. They even tried to pull him off his stretcher. Uncle Earl covered his face with a newspaper and a sheet. They tried to pull the sheet off and take his picture. Uncle Earl was all upset, just a cussing and raising hell. If they had left him alone he would have given a story."[118]

Long, on the gurney, realized he had left his dentures behind and sent someone for them. While waiting he spoke with a reporter, telling him that his doctors wanted to check his kidneys, stomach, and heart and the effects of the ptomaine poisoning that had overcome him. Asked whether he thought McSween was as tired as he was, Long said, "He's young. He can take it."

"I don't think anything is wrong," he maintained, but he was going to go to the hospital to rest. "I'm very proud and happy and thankful because I won my home district," he said.[119]

"We couldn't hardly get in the hospital for the reporters," Littleton remembered. Dr. Parrott and Dr. Worley put him to bed "and went to work on him." Dr. Parrott's notes on Long's condition at admittance said "heart sounds are very distant. Head, neck, chest, and abdomen examined. Remainder of physical exam not done due to the critical condition of the patient at time of exam." In his notes on Long's medical history, Parrott wrote that he had had "the usual childhood diseases" and that "Patient had a rather severe coronary several years ago and apparently recovered. The Patient has a past history of headache, severe bronchial cough with shortness of breath for the past several years, and expectorates large amounts of frothy material, particularly in the mornings upon arising. This has gradually increased in severity until the present time."[120]

The Baton Rouge *Morning Advocate* the following day trumpeted, "Earl Long Wins For Congress—Former Governor Goes to Hospital Following His Political Comeback—Earl Kemp Long, the Pea Patch philosopher, won a seat in Congress from the Eighth District of Louisiana Saturday while flat on his back and under sedation in a sick bed." In the final returns from all 316 precincts, Long had 38,966 to McSween's

Table 1 Results of Earl's 1960 Primary Runoff		
	Long	McSween
Avoyelles	6,796	5,484
Grant	2,977	2,178
LaSalle	2,264	2,124
Natchitoches	4,298	3,595
Rapides	12,004	13,955
Sabine	3,393	2,665
Vernon	4,304	2,320
Winn	2,930	2,055
Totals:	38,966	34,376

34,376, a margin of 4,590. He carried every parish but Rapides and lost it by only about 2,000 votes. His biggest margin was in Vernon Parish, which he won 4,304 to 2,320.[121] Table 1 shows the results.

In later years, McSween engaged in much introspection about his defeat. In 1999, in a letter to this writer, he said that many politicians who supported him in 1958, including Bill Dodd, John McKeithen, and Camille Gravel did not help in the 1960 race. He said he was unable to hold onto them because "their intensity of feeling had dissipated," and he had failed to spend time cultivating them. McSween said, "I ran myself ragged from the time of the 1958 campaign through the 1960 campaign," to no avail.[122]

"Earl won owing to the failure of strategy and tactics in my campaign," McSween acknowledged.

> Bill Dodd and Joe Arthur Sims made a lot of difference in the second primary for him—both superb stump speakers and of more consequence than those engaged in his campaign's entertainment. Although I assume responsibility for this breakdown, I did not hold control. I should have retained control but delegated much. You know that political campaigns compare to military campaigns and football games: they don't proceed as planned. My using two sound trucks for stump speaking in 1960, as in 1958, an anachronism, conveyed a voice not the same as those over radio and TV. Stump listeners wanted entertainment and ridicule. When this was reported in the press it did not sound like me—didn't sound appropriate for me. Moreover, I should have

> taken a different approach toward a sick former governor by showing a more delicate/kind form of ridicule not apparent. All of these aspects presented dilemmas that I did not resolve in my mind at the time. Also, I had to listen somewhat to contributors who were applying a form of the Golden Rule, I regret to admit.[123]

McSween said, "I realize now that I didn't have my heart in the 1960 campaign, so disillusioned I was, inter alia, not only about living in Washington, with wife and children ages eight, six, and one, the latter not yet born when I was first elected in November 1958, but with the insatiable demands of the political right, political naivete of many on our side of the bi-factional divide, the reality that one in politics must devote all one's time to it, and other factors on a long list."[124]

McSween was not prepared to devote "all one's time" to politics, but that was what Earl Long had been doing for over thirty years. McSween was confident that Long would not survive the campaign and would die before the first primary. To his own dying day, he insisted that the "medical grapevine" had been adamant that the strain of the campaign would kill Long.[125]

Adras Laborde wrote in his political column that Long made "a comeback from what many had believed was political entombment," counted out by everyone but himself. "Unquestionably, Mr. Long's unbelievable durability on the campaign trail, his challenging ardor on the stump, his flippant—if careless—oratory, has placed such cardinal human emotions as sympathy for the underdog or compassion for the downtrodden—all paid off in votes that spelled victory, to the surprise of political savants," including himself.

Laborde said that McSween's "inability to match punch for punch in the bare-knuckled campaign was a major factor in his defeat. Some will argue that McSween launched the attempt to answer Mr. Long in kind too late; others will argue that he should never have tried in the first place because it was strictly out of character for him."[126]

With his immediate treatment diagnosed as necessary rest, Long was made comfortable in his hospital room. Clem Huffman, W. K. Brown, Jay Chevalier, and others were in and out, and Easy Money Littleton was a constant presence. Blanche Long came to Alexandria and visited him twice on Sunday, August 28. "I just wanted to see how he's getting along," she said. "He looks well, his color is very good. He talks quite easily now."[127]

Telegrams poured into the hospital, congratulating him on his victory and wishing for a speedy recovery. They came from friends and other politicians, as well as from national figures that included former president Harry Truman and Senator Stuart Symington.[128]

Dr. Parrott told newsmen that there was no reason to alter his original diagnosis of exhaustion and dehydration caused by overwork and food poisoning. Parrott said that "Long is very happy. That election victory gave him a shot in the arm." He put up no-visitors and please-don't-knock signs on the third-floor hospital room, saying "I want him to rest here several days." To guarantee that, he had Long's clothes removed from the room.[129]

Long's campaign speakers were overjoyed at the outcome of the election. Bill Dodd, addressing Mr. and Mrs. Albert A. Fredericks as his "Partners in Crime," wrote "now that we have succeeded in sending our dear beloved leader to Washington, we can turn our energies to lesser projects." Dodd believed that Russell Long had not only failed to do anything to help his uncle but preferred for McSween to win. He told them, "My mouth is watering like a street sprinkler with the anticipation of reading about or, if my strained budget will allow, being on hand in person to see the installation of Uncle Earl with his sweet little nephew in the audience. I can lick my chops with a warm feeling of satisfaction over the way his soft little feminine hands will tremble as he clasps and unclasps them while the Old War Horse is being saddled for the dash to National Fame and Glory in the Washington Sweepstakes. I can see him drop his pari-mutuel tickets on McSween as the loud-speaker announces that Uncle Earl has won and is led to the winner's circle."[130]

Dodd predicted that with Uncle Earl there, "The halls of Congress may not smell so sweet to the society bugs; the members may waterproof their pants legs; and individual glasses may become the fad, but no one will complain of dullness. No one will go to the cloak room, except to change clothes, when our Champion takes the mike. Unless I'm badly fooled, Uncle Earl will place his brand on the National Capitol, his mark upon its leaders, and his common sense upon its doings."[131]

Long had made several bets on the election, and he was eager to collect them from his hospital bed as his strength began to return and he felt better. There were several stories about the wagers. In one, several days before the runoff he spent the night in the room he kept at the Hot Wells Resort motel. He loved to go to the spa for mineral baths and massages and kept changes of clothes in his room. The front porches of the motel rooms were separated by concrete walls, and that morning a family staying next door heard a man on his porch talking loudly. Tom Leeper said, "We soon figured that he was on the telephone placing bets on the election, and finally that it was Uncle Earl himself. We listened with amusement until our oldest boy could not restrain himself and ran down the steps to see what was going on. He quickly returned, bursting with excitement, and announced that the caller next door was sitting on his porch 'in his underwears.' We listened a while longer and determined that Earl was betting on himself."[132]

On Monday, August 29, Long wanted to collect a substantial bet that Charlie D'Amico, an old friend who owned the Sportsman's Lounge, was holding for him. D'Amico's place was a restaurant and bar that was popular with the courthouse crowd in Alexandria and ran a handbook upstairs.[133]

With Long regarded as an underdog in the primary, Tullos oilman Glen Lowe bet him $5,000 that he would lose by five thousand votes in the first round. Long covered that bet and bet another $5,000 that he would win by five thousand votes, so they had a total of $10,000 riding on the outcome. When Long ran four thousand votes behind McSween in the primary, neither bet won, so they agreed to let it ride for $10,000 each on who won the runoff. D'Amico held $20,000 on that bet in his safe, plus $4,000 more for side bets Long made.[134]

"Feel like walking?," Long asked Littleton. "Go to Charlie's." Easy Money thought Long wanted "something good to eat" and asked what he would like; Long said he wasn't hungry but to get something for himself when he picked up a bag from D'Amico; he called D'Amico to tell him he was sending Littleton over. Littleton said that when he walked into D'Amico's, "Charlie got up and got me a paper bag" and accompanied him (Littleton) back to the hospital.[135]

Many years later D'Amico described the scene, saying "Earl spread the money all over his hospital bed, counted it, stuffed it in his pillowcase, and laid down on it." Long then called Bob Levins, an officer with Rapides National Bank, and asked him to come to the room. When

Levins got there, they recounted the money, in stacks of bills of different denominations, and verified the total. Long told Levins to put the money back in the bag and put it in the bank. D'Amico thought Long did not want to deposit it in an account, but only wanted it held in safekeeping until he could get it.[136]

While Long was getting the paper sack of cash, Dr. Parrott issued a medical bulletin stating that he was "much improved" and should be able to leave the hospital in two or three days. Parrott again did not disclose that Long had suffered heart failure, and news stories continued to say that he was recovering from ptomaine poisoning and exhaustion. Dr. R. B. Wallace Sr. said his examination of Long "found him doing very well. He looks well, his color is good, and he is definitely improved. I would say his condition is satisfactory." Dr. Parrott told newsmen that there was no reason for him to alter his diagnosis of exhaustion and dehydration caused by overwork and food poisoning.[137]

Reporters continued to seek information about Long's condition. A Wednesday, August 31, Associated Press story was headlined "Rumors Claim Long Suffers Heart Attack—Physician Refuses to Confirm or Deny Reports on Illness." It said that "persistent reports that former Gov. Earl K. Long had a heart attack today could not be officially confirmed or denied. One physician who said he was not the authorized spokesman said Long 'is doing all right, under the conditions; he ate a good supper and feels all right.' He would neither confirm nor deny that Long had a heart attack." Dr. Parrott, the only physician authorized by Long to report on his condition, was out of town and unavailable for comment, but attendants at the hospital denied that he had suffered a heart attack.[138]

Long sent Littleton for newspapers every day. He must have been pleased with the editorial in the Baton Rouge *Morning Advocate* on September 1. It was probably written by Margaret Dixon, the dean of Louisiana political writers and managing editor of the newspaper, whom Long called "Miss Maggie." Her weekly column, The Capitol Beat, covered the state political scene and was must reading for anyone in state politics. Long and Dixon were fond of each other, and the governor appointed her to the LSU Board of Supervisors. When, in 1959, his leaders stepped in to end his rant before a joint session of the legislature, Mrs. Dixon led him from the podium to his office behind the chamber. In Galveston, she learned where Long's room was at the hospital and joined other journalists in throwing rocks up at the window to get his attention. He yelled out that he was not crazy and asked them to get him out of there.

Titled "The Wizard of Winnfield," the editorial said that he should be "placed high on the list of major political phenomena" because

> crushed to earth, he rises again, like the legendary wrestler Antaeus, who was invincible so long as he touched the soil. And no Hercules has yet appeared, capable of keeping him off the ground long enough to end his public career. His congressional victory has been the cause of some astonishment and dismay in Louisiana and will be the subject of much comment, not all of it kind, in other parts of the country. But as Earl Long makes no apologies for his vicissitudes, his troubles and his antics, so widely reported, neither do those who know him best make any apologies for him. They advise, instead, that when Earl Long reaches Washington, his voice, hoarse and rasping though it is, will be the voice of long experience and considerable political acuity. It will be the voice of a man who knows what a lot of people want and how they think, of a man whom those same people believe to be sincerely interested in their well-being.
>
> They will find in Earl Long a brave man, a man of what some people call incredible gall and others call incredible nerve, who often has dared to say what others thought but feared to say, and who has not stood aside from formidable opponents and heated controversy. They will find an extraordinarily blunt and plain-spoken man who almost always means what he says. Whatever may be said about Earl Long, it cannot be said that he is mealy-mouthed, hypocritical, or holier-than-thou. He is not deceptive or secretive. Those who face him know how he stands, even if they don't like it.
>
> They will find a man of incredible endurance, inexhaustible energy, and strong determination. His energies at times may have been misdirected, but he never has been saving of them. He has been totally oblivious to exhaustion, frayed nerves, and apparently crumbling health. Even the distant spectator finds his campaigns exhausting to watch. It's hard to keep a man like that down.
>
> Washington will see in Earl Long a man who is the antithesis of everything in which the hidden persuaders, public relations experts, television advisers, and makeup specialists of Madison Avenue believe. The latter will see a man in a plain state, unvarnished, unhomogenized, unadvised, not propped up by

> anybody, and speaking without ghost writers or prompters. The sight should be good for their souls.
>
> Gov. Long's career in Congress will depend on his ability to retain his energy and equilibrium, a task which even he must admit becomes more difficult when advancing age and ill health are combined. He has done many astonishing and shocking things. He may do others. But his political victories do not reflect conditions unique to Louisiana, nor always credit to Louisiana. They are not without reason—reason that has meaning to all others who seek elective office in any part of the country.[139]

On Saturday, September 3, Dr. Parrott said that "last night he looked pretty good when I saw him. His color was good. I think he's exhausted. You know he conducted a hard campaign for a man his age. He almost beat himself to death."[140]

Long received Associated Press correspondent James McLean, whom he thought had always treated him fairly, in his hospital room on Saturday, September 3. McLean said he "remained flat on his back, breathing under an oxygen tent. Long said he hoped that Governor Jimmie Davis could keep public schools open, although he was under pressure to close those in Orleans Parish in the face of integration of the first grades of two schools to start November 14. "I'm glad he's in there instead of me," Long said. "He's got two college degrees. I have none."[141]

McLean described Long as "indestructible." Sleepy from sedation, Long said, "I tell myself I'm leaving the hospital Tuesday. I'm the doctor. I understand my case as well as anyone." He said two friends, Dr. Robert Bernhard, a heart specialist who had treated his 1950 heart attack, and Dr. Edgar Hull, had come from New Orleans to see him and "they keep telling me to rest, to take it easy. If you leave it up to those doctors, they'll have you resting for the rest of your life. I haven't felt bad since I've been here, and I feel a whole lot better today." Long's physicians had ordered complete rest for him, with very few visitors. McLean said Long had personally granted permission for his interview, and "while there have been reports that Long suffered a heart attack after a rough campaign trail, physicians have neither confirmed nor denied the report."[142]

Long said he was looking forward to going to Washington. "I'll be there and I don't intend to keep my mouth shut," he said. "There are too many federal agencies but not enough to give the people what they need." He told McLean on parting, "I think I'm kind of a statesman-like politician. A politician is misunderstood. He is a man capable of doing something for the people. That's what I tried to be."[143]

Although his doctors tried to restrict the number of visitors, Long enjoyed seeing his old sidemen and told Littleton he was taking them all to Washington with him.[144] Blanche visited again and said that "when he had the heart attack and was hospitalized, I went up to see him immediately. He had refused to allow himself to be hospitalized until all the votes were counted and he was sure he'd won. He said if he died, he was going to die right there in bed and didn't care so long as he knew he'd won the election. By the time I got there, his voice was so gravelly and hoarse that he could hardly talk. Some of the time in the hospital he'd be as nice and sweet as he could be; then he'd just go completely off. He'd yell and scream. On the Sunday afternoon before he died, he was screaming and hollering like that, carrying on just like a wild man. But I stayed with him until he died."[145]

Littleton stayed in the hospital room, sleeping on a cot. He said that on one of Blanche's visits "they had a cuss fight and Earl yelled at me, 'Easy Money, get her out of here.'"[146]

W. K. Brown said that Long was "very tired but sharp and alert" on his visits. "One night he asked me to call the returns out to him and it was amazing how he knew the wards and precincts and the location of them. He remembered very well the Glenmora precinct." Brown said that on Sunday, September 4, "I went to see the Governor and Congressman McSween was outside in the hall writing a note to give Earl. Harold saw me and asked me to give it to the Governor as he was in a hurry to get back to Washington. I went in and gave the note to Earl and he told me immediately to go get Harold and have him come in to see him. I tried to locate Harold in the hospital and he was already gone. Earl was disappointed because he wanted to talk to him."[147]

On Monday, September 5, 1960, Littleton was keeping watch in the room when Long awakened. Easy Money said that "he drank a full cup of coffee, smoked two cigarettes, and ate two bars of Almond Joy, but took the almonds out. He said 'Easy, call Ray Ellington and tell him to come up here. I want to send him to Shreveport to pay the literature bill.' I went out to the nurses' station and used the pay phone to call Ray. I went back to the room. I said 'I'm gonna shave you, alright?' He said 'yeah.' I shaved him," and then "he coughed and strained, couldn't catch breath."[148]

Easy Money told newsmen that "they sounded like gasps. It was a funny racket. I saw he was in sort of a strain. I went outside and called the nurse. She went and looked at him and said, 'He's going,' and she called the doctor. And then he died. He just died."[149] A few years later, Littleton remembered that "he turned blue. His eyes open. He done died. I put my hand under his head to keep him up. He didn't suffer or scuffle. That was the easy way. He went easy."[150] In another interview, he said that Long suddenly moaned and "I held him up in my arms. His head flopped over to my chest and then he groaned and died."[151]

Dr. Parrott recorded that Long died at 7:10 a.m. of acute coronary thrombosis.[152] He said that the massive heart attack caused a complete occlusion in one of the channels of the heart, blocking the blood supply.[153]

The *Daily Town Talk* rushed out an extra with a huge "Earl Long Dies" headline announcing his passing.[154] The Winnfield newspaper reported that "the moon eclipsed, it is rumored, the night Huey died. Monday night, after Earl's demise, the lovely orb again shyly took refuge from view."[155]

In 1993, Jay Chevalier said that he rushed from his home to the hospital after hearing a radio news bulletin that Long had died. He told a lurid story of going to the hospital mortuary with Dr. Parrott and holding Long's heart in a jar of formaldehyde in his hands. Littleton was very upset at Chevalier's interview and obtained Blanche Long's authorization for him to obtain copies of the medical records from Rapides Regional Medical Center, successor to Baptist Hospital. The hospital noted that a number of pages were illegible due to the age of the records but that most could be identified by the procedures done. The letter from Joy Hollis, director of the hospital's Medical Records Department, was also signed by Dr. John A. Worley, the cardiologist who had treated Long. The letter said "it might be noted that the patient did not have an autopsy performed at the time of his death."[156]

Littleton and several others said there was no autopsy. However, Jay Chevalier maintained that there was one and that Dr. Parrott pointed out the areas of damage from the 1950 heart attack and the 1960 one.[157]

Dr. W. L. Ryder, Rapides Parish coroner, said that his office did not perform an autopsy since Long died in the hospital, under a physician's care. "It was not a coroner's case," Ryder said, "and the autopsy was performed by the hospital."[158]

Perhaps the final word on the autopsy came from Dr. Parrott, who told the Baton Rouge *State-Times* that he performed the autopsy at the hospital morgue shortly after Long died. The news story stated that "Dr. Parrott said the autopsy showed evidence of a gall bladder disturbance and a long history of gastronomic trouble." He said there was "a sizable scar from the 1950 heart attack, but it was on the other side of the heart from the scar tissue resulting from the last attack." Dr. Parrott said the final attack caused a "tremendous occlusion" of the heart that a man "in the best of health" might have been able to survive but that Long "just was too worn out physically to make it." Dr. Parrott said he had tried on several occasions since 1950 "to get Earl to have various tests made for gallstones and everything else, but he was always too busy." He said he had not examined or treated Long for a number of years until the last heart attack.[159]

Crossing Huey

Earl helped run Huey's campaigns for governor and senator, but they fell out when Huey would not support him for state office. Earl appeared as a witness against Huey's organization in the Overton hearings and was cross-examined by Huey, shown asking Earl to identify a document in 1932. Courtesy Trice Political Photographs Collection, Louisiana Research Collection, Tulane University.

Together Again

Two years after the Overton hearings, Earl and Huey had patched up their relationship, and Earl was an adviser to him during a series of seven special sessions of the legislature that consolidated Huey's power. This 1934 photo shows Earl conferring with Huey at the dais of the state senate. George W. Wallace, executive counsel to Governor Oscar K. Allen, is seated on the left. Courtesy Trice Political Photographs Collection, Louisiana Research Collection, Tulane University.

The First Oath
Earl Kemp Long was governor of Louisiana three times. He first took the oath of office on June 26, 1939, upon the resignation of Governor Richard Leche (center). Earl's wife Blanche Revere Long is on the left. Louisiana Supreme Court Associate Justice John R. Land administered the oath. Jack McGuire Collection.

The Second Oath
Earl Long won election to a full term as governor in 1948. He was sworn in on May 11, 1948, at the LSU Football Stadium by Judge Casimir Moss of Winnfield. Moss had defeated Earl's brother Julius in a race several years earlier with Earl's support. Earl and Julius never reconciled.

The Third Oath
Long won a third term as governor in the January 17, 1956, primary over a large field. Louisiana Supreme Court Chief Justice John B. Fournet (left) administered the oath of office on May 12, 1956. At that point, Long was the first governor in Louisiana history to hold the office three times. Courtesy Earl K. Long Papers, Mss. 3126, Louisiana and Lower Mississippi Valley Collections, LSU Libraries, Baton Rouge, Louisiana.

Basking in the Sun
Earl Long and his wife Blanche on Inauguration Day 1956 on the steps of the Louisiana capitol prior to Long's taking the oath of office for his third term as governor.

Peak Long
On May 12, 1956, three Longs held state or federal elected office in Louisiana. US Senator Allen Ellender (left) joined US Senator Russell Long (Huey's son), Governor Earl Long, and Eighth District Congressman George Long on the inaugural platform in what *Time* magazine called "Louisiana's monumental living tableau to Huey."

Pea Patch Farm
Earl Long's beloved Pea Patch Farm outside of Winnfield was his home when he was not living in Baton Rouge. It served as his retreat as well as the base for his political operations in north-central Louisiana. Courtesy Robert Gentry.

Clem Huffman
Clem Huffman spent over twenty-five years working for Earl Long. He ran the Pea Patch Farm from 1934 until Earl's death. He displayed a painting of the Pea Patch Farm when he received the Friend of Earl K. Long Award from the Louisiana Political Hall of Fame. Courtesy James Ronald Skains, *Piney Woods Journal*.

Linda Huffman
Earl and his wife Blanche were childless. Earl doted on Clem Huffman's daughter Linda, loving her as if she was his own. She has no photos of her with Earl but treasures her memories of him today. Courtesy Linda Huffman Cox.

Working the Phone
The Pea Patch Farm was Earl's respite, but he was never away from politics. He's shown here working the phone in the living room of his house on the farm in the 1950s. Courtesy Earl K. Long Papers, Mss. 3126, Louisiana and Lower Mississippi Valley Collections, LSU Libraries, Baton Rouge, Louisiana.

Before the Storm

Governor Earl Long (right) and former governor Jimmie Davis (left) flank Claiborne Parish segregationist State Senator Willie Rainach at a May 1959 event in Shreveport. Rainach, who chaired the legislature's Joint Legislative Committee on Segregation, led the White Citizens' Councils' efforts across the state to purge black voters from the registration rolls. Davis, who would succeed Long after the 1959–1960 elections, supported the Rainach effort. Long opposed it because it was an attack on part of his political base.

Intemperate Remarks

On May 26, 1959, Earl Long appeared before a house committee meeting in the Louisiana house chamber speaking in support of his amendments to liberalize voter registration laws and to block purges of black voters that were being pushed by the White Citizens' Councils. During heated exchanges, Earl lost his temper. His appearance before a joint session of the legislature the next day, when he again lost control, prompted Blanche Long to forcibly take him to a mental hospital in Galveston, Texas. Courtesy the Louisiana Collection, State Library of Louisiana.

Governor in Exile

After being held against his will for two weeks at the John Sealy Hospital in Galveston, Earl Long successfully petitioned on June 15, 1959, for a habeas corpus hearing, signing his petition "Earl K. Long, Governor in Exile by force and kidnapping." He was escorted from the hearing during a noon recess. In a compromise with his family, he agreed to go to Ochsner Hospital near New Orleans for rest and treatment.

Back to Louisiana

Governor Earl Long stopped to talk with newsmen before boarding a Louisiana National Guard plane to fly from Galveston to New Orleans on June 18, 1959. Blanche Long, who had been watching the scene from a window on the plane, returned to the tarmac to guide him away from the reporters and photographers.

The Basement Hearing

Long left Ochsner Hospital in New Orleans the morning after he arrived, saying he would take his rest at the Pea Patch Farm. Blanche Long signed commitment papers in Baton Rouge. East Baton Rouge Parish sheriff deputies intercepted Earl's car and took him to the basement of the parish courthouse, where the coroner and a psychiatrist interviewed him. The coroner signed the papers for a judge to commit him to Southeast Louisiana Hospital in Mandeville. Captain Herman Thompson, East Baton Rouge sheriff's office chief of detectives, is shown trying to convince Earl to leave the state police car in which he was traveling and get into the sheriff's vehicle. When the governor refused, he was dragged kicking and screaming from the car by six deputies and taken to Mandeville. Courtesy State Library of Louisiana, Louisiana Section.

A Free Man

Earl Long won his release from Southeast Louisiana Hospital at a court hearing on his petition of habeas corpus on June 26, 1959. He called a meeting of the State Hospitals Board immediately prior to the hearing. It dismissed the officials responsible for holding him, their replacements ordered his release, and the case was dismissed. He went to the Pine Manor Motel outside Covington where he met the press with a sheet draped across him.

Western Swing
After a panel of doctors he called to his side said that he had suffered a nervous breakdown brought on by overwork and a series of small strokes but was not mentally ill, Long decided to embark on a vacation consisting of a tour of horse race tracks. Hounded by photographers and their flashbulbs, Long resorted to putting an airline pillowcase over his head with a hole cut so he could see where he was going when he arrived in Fort Worth, Texas, on July 11, 1959. The photo garnered worldwide attention.

A Friendly Face
Governor Long arrived in El Paso on July 16, 1959, on his tour of western horse race tracks. He was greeted there by his cousin and longtime aide David Bell, who also served as the state commissioner of veterans affairs.

Not-So-Special Session
Rested and reinvigorated, Long returned from his western swing and jumped back into the fray by calling a special session of the legislature. When his allies rebelled and adjourned the session twenty minutes after it convened, he took the microphone in the senate, saying "I'm not especially mad at anybody" and apologized for his outbursts in May. Courtesy State Library of Louisiana, Louisiana Section.

The Subject and the Author
Earl Long ran for lieutenant governor in 1959 on a ticket headed by James Noe. Jack McGuire, then a high school senior working on a paper about him, met with the governor at a speech in New Orleans.

Their Last Tangle
DeLesseps S. "Chep" Morrison, the reform mayor of New Orleans, was the antithesis of Earl Long. In the last days of Earl's final term as governor, French President Charles de Gaulle visited New Orleans. When Long left his seat at a luncheon to whisper to Morrison about the welcome remarks he would give, the mayor told him to "keep it short, no more than five minutes." Long spoke for three minutes and said afterward, "I gave that two-bit mayor two minutes back."

Blowing the Hunt Horn
Earl Long liked to say that he was born a country boy and remained one throughout his life. One of the things he loved to do was hunt wild hogs. He's shown here blowing the horn signaling the start of a hunt near the Pea Patch Farm. His hometown of Winnfield now celebrates Uncle Earl's Hog Dog Trials each year. Courtesy Louisiana Political Museum and Hall of Fame, Winnfield, Louisiana.

13.

IN UNCLE EARL'S WAKE

Blanche Long took charge of the funeral arrangements and acted as the next of kin and principal mourner despite their separation. Long's survivors were her, as his estranged wife; one brother, Julius Tison Long; four sisters, Mrs. Robert Wesley Davis, Mrs. Olive Long Cooper, Mrs. Clara Long Knott, and Mrs. Stewart S. Hunt; and six nieces, four nephews, nine great nieces, and ten great nephews. Long's body was taken to Hixon Brothers Funeral Home in Alexandria, where it was prepared for viewing in a large bronze casket with an oval glass sealer on its rounded top. The first mourners came that evening, and before the home closed, one thousand people had paid their respects and offered condolences to Blanche Long, Russell Long, and other family members. Blanche said, "I really think he would have been elected governor again even if he was in a rocking chair." Russell refused requests by photographers to pose by the casket. "I feel that this is a personal thing," he said. "It just wouldn't be right." Speedy said, "He wore me out. He went into the campaign with all the vigor of a young man. He felt he knew the district and could best represent the people. One of the last things he told me was he didn't understand why people he had helped were opposing him. I think this worried him. I think it was on his mind a lot right at the last."[1]

Blanche reflected that "politics was his life. He did what he wanted to do most. He realized he was sick—extremely sick—but hoped that he would live until the election was over. He wanted to win this election more than any other one. He did. He was happy. If he had lost, everyone would have said the defeat killed him."[2]

There was some confusion about whether Long would be taken to Winnfield or to Baton Rouge. Blanche called Governor Davis to request that Earl be laid in state in Memorial Hall of the capitol. Davis assented and offered any assistance the state could give in providing appropriate honors.[3]

On the funeral motorcade's 120-mile trip from Alexandria to Baton Rouge, motorists pulled to the side of the road in respect as it passed. A news story said that "scores of pedestrians watched" as it passed through small towns and rural intersections: "Onlookers removed their hats, Negro field workers paused to stare, a farmer stood on his tractor, motorists pulled aside when warned by the flashing lights of the oncoming cars" in a gesture of respect.[4]

Long's body was taken to the great hall of the capitol, where Huey had rested twenty-five years before. Over twenty-three thousand people passed by the open coffin. Emile Comar, a political writer for the New Orleans *States-Item*, wrote a moving story about the scene: "He could have called hundreds of them by their first names, inquired about uncles and aunts, remembered the maiden names of married women, remembered a joke on a political worker. The people moving in the line chatted; legislators, officeholders and their friends conducted private get-togethers. At times the whole thing took on the air of a political rally, but a quieter rally than Earl liked."[5]

The Baton Rouge *Morning Advocate* reported that "big shots and little guys, neatly dressed businessmen and Negro capitol janitors, young women and old, filed slowly past Long's bier." Former Governor Dick Leche came, as did Abraham L. Shushan (chairman of the Orleans Levee Board under Huey, O. K. Allen, and Leche). Leche, Shushan, and Seymour Weiss had gone to prison in the Scandals that rocked the state after Huey's death. Shushan and Weiss "sent a tremendous blanket of purple and white orchids that covered the lower half of the casket like a fairy tale quilt."[6] The United Press International reported that "Louisiana's greatest pilgrimage of mourners since the death of Huey Long filed past the ashen remains of Huey's little brother Earl, gaudiest of an untamed breed of politician."[7]

Long's pallbearers were his nephews and grandnephews, Senator Russell B. Long and his brother Palmer Reed Long; James Long, son of Julius Long, the only Long brother still alive; John Ducournau, grandson of Long's sister, Mrs. Olive Long Cooper; John S. Hunt, son of another sister, Mrs. Lucille Long Hunt; Paul Revere, a nephew of Blanche Long; Robert V. Parrott, son of Long's niece, Mrs. Charlotte Long Parrott; and Jerry Menefee of Monroe, son of Long's close friend, J. M. "Pete" Menefee. The honorary pallbearers included Governor Davis and the four living ex-governors, Sam Jones, Robert Kennon, James A. Noe, and Richard W. Leche.[8]

The services held at the First Baptist Church in Baton Rouge were presided over by the Reverend J. Norris Palmer, who had baptized Long in 1955. "Earl Long has passed from our midst, not as he would have chosen," Palmer said in a eulogy. "He wanted to fight on and serve on." Palmer said that he baptized Long after he left the governor's office in 1952, recalling that "he made it clear that he wanted no publicity. He waited to join between his periods of service to the people and he was deeply grateful that I did not call attention to his presence in the church. He said he did not come to church for that." Palmer said, "Thousands will remember Earl Long's consuming passion—to do all he could for people of modest or below average income. No one can question his sincerity or his desire to help which continued to the day of his death. Another characteristic I must mention is that of generosity. His well-known attitude to money has been expressed frequently. He was never happier than when he could give something to somebody."[9]

Palmer quoted the poet Will D. Muse, who wrote, "The fight is done, please let me all alone, quietly here, for I am weary. Do not try to waken me. It is not best. Leave me alone, the fight is over." He closed by reciting "let me live in a house by the side of the road and be a friend to man." A choir sang Long's favorite hymn, "In the Garden," at the conclusion of the services. His favorite words from it were "I come to the garden alone, while the dew is still on the roses, and the voice I hear falling on my ears, the Son of God discloses. And He walks with me, and He talks with me, and He tells me I am His own, and the joy we share, as we tarry there, none other has ever known."[10]

There were over one thousand people in the church, including political allies and adversaries. Blanche Long, sitting with Russell, cried when the choir sang "Precious Lord, Take My Hand." The news stories listed the names of dozens of the attendees; one noted that "a cluster of about 30 Negroes participated in the services from the rear balcony."[11]

After a long procession to Winnfield, the casket rested in the little church that his mother had founded, while hundreds came all through the night to say their farewells. The local paper estimated there were from two to three thousand people at the burial the next day.[12]

On September 8, 1960, exactly twenty-five years to the day after Huey Long was shot, Earl Long was buried in the red clay of Winn Parish, in the plot of the old family homestead that he had set aside when he donated it to the city of Winnfield for a park, with instructions that there be swings for children and benches for old people.[13] Dupre Litton said "his actual burial place is located where the bedroom was located when he was born."[14] On July 4, 1963, a statue of Long was unveiled at the Earl K. Long Memorial Park before a crowd of one thousand people that included family members, friends, and a large number of public officials.[15]

One reporter wrote that "Mrs. Blanche Revere Long, the ex-Governor's widow, bereaved and near exhaustion from the four-day wake, sobbed through the rites." Dr. W. L. Holcomb, the pastor, performed the committal ceremony. "He won the election, but lost his life," Dr. Holcomb said. "He went down fighting. No doubt, this is how he wanted it." Bill Lynch, a longtime political reporter, wrote that "hundreds of neighbors clad in overalls, and fellow politicians, sweating in ties and coats, were here to attend this final ceremony."[16]

Ed Clinton wrote in the Baton Rouge *State-Times* that "Earl Kemp Long made his final journey here to the little town and farm grounds he could never forget, even at the peak of power which comes to a Governor in the Mansion in Baton Rouge. The three-time Governor of Louisiana was home for good in the rolling red hills of North Louisiana which had produced him." He said that after the brief service the casket "was lowered into the grave dug in the red clay of the Winn Parish hills." Clinton noted that Governor O. K. Allen was buried a few blocks away, and he wrote that prior to the graveside services, there were many callers at the church before the casket was moved to the burial site, but there was one difference, "a concession made to the doctrine of segregation. Callers at the capitol took their places in line regardless of race, creed, or color. Here, Negroes were required to enter through the back door of the church and await their chances to file past the bier. The few Negroes who attended the graveside services stood in detached groups, most of them across the street from the park."[17]

State Representative W. K. Brown said that some of Long's friends wanted to bury him on the state capitol grounds, by Huey, and they took that up with Blanche during the visitation at the funeral home. A headline in the Baton Rouge *Morning Advocate* on September 6 said "Body to Rest at Capitol with Services Held at First Baptist—Former Governor May Be Buried On Capitol Grounds Near Huey." The story said permission for interment in the Sunken Garden would require legislative approval, and a poll of members was underway."[18]

Brown said that "I went to Hixon Brothers and told Mrs. Blanche that the Governor did not want to be buried on the capitol grounds. She asked me how I knew that. I told her he had told me that and that he had a will made out to that effect. I told her Mr. Sam Wells, District Attorney at Colfax had the will. She asked me to ride with her out to Mrs. Parrott's house and call Mr. Sam Wells which I did. He told me he had the will at the courthouse in the vault and he would go and get it and bring it on down for Mrs. Blanche to read. After she read the will she said she would honor the will and the Governor would be buried in Winnfield."[19]

Brown confused the donation of the Long family property in Winnfield—which Wells had prepared and witnessed when Long signed it on August 23 at the farm—with a will. The deed reserved a small plot for burial of members of the Long family that Brown and others took to mean that he wanted to be buried there. None of the participants apparently recalled the July 2, 1959, press conference on the back porch of the farm home during which Long said that he expected to die in Winnfield and be buried there. It was, however, generally accepted that he wanted to be buried there when he reserved a parcel in the park for family members.

14.
LOUISIANA REACTS

The news coverage of Long's death and funeral was extensive. The reporting included photographs and film from his career and tributes and reminiscences from friends and foes.

Camille Gravel said that Long's death "closes the amazing career of the most aggressive, determined, and resourceful man of politics ever known to Louisiana and perhaps in any other state. I regret his passing. He has been much to Louisiana. Never neutral, ever partisan, those of us in politics knew him either as a formidable foe or potent ally."[1]

Dr. Robert Bernhard said that "he wasn't keen on following doctors' orders, unfortunately. All the hurting he did was mostly to himself."[2]

James McLean, the Associated Press correspondent who in the hospital had the last interview with Long, wrote that "on the stump, Earl was a rural bombshell, with his rumpled clothes, coarse words, hoarse voice, and his way of dynamiting a foe with his fuse-like tongue."[3]

The Baton Rouge *Morning Advocate* noted Long's passing in an editorial that called him the "miracle man of Louisiana politics" in tribute to his remarkable political comebacks. It said that

> Earl Long died not in a moment of confusion and defeat but in a moment of satisfaction and victory and happiness, an end that many men might envy and one that even his worst enemies will not begrudge him. He died quietly and even peacefully, an end that was in marked contrast to a life that was filled with controversy.
>
> In a way, Long died at one of the many peaks in a remarkable career. When he left the governor's office last May after having suffered a defeat at the polls when he ran for lieutenant governor and after confinement in two mental hospitals within a year, many wrote him off. But the old war horse tricked them as he had done so many times before. He got into a political rough-and-tumble of the kind he loved best and he won, proving himself once more a

> factor in Louisiana politics as he had proved himself time and again in the past. His death is probably directly attributable to that campaign. It was bitter and vicious and grueling but Earl Long was in there fighting until the votes were counted and he had proved the winner. It was a source of satisfaction to him and his loyal followers in the state. Indeed, many of them were already writing him in as Louisiana's next governor.
>
> Earl Long himself loved politics. He had plans, and many of them, for Congress. His career will go down in Louisiana's history as one of the most remarkable in the state's political history. Now that fiery spirit is at rest. No other politician on the scene today was able to command such loyalty and such devotion as Earl Kemp Long inspired among a large segment of the state's voters.[4]

Margaret Dixon wrote the album liner notes for a recording of excerpts from Long's speeches and interviews. "What kind of Congressman Earl Long would have made must remain a matter of conjecture," she noted,

> but as one who covered the political scene in Louisiana over the three periods he held the post of Governor and who watched his activities with a reportorial eye for a quarter of a century, I say without fear of contradiction that he would have livened up the staid congressional halls.
>
> I have been called a captive newsman insofar as Earl K. Long is concerned. That I deny, but I freely admit I was a captivated one. To me Earl K. Long was the most fascinating, funniest, wisest, best informed and thoroughly delightful politician I have ever known. He liked to call himself the last of the red hot papas in politics and to say that after he was gone the breed would vanish from the earth. I agree. There never was and never will be another Earl Kemp Long.
>
> Unfortunately Earl Long did have a breakdown. I am unable to say what was wrong with him but the most logical explanation I have heard was that he probably suffered a series of small strokes which, I am told, cause an exaggeration of one's usual conduct. Well, Earl Long's conduct was never usual but to me Earl Long's breakdown was one of the great tragedies of American politics. Here was a man dedicated to public service, who regarded Louisiana as his child. If something was right for the state, Earl Long never hesitated although he might hurt himself in the process. Persons outside of Louisiana who base their opinion of Earl Long entirely on newspaper accounts of his

> activities are at a loss to understand the hold he had on the people of Louisiana. His election to Congress is perhaps the best illustration of the affection in which he was held because it was gained after he had been in and out of two mental hospitals and after he had done many things which would have wrecked a lesser politician. But Earl Long knew his politics and he knew his Louisiana. His quips were legendary, his invectives widely quoted, and his remarks, both public and private, had his listeners rolling in the aisles. His frankness was sometimes embarrassing but his word was good and his political followers knew it.
>
> Earl Kemp Long was without inhibition. He loved to play the races and he did. He said frequently he was no "goody-goody" and although he cussed a bit on occasion, he had a genuine kindliness about him. In the midst of racial controversy, he never exploited the Negro and his interest in providing benefits for the poor and needy was genuine, going far beyond the getting of votes. In fact, Earl Long's breakdown came when he was fighting to keep the segregationists from removing Negroes from the voting rolls, a fact that has been overlooked in the northern press although it should at least have guaranteed him a place in the liberal sun.[5]

Dr. T. Harry Williams, the Louisiana historian, said Long was not particularly interested in going to the House of Representatives, and that he ran for Congress "only to demonstrate that he was on the comeback trail to the governor's chair. At the time of his sudden death he gave every indication that he would win an unprecedented fourth term." Williams said that "Earl had a genuine concern for poor people and believed that government—and with him this meant the state—should act to improve their lives. He, and also Huey, realized that Negroes were poor people, the poorest of the poor, and had to be included in any program of social uplift. It was an awareness that set the Longs apart from virtually all other Southern popular leaders, who saw the blacks only as a vague group on the fringes of white society or as a menace to be conjured up at election time."[6]

When Governor Davis came from his office behind Memorial Hall to pay tribute to Long, as he lay in state, for being a "kindly, Christian man," Davis was accompanied by his public safety director, Murphy Roden. A bodyguard for Huey, on September 8, 1935, Roden grappled with and shot Dr. Carl Austin Weiss, the assassin, in the corridor outside the governor's office after Huey was fatally wounded. Davis said he was not surprised by Long's death "because he was a hard worker and he just worked himself to death in the campaign. He was a man who wouldn't quit."[7]

A Negro woman, Lula Stull, who said she was Long's age, sixty-five, mourned him as she waited to pass by the casket. She had sat in Memorial Hall for many hours so that she could be first in line. "I felt we have lost a great man," she said. "The Lord wanted something good, that's why He took him."[8]

Blanche Long said her husband "enjoyed running for governor, but he didn't enjoy being governor," a statement that surprised many who had served with him. Dr. M. O. Miller noted that while Earl had ranted at Russell publicly when he was committed, he told Miller privately that he still admired Russell and "was proud of him. He felt Senator Long was capable and told me many times Russell was just as good as his father."[9]

Russell Long, who had sent a telegram to the hospital congratulating his uncle on election night, said "I am deeply grieved at the passing of my uncle. He made the state a good governor during his three terms and served with distinction in several other important capacities."[10]

Among many other officials, Congressman Otto Passman stated that "few public officials, if any, ever worked harder for the masses and delivered in greater measure to the underprivileged and unfortunate than Earl K. Long. Doubtless historians will record him as one of the great humanitarians of his time."[11]

Theo Cangelosi said of his former client, "He could conquer all, by the volatile force of his own personality, but even he could not control Old Earl. Earl possessed more raw courage and determination than any man I ever knew or read about. Tough odds meant nothing to him. Frank and open to a fault, Long detested hypocrisy. I didn't know Huey like I knew Earl, but Earl had absolutely no give-up in him at all. The pressure was never too great for Earl, but Huey apparently had his breaking points. It's well known that during the impeachment process, Huey wanted to resign as governor. Over the years you could pick that up from insiders. Earl primarily was responsible for persuading Huey to stay in and gut it out."[12]

Edgar Coco believed his old friend's situational awareness was without equal in politics: "Earl Long could see through a situation better than anyone. He'd rule by confusion. He never would let us organize.

He wanted to be damn sure no one else called the shots. Earl was closer to the ordinary people than Huey. Earl really knew the poor people, the little people. He'd go back in the woods to shake hands with them, white or Negro."[13]

"Earl Long did so many great and wonderful things for the folks in Louisiana, but so many people have forgotten all about them," Clem Huffman said, recalling his longtime friend and employer. "Homestead Exemption was one of the greatest things he ever did. I remember that my Dad lost 40 acres of the finest land you ever saw, down around French Forks, because he couldn't pay $12 in taxes. Another great thing was the Old Age Pension. When he started going around talking about giving all the old folks $50 a month I told him that he better not promise the people that unless he could really do it. He told me, 'Clem, if I have to sell the State Capitol I'm gonna give them an old age pension.' Earl did a lot of other good things like school books, school lunches, and school buses. He was a wonderful friend to the working folks and the poor folks."[14]

Huffman said he was with the governor for twenty-five years and was certain that "Earl Long never went crazy. In his last two years he had two heart attacks and several light strokes. Earl was just an old worn out politician with health problems. But you have to remember that Earl won his last race."[15]

Former Governor Robert Kennon told newsmen that "while we did not agree politically at all I never had a personal dislike for him. While we were of different political philosophies, I found much to admire in him, particularly his tremendous energy and willingness to fight against all odds. I believe that if Earl Long had to go, he would have rather had it this way—in the midst of success in the political arena."[16]

Dr. Felton Clark, president of Southern University, the largest land-grant Negro college in the South, noted that Long, "within the framework of his political outlook and philosophy, showed an active sympathy for the education of Negro people. He did so in big and little things, and with blunt, sudden speed." Dr. Clark recalled a visit to the mansion to seek additional funds. Long received him, told stories for an hour, and then asked, "Well, what do you want?" The educator said "Five million dollars." Long responded, "All right, I'll give you the five million dollars," and that was that.[17]

Bill Dodd said that Earl "knew no equal in the field of practical politics. He planned his campaigns like Robert E. Lee and fought his battles like George S. Patton, never using a cannon on a flea or a flyswatter on an elephant." The story said that despite their prior political differences, he gave Long, "desperate for a political comeback, a helping hand in the congressional contest" for old times' sake. Dodd said that "Earl gave more to the people than any of us. He gave his life."[18]

State Representative W. K. Brown of Grant and Rapides Parishes delivered a eulogy on the floor of the Louisiana House of Representatives during the next session in which he said Long

> was a fighter who died because he would not quit the political fight, even to preserve his health and prolong his life. Earl Long loved politics and devoted his life to politics and public service. He was truly "the last of the red hot papas," as he was fond of referring to his brand of campaigning. It is somehow fitting that the miracle man of Louisiana politics should have died in a moment of satisfaction, happiness, and victory, having again accomplished a political victory as remarkable as any in a political career unparalleled in the annals of politics. Now that fiery spirit is at rest, and his body is returned to the red clay hills from which he came. Yet his name and his memory live on and will live on as long as there are men who can recall his impassioned oratory, and it will live on as long as the governmental philosophy he established continues to function.[19]

15.
LOUISIANA EDITORIAL REACTIONS TO EARL LONG'S DEATH

The New Orleans *States-Item* reviewed Long's career the afternoon of his death, describing how he would "revel in the hurly-burly of legislative sessions, when he spent most of his time in one of the houses or in the hotel lobbies where legislators were congregated. His favorite posture was to stand with his feet slightly apart. He always carried his big, broad-brimmed hat in his left hand, resting it on his hip. The coat gaped wide. Long was willing to pay for expensive suits and shoes, but he was a picture of sartorial carelessness. As he talked with first one and then another, his eyes darted from one side to the other. He always knew who was entering a room and who was leaving. He had a way of turning abruptly and walking off when he was finished with a conversation. 'Otherwise they'd drive you crazy,' he once explained."[1]

"He liked plain food, plain living," the story continued. "The Mansion was a little pretentious for him, and his idea of comfort was to retire to the small, tin-roofed house—Mrs. Long called it a shack—at the Winnfield farm and loll, shirtless, in a rocking chair. He had a Negro cook to prepare the pork, grits, eggs, turnip greens, and other fare that he relished. 'Uncle Earl' was a betting man. He made frequent appearances at the Fair Grounds during the season, hauling out a roll of hundred dollar bills when he wanted to get down a bet, and that was on every race. He enjoyed junkets to Louisville for the Kentucky Derby and to Baltimore for the Preakness. While he liked a drink, he did not have a reputation as an imbiber."[2]

The Baton Rouge *State-Times* said that Long had "kept going on borrowed time for a year or more" and had made "a most astonishing comeback whose achievement was possibly the motivating force that kept him going for the past year" for "a victory that cost him dearly in the effort." The newspaper suggested that

> the historians of Louisiana will deal more kindly with "Old Earl" than did many of his contemporaries. The history of his two [full] terms in the governor's office will deal more with some of the social legislation he pushed through and less with some of the fiery episodes that sometimes shocked the state. The drama of his illness of a year ago will not be forgotten, but memory will tend to see him more in the light of a person who was temporarily ill and thus entitled to sympathy. Controversial, colorful, energetic, imbued with a belief that he had the primary political power in Louisiana to help the "poor folks," Earl Kemp Long was of a mold that has since been broken. We are not likely to see his type again in Louisiana. And with his death will go the last person who could bring together the diverse groups that became known so long as the "Long" faction in Louisiana politics. While many have differed with him in politics, their present thoughts will dwell more on his remarkable abilities and solid achievements.[3]

Uncle Earl's old adversary, the *Times-Picayune*, noted in an editorial that "few political leaders had as many ups and downs or attracted as much public attention as did Earl Kemp Long, three-time governor of Louisiana." After a brief review of his career, the paper said,

> Many of the official acts of the late governor were those of a spoils politician. He believed in big pay rolls and large numbers of jobs for his followers. His record, however, was not without its credits. As an example, when legislative efforts were made to restore to the governor practical control of Louisiana State University, Gov. Long ended the attempt. His attitude was, "LSU is doing all right under the present setup. Don't disturb it." More than a year ago, when he performed many unusual acts, this newspaper expressed the opinion that such actions were the result of illness. Some doctors who examined him agreed; others did not. He was a participant in several escapades which brought no credit to Louisiana. We still believe that this was not the conduct of a healthy Earl K. Long. "Uncle Earl," as he was affectionately known by thousands of men and women, will be widely mourned.[4]

Its afternoon sister, the *States-Item*, acknowledged that most of its editorial comment about Long was "of a critical nature" but said that was done "while Earl K. Long lived, while he had the opportunity—which he frequently exercised—to speak in his own defense and to criticize the newspapers for being critical of him." The editors said

> now that his voice which was familiar to thousands of Louisianians for more than two decades is silenced, we feel it proper to be guided by the classic Latin advice: *de mortus nil nisi bonum*—of the dead be nothing said but what is good. Accordingly, we note that in the death yesterday of former Gov. Earl K. Long, Louisiana lost one of its most colorful political figures whose support at the polls reflected extraordinary popularity over a broad span of years. Among many of our citizens he will be remembered as the advocate of more liberal old-age pensions, of free school lunches, of general welfare assistance. Their image of "Uncle Earl"—as he liked to call himself—will always be the one which pleased his tired old heart, that of champion of the common man.[5]

The *Shreveport Times*, in a particularly uncharitable editorial, said that "Earl Long will occupy a big chapter in Louisiana's history. Perhaps he will be viewed better in retrospect many years from now than by some at present. And perhaps some who have viewed him favorably, despite his personal conduct, will view him less favorably. He died to some extent as he had wished—after a political victory. But he died quietly where he would have preferred a spectacular end. Undoubtedly the physical trials and tribulations of the congressional primary campaign took their toll. But the real toll was taken over many years. It cannot be said that Mr. Long died as a martyr, for he did not. He died because, knowing his own ailments, he refused to carry on in a manner that might have prolonged life. The time came when the heart was too tired to go along with the body."

The newspaper claimed that Earl's consuming desire was for history to regard him as "greater" than Huey and accused him of a "willingness to take almost any means to gain an end." It dismissed his 1948–1952 administration and said that he squandered the opportunity "to go down in history as perhaps Louisiana's greatest Governor of all time." After returning to office in 1956, "Once more opportunity beckoned but again Earl Long failed to answer the call. This time he brought not only criticism and ridicule upon himself but upon his state—from over the whole nation." Acknowledging Long's "smashing victory" in his last campaign, the newspaper said that "to him, this may have been Earl Long's greatest victory, for it came when he had to win or become a political has-been. That would have broken his heart—perhaps been even more devastating physically, for few men in history have been as thoroughly consumed by personal ambition as Earl Kemp Long."[6]

The *Shreveport Times* noted that Long's death "was not only front page news throughout the nation but drew editorial comment from coast to coast." The newspaper ran extensive excerpts, most unfavorable.[7]

16.
NATIONAL EDITORIAL REACTION

Across the country, newspaper editorial reaction to Earl Long's death tended generally to respond to the caricature of the man. For example, the Baltimore *Evening Sun* wrote that "he had a rich, rascally charm which, for his purposes, served as well as statesmanship. Up to the end Louisiana voters thought so too. They kept him at or near the state's political controls for 25 years and, but for the collapse of an understandably overworked heart, were about to launch him at 65 on a new congressional career." It noted that

> of his enemies Long asked no quarter and gave none. The important thing to this peppery, coarse-grained up-countryman with the sharp political wit was the friends he managed to amass. His appeal was squarely to the underprivileged. He delivered substantially and, in return, those who had been shut out for a generation from Louisiana's tight Democratic circle were willing to give Ol' Earl nearly anything he wanted. Earl Long lacked Huey's vaulting and spine-chilling ambition but he was still no model for earnest young politics students. He was tricky and truculent by turn, a demagogue of the clearest stripe. Last year there were even official suggestions that his mind was giving way. What is not so generally understood, however, is that Earl Long may turn out to have been one of the earliest symbols of a new political generation in the Deep South, a living demonstration that a man can put aside racism and labor-baiting and still hold tight to his political power. Ol' Earl was an oddly spiky branch on which to look for so tender a political bud, but political historians may eventually decide that the bud was there.[1]

The Birmingham *News*, in a mean-spirited assessment, hailed his passing: "Death early yesterday ended the madcap career of Louisiana's former governor, Earl Long, and saved the people of his state and the whole country, for that matter, much further embarrassment." It said

Long's victory "came as a shock and surprise and started much speculation on what might happen when he got to Washington" and noted that "Earl Long was crude and uncouth even before his mental breakdown last summer but he, like his brother, Huey, was something of a hero to the back-country and cross-roads. Let us hope he was right when he called himself 'the last of the red hot poppas.'"[2]

The "Old Stump Jumper Runs Final Race," the Atlanta *Constitution* editorialized. "Probably the only inevitable thing in the life of Earl Long was death," it noted.

> Opponents, reformers, and lunacy warrants could not keep him out of office. Misfortune could not frustrate him and reason could not predict him. He had just been elected to Congress when his driven body gave out. Now he lies in state in the Baton Rouge Capitol near the spot where an assassin's gun stilled his brother, Huey. And the state of Louisiana, enormously rich in resources but egregiously abused by its politicians, says goodbye to one of those colorful men it could not help but elect. Let it be said that there was a good deal of brash honesty in Earl Long. His cunning was sometimes turned to good purposes. His colorful courage in adversity made him a monument of audacity. But the kind of politics he practiced was not fitted to this era in a South that is sated with barnstormers and starved for responsible leaders. All honor to the old stump jumper. Louisiana loved him to the last. It is just as well that she will not look upon his like again.[3]

The Dallas *Morning News* said that Long's "peaceful end was not the way he had lived. He was tempestuous, bold, adventuresome, courageous—and, at times, crude. His death, perhaps, is a blessing. In January he was due to go to Congress, and the seriousness of the times demands more than Long was able to give. He was a sick man, obviously. No one can say how he would have acted in the House of Representatives. But every little mistake, every breach in good manners, would have been seized upon by the prejudiced liberals of the North to make the South look ridiculous. It would have been unfair to Long, to Louisiana, and to the South."[4]

"His opponents toppled 'Ole Earl,' as he liked to be called, from time to time but he always came back to power and came back with characteristic flamboyance," the Norfolk, Virginia, *Pilot* noted. "He was again riding high when death took him. What happened was one more demonstration of what the Long name means in Louisiana. 'Ole Earl' won while flat on his back in a hospital."[5]

The Arkansas *Gazette* said that

> compassion demands its due in the passing of any human being, and perhaps especially so in the case of a man as human as Earl Long. Yet in full candor, there must be general relief in the removal of Mr. Long from among us before he took his seat in the 87th Congress. Earl Long's death could hardly be described as a personal blessing which removed him from suffering. Certainly he was at times irrational, even near the point of madness, but it must be conceded that few men have enjoyed mental illness so much. It was nevertheless a blessing for the country to be spared the spectacles which Mr. Long would inevitably have created in Congress, on a bigger stage than he had in Louisiana during his recently expired term as governor. There may be a temptation to contemplate the divertissements that might have been offered in the House by the man who, as governor of Louisiana, almost shoved the visiting President Charles de Gaulle into the cherries jubilee. Yet these are, veritably, the most critical times mankind has ever faced and in the seat of the American government great decisions will be made. The causes of this country and of free peoples everywhere could not but sustain some damage in the sight of democracy working to send so capricious and irresponsible a figure as Earl Long to the Congress of the United States.[6]

"It was always hard to tell how much of him was real and how much was hokum," the Charlotte, North Carolina, *Observer* said.

> The real rarely showed. The real was implicit in a guy who peddled hardware by day and went to school at night until he was able, at 31, to pass a bar examination and to become, in the words of his associates, an able attorney. He called himself "a jackleg lawyer." He called himself "the last of the red hot papas," and though that, politically, was part of the hokum, he was, politically, hot as a pistol. He took up where his brother Huey, the late, unlamented "Kingfish" Long, left off—and there were some who claimed that Earl improved on the act. A strict segregationist, Ol' Earl somehow managed to carry the Negro precincts. And if he gave away a lot of groceries in order to do so, his disciples never suffered from malnutrition. His critics said Ol' Earl

> was crazy, and nobody can deny that he did some crazy things. "If I'm nuts, I've been nuts all my life," he insisted. "And I'm not quite as dead as they said I was." It was part of the hokum. Until this week, it was part of the public image of a guy named Earl Kemp Long of Louisiana.[7]

The Houston *Chronicle* noted his "Death on Eve of a Triumph" at the end of his "roller coaster political career." It recognized his "astounding capacity for inspiring loyalty in his many followers and an equal capacity for evoking strong revulsion among those who disagreed with him politically. Perhaps Louisiana politics, among the stormiest in the nation for more than 30 years, will be quieter in the future now that Earl Long is gone."[8]

The Des Moines *Register* editorial was headed "The Last Hurrah for Earl Long" and said that "Earl Long's career was not as spectacular as Huey's, although it was rambunctious enough. Even Huey never equaled those nightmarish months last year when Earl Long was in and out of mental institutions, traipsing around the country living it up, and fighting so desperately to hold onto the governorship." It noted his "comebacks" from defeats and said that his "formula for achieving public office, which he copied from his brother, was based on a real talent for Southern backwoods public speaking, on the use of the spoils system, on promises to the 'little people' and attacks on 'The Interests.' He bought off opponents by giving them lucrative jobs, chose his enemies as well as his friends with care, and turned his moral vices into political virtues. He was a clever, if not an intelligent, man, utterly uninfected with ideology. He believed only in victory, and he knew how to achieve it in his backward state. His type of politician is going out of fashion even in the rural south."[9]

"Long's Career Reflects on Voters," the Chicago *Daily News* said, writing that "he was sometimes criticized on his home grounds for 'undignified' conduct, which was about like criticizing a hog for bad table manners. His career confirmed the fears of the early critics of democracy that the voters would not invariably show discrimination in their choices. His idea of progressive government was a lavish welfare program of bonuses, free lunches, charity hospitals, and abundant free entertainment. 'Ol' Earl' used to describe himself as 'the last of the red hot papas in politics.' We wish we could believe it."[10]

17.
SETTLING UNCLE EARL'S ESTATE

Friends and foes, newspaper editorials and commentaries all discussed Long's legacy. Blanche Long acted quickly to claim the material aspects of it. She had a will he had made in 1955 that left everything to her, and she took control of the Estate of Earl Kemp Long when rumors of a will executed after their separation surfaced. (The "Estate" is the legal name of the document and court filing, and it was the legal entity Blanche administered as executrix.) She also sought possession of his personal property and monies owed him.

Rumors and innuendo that trailed the Longs had it that both Huey and Earl had amassed massive personal fortunes that they somehow kept hidden from the public and investigators who tracked them. The scandals that erupted after Huey Long's assassination in the 1930s toppled many of Huey's cronies, but Earl emerged unscathed despite the fact that, as Huey's brother and the heir to his political organization, he was a ready target for investigation. Huey, Noe, Seymour Weiss, O. K. Allen and several minor figures had formed the Win-or-Lose Oil Corporation and secured valuable oil leases from the state. They and their families have received tens of millions of dollars over the years from lease royalties. Rumors that he, too, had cashed in followed Earl for the rest of his life. With his death, his estate became a matter of public record. Unlike Huey, Earl Long left a very modest estate, most of which was derived from small parcels of real estate he'd bought over the years.

Whatever was there, Blanche—armed with Earl's 1955 will—was determined to get everything he owned. Charlie D'Amico said that several days after Long's death, Blanche, accompanied by "a young man," visited him at his restaurant. She said that she had come across evidence of the election bets in Earl's papers and asked about the money. D'Amico told her that he had not seen it since turning the bag over to Earl in his hospital room. In 1989, Bill Carter wrote a column in the *Daily Town Talk* titled "Long's Last Wager" that described how the money was brought there and mentioned her visit to D'Amico. It came to Blanche's attention, and Carter said D'Amico told him Blanche wrote a letter to him denying the incident ever took place. She knew nothing about the bet and had never heard of him, according to D'Amico, and said she came to Alexandria after Earl's death only because one of his sisters asked her to. "D'Amico was not upset by her denial," according to Carter, "but he assured me he had witnesses to her visit. But if the money ever showed up again, he did not know about it."[1]

Ellis Littleton said that Blanche got the money from the bank several days after Earl's death. He said that it was not deposited in an account in Long's name but was put in the vault, in the paper sack for safekeeping, until he could get it. "Miss Blanche got that $24,000 and she got just about everything else that the Governor had," Littleton said.[2]

Easy Money said that Long, whom he felt loved him like a son, told him in one of their hospital conversations that he wanted to set him up with "a real place of his own" at his home in Deville. He told Littleton that he wanted him to have a bull and several cows that were being held for him at an auction barn in Alexandria, a number of rolls of barbed wire at the Pea Patch to make a pasture for the cattle, a pickup truck, and the 1960 white Buick that Easy Money drove during the campaign. Littleton said that several days after Long died, Blanche asked him to meet her at the Holiday Inn in Alexandria. She was accompanied by "a young man," probably the same one D'Amico said was with her, and told him that she heard he had been talking about Earl's promised gifts to him. She said that she was taking everything except several rolls of the barbed wire that he could have.[3]

Littleton was disappointed that he would not receive what Long had promised. "There was nothing in writing," he said, "but there were four witnesses in the room that day," including a man from the auction barn "who told me which bull and which cows I was to get." He said he could not fight Blanche because "I just didn't have enough money to hire a lawyer. I didn't know how to handle it."[4]

While Blanche Long moved quickly to establish herself as Earl's heir and executrix, several members of his family sought to contest the will she had and search for a later one. Littleton said that when Earl got out of Southeast Louisiana Hospital, after filing for separation, he was "so mad at her for putting him in the insane asylums that he wrote up a new will." On September 9, 1960, Olive Long Cooper and Clara Long Knott, Earl's sisters, and John Ducournau, a great-nephew, filed a court petition in which they said "they are reliably informed and believe and therefore allege that the late Earl K. Long left a last will and testament executed within the past twelve months, which will is in full force and effect and is valid in all respects." They asked that a search be made among his papers and effects and any bank boxes owned by him to find the will. The court ordered that a search be made "particularly among the personal papers and effects of the late Earl Kemp Long in his home" and for any bank boxes.[5]

Blanche Long responded three days later by stating that Long left only a will dated February 16, 1955, which she filed for probate in Eighth Judicial District Court in Winnfield, asking that she be confirmed as testamentary executrix and that an inventory of the property left under terms of the will be made.[6] A news story said that "another will, claimed by relatives to have been written in 1959, has not been found."[7]

Whether there was another will that would have affected Blanche's standing as the sole heir was never determined; none was ever found or produced. Earl's 1955 will naming Blanche his sole heir did not have any reference to any further disposition of his property other than a provision that he wanted the old Long family parcel to be donated to the town of Winnfield "for use as a memorial park." There was no mention of reserving a small plot within it for burial of members of the Long family. W. K. Brown had said District Attorney Sam Wells was holding a will that stated that he wanted to be buried in Winnfield and that at his request Wells brought it to Blanche at Mrs. Parrott's home. He said that after reading it she said that Earl's wish to be buried in Winnfield would be honored. As previously noted, however, Brown confused the Act of Donation of the Long family property that Wells had prepared with a will. It did not specify that he wanted to be buried in Winnfield but it did reserve a small plot within the property for burial of members of the Long family. Presumably Long's niece, Mrs. Parrott, looked at it with Blanche, and if it was actually a will, subsequent to the 1955 one, she would have made that an issue in her request that a search for another will be made.

Judge H. L. Allen ordered that the 1955 will submitted by Blanche be accepted the same day she filed it, on September 12, 1960, after W. Bryant

Parker and Wilma R. Lockhart appeared to testify that they had witnessed it and identified the document presented to the court as the one that they had witnessed. Blanche was confirmed as executrix; Kenneth Watts, a notary public, was appointed by the judge to take the property inventory, with assistance from appraisers appointed by him; and Clem Huffman, Long's farm manager, was appointed caretaker of the farm, cattle, and other personal property in Winn and Natchitoches Parishes.[8]

Long's testament directed that all of his just debts be paid; that he bequeathed to Blanche Revere Long all of his property, except his undivided interest in the "old home lot" on Maple Street in Winnfield, "which it is my desire and it is my understanding that my brothers and sisters desire to dedicate this property to the town of Winnfield for use as a memorial park"; and that Blanche be appointed testamentary executrix of the will.[9]

On October 6, 1960, Kenneth Watts reported to the court that he had not found any lock boxes in Winn Parish. He also said that a search of the farmhouse found no papers, documents, stocks, bonds, or other assets among the personal effects.[10] Long also left properties in East Baton Rouge, Rapides, and St. Tammany Parishes, and the court appointed notaries public there to inventory them.

On October 20, 1960, the inventory of Long's property in Winn Parish was submitted to the court. It included the Pea Patch farm property of 320 acres, bought in 1937, valued at forty dollars per acre, for $12,800, of which Long's one-half community interest was $6,400; an additional tract of three acres "where the residence of the deceased is located," valued at $1,000, with his interest $500; an eleven-acre tract, valued at $1,662.50, with his interest $831.25; a twenty-five-acre tract valued at $1,275, with his interest $637.50; an eighty-acre tract valued at forty dollars per acre, for $3,200, with his interest $1,600; one-half interest in eight acres, at forty dollars per acre, for total of $1,600, with his part $800; and a 10/12 interest in forty acres, for $1,330, with his half $665.[11]

Long's personal property included "household furniture, located in dwelling house known as the home place, including two electric refrigerators, two electric deep freezers, and all other living room, bed room, kitchen, and other furniture and chairs, appraised at $2,500.00," with his one-half community interest of $1,250. The balance of the personal property included an International brand flat body truck appraised for

$1,250; a 1958 Ford pickup truck, valued at $1,000; a tractor and disc, at $500; nine head of horses and mares appraised at $1,000; one mule, for $50; one hundred head of cattle and calves, at $10,000; one hundred goats at one dollar each, for $100; forty hogs, at $5 each, for $200; and fifty chickens and ducks, at one dollar each. The total value of personal property was $16,600, with his half $8,300.[12]

A Winn Parish tract of 33.25 acres was appraised at $50 per acre, for a total of $1,662.50, with his one-half $831.25. Another tract of 25.50 acres was appraised for $1,275.00, with his half $637.50. A tract of eighty acres was valued at $3,200, with his half $1,600. Another tract of forty acres was valued at $1,320, with his half $665. Blanche sold two parcels in Winn totaling 154 acres to Tremont Lumber Company for $11,850 in 1963, while a forty-five-acre tract in Rapides Parish was sold for $7,500. A six-acre tract in Grant Parish was sold for $300. A lot in Concordia Parish was sold for $350. A parcel of over one hundred acres in St. Tammany Parish, on Bayou Lacombe, was sold for $12,500.

The recapitulation put the total inventory of real estate and personal property in Winn Parish at $39,467.50. His one-half community interest was $19,733.75.[13]

The community property in East Baton Rouge Parish included cars and station wagons used as sound trucks. There were a 1960 Dodge Station Wagon, $1,800; 1960 Buick Sedan, $2,600; 1960 Mercury Sedan, $1,800; 1959 Chevrolet Sedan, $900; 1959 Ford station wagon, $1,400; another 1959 Ford station wagon, $1,400; 1959 Mercury sedan, $1,500; 1960 Ford station wagon, $1,500; and another 1960 Ford station wagon, $1,500.[14]

The balance in the Estate of Earl Long checking account in the City National Bank of Baton Rouge was $468.21. An "Earl K. Long, Campaign Account" at the Bank of New Orleans contained $288.87. Certificates No. 343 and No. 357 for fifty shares each in the Times-Picayune Publishing Company were valued at $12,600.[15]

The property in East Baton Rouge Parish was valued at $27,757.08. His one-half interest was $13,878.54.[16]

Blanche secured court approval to sell all the vehicles and livestock at private sale for not less than the appraised values.[17] On May 17, 1962, she secured court permission to sell one share of the Sherwood Forest Country Club, eight shares of International Paper Company, and one hundred shares of the Times-Picayune Publishing Company.[18]

It was ironic that Long was a stockholder in the publishing company. He called the newspaper the "Times-Pick-On-You," and on several occasions, visitors to his office found him eating ice-cold watermelon at his desk and spitting the seeds on a copy of the paper spread on the floor. Walter G. Cowan, who retired as managing editor of the paper after a distinguished career in journalism, said that Long probably acquired his stock when shares were offered to the public for a brief period in the 1930s. Cowan said that when he was night editor of the New Orleans *States*, the morning paper's afternoon sister, Long would often call to complain about stories. Cowan said that "he would start off saying how terrible we were, and all the awful things he hoped would happen to us, but then he would let out a little chuckle and say that he still wanted us to do well and make money since he was a stockholder."

When Long was traveling and called the paper to get the latest race results, Cowan had Long's calls routed to the news desk for an interview before he could be transferred to the sports desk.

There were a number of claims against the estate by people who had served Long in the campaign and were not paid before he died. Joe Arthur Sims filed suit against the estate in May 1962 to recover $36,012 that he claimed was due him for fees, loans, and expenses incurred during the campaign. Sims said that he was due $25,000 in attorney fees promised him by Long after his release from Southeast Louisiana Hospital, $8,500 for a loan, and $2,500 for expenses in the campaign. He said that he wrote Mrs. Long in October 1960, a month after Long's death, explaining the expenses, and she responded that the claim would be considered but took no further action on it.[19]

Leroy Chandler, a motel and bar operator, filed a claim for $3,000 that he said Long borrowed from him on August 3, 1960, as well as charges at his motel of $88 for telephone calls; $106 for lodging; and $47 for merchandise, food, and drinks. The $3,000 claim was represented by a ninety-day note held by Rapides Bank & Trust Co., "the proceeds of which were delivered to Earl K. Long, said note being signed by Earl K. Long and endorsed by Leroy Chandler." Chandler said that Security National Bank now held the note and had made demand for payment.[20]

J. D. Harkins, who did business as Harkins Sand & Gravel Co. of Alexandria, filed a claim for $2,736.00 for rental of a truck and driver for 456 hours at $6 per hour from June 15 through August 20, 1960.[21] On

July 12, 1961, C. J. Ellington of Natchitoches Parish filed suit against the succession (the legal proceeding to settle the estate) for $540 due for grazing eighty head of cattle owned by Long at pasture rental of $1.50 per head per month for the period April 1 through August 15, 1960. He said that his attorney had filed a claim with a sworn statement of the account to Blanche Long and her attorney on March 1, 1961, but had received no response. Blanche answered the petition on July 19, 1961, denying the claim.[22]

On July 18, 1963, Dr. R. U. Parrott filed suit against the succession of Earl K. Long for $1,225. Dr. Parrott claimed that he "incurred expenses for hospital care and treatment and for prescriptions and drugs for the late Honorable Earl K. Long while in the throes of his last illness from which he died." He said that itemized statements had been sent to Blanche Long on many occasions but that she had disregarded them.[23]

The Internal Revenue Service claimed that $59,110.27 was owed in back taxes, interest, and penalties for 1956 through 1959; the government waived the penalties and settled for $34,391.46.[24] The principal items at issue were monies that Long regarded as campaign contributions but which the government said were personal income. He maintained that since he was always running for office, any money he received was a campaign contribution.

When Mrs. Long sought authority from the court for the succession to settle with the IRS, her petition stated that

> for some time prior to decedent's death the United States Treasury Department, Internal Revenue Service, has been investigating the income tax liabilities of the decedent and your Petitioner for the years 1956, 1957, and 1958; that further the said Internal Revenue Service has investigated the returns filed for the year 1959, and, according to the Internal Revenue Agent's report a proposed assessment for all of the four years 1956 through 1959 was made which would amount to additional taxes, penalty and interest in the amount of $59,110.27; that prior to decedent's death he and your petitioner had employed George R. Blue of the firm Beard, Blue, Schmitt and Treen, New Orleans, Louisiana, to represent them in connection with said investigation and have been acting in such capacity since decedent's death; that the attorneys have reached an agreement with the Internal Revenue Service to settle the tax liabilities for the years above stated under the terms of which an additional tax

> assessment in the amount of $28,622.45 would be agreed upon and the interest thereon to May 15, 1961, would amount to $5,769.01 or a total proposed settlement with interest to May 15, 1961 of $34,391.46 in lieu of the assessment as proposed by the Agent as above stated.[25]

On June 8, 1960, Mrs. Long sold the home she had built on the Capitol Lake, described as "lavish," and at the same time purchased her buyer's smaller and less desirable home. The Long home was on Ted Dunham Avenue, known as Millionaire's Row. A news story reported that "federal agents were probing construction of the home, with contractors and subcontractors being questioned on transactions in connection with the new home," as well as how the property on which it was built was acquired.[26]

On July 7, 1958, Mrs. Irene Revere Simon, Blanche Revere Long's sister, had sold Lot 1 in Capitol View Subdivision to Blanche and Earl for $5,000. It measured 140 feet front on Ted Dunham Avenue by 167 rear and 304 feet deep. It had been acquired by Mrs. Simon in 1956.[27]

On August 25, 1958, North Baton Rouge Development Co., Inc., sold a tract containing 30,450 square feet to the Longs for $3,045.[28] This gave them an oversized lot on which the home was built. The contractor was George Caldwell, who went to jail in the Louisiana Scandals for corruption while he was in charge of construction projects at LSU.

On April 15, 1959, the Longs took out a $40,000 mortgage with Florence Overby, a notary public, representing any future holders of it, payable on demand at the American Bank & Trust Co. The notary for the transaction was Theo Cangelosi. The witnesses were J. P. Simmons; a state police officer; and Wilma Lockhart, Long's secretary.[29]

On June 8, 1960, Blanche and Earl Long sold the two properties to G. Harold King for $140,000. Lot 1 and the additional tract were designated as Lot 1-A of Capitol View Subdivision.[30] Earl had been enjoined by Blanche from disposing of any community property following their separation. To facilitate the sale to King, they agreed to modify the court order so they could jointly sell the property.[31] Long left the primary campaign to sign the sales papers in Baton Rouge.

On June 9, 1960, Blanche Long paid G. Harold King $42,500 for a lot and house at 605 Camellia Avenue in Roseland Terrace Subdivision. The sale stated that she was purchasing the property with her separate funds, which Earl acknowledged.[32] Since they were not divorced, the notary for the closing should have required Earl to appear to acknowledge his wife's transaction, but he failed to do so. On June 29, 1960, at Blanche's request, Earl again left the campaign to sign an instrument in Baton Rouge stating that he had no interest in the property she had purchased and that his declaration would have the same force and effect as though he had appeared and executed the act of sale.[33]

The total amount that Blanche Long spent on the Capitol Lake house is not known, but apparently any gain on its sale was addressed after she bought the Camellia Drive house. Since she bought it with her separate funds, it was not part of the estate of Earl K. Long.

Everything that was reported in the succession did not amount to very much for Earl's share of their community. However, there was a significant amount represented by notes for loans to the Matthews family by Earl that Blanche found.

Frank and Ruth Mathews, who were close friends of Long, owned King Lumber Company in Alexandria and Matthews Lumber Company in Mansfield. Described as wealthy, they had a home in Alexandria and an elaborate lakeside camp where Long sometimes spent the night. He may have loaned them money after their sawmill burned down, one supporter said, although if they were wealthy, another wondered, why did they need to borrow money from Long? Several of Earl's supporters said that they gave or sent him envelopes with cash repayments during the campaign.

Mrs. Long filed suit, as executrix of the estate, for $160,000, alleging that Mr. and Mrs. Matthews and their son, James Roy Matthews, had not paid three notes for loans obtained from Long in 1960. Frank Mathews, at the trial, acknowledged that he received the money and used it in his lumber business but claimed the indebtedness had been paid.[34]

The three notes were for $46,000, dated June 12, 1960, signed by Frank Matthews and Ruth Matthews; $64,000, dated June 13, 1960, signed by Ruth Matthews; and $50,000, dated June 18, 1960, signed by Ruth Matthews and James Roy Matthews. Mr. and Mrs. Matthews could not prove that they had paid the notes in full, but they were credited with several payments, including $5,000 in cash turned over to Jay Chevalier to give to Long and credits for lumber and millwork supplied by Matthews Lumber Company for the house Mrs. Long built.[35]

Mrs. Long found two of the notes in Earl's papers. The third was in possession of his sister, Mrs. Stewart Hunt of Ruston, who had no claim on it.[36]

Mrs. Long and her attorney, Clint Pierson, met with Mr. and Mrs. Matthews in early December 1960 to discuss the notes and to ask them for "copies of any receipts, checks or other instruments representing payments claimed by you to have been made against these notes." Pierson wrote that "in the event that no checks or receipts were available then I stated that I would require an explanation of the time and place and how the alleged payments were so made." He wanted to hear from them at the earliest possible date "as we have to wind up the affairs of the late Governor Long's succession as well as make the necessary tax returns in connection with his affairs."[37]

On April 6, 1961, having received no response from Matthews, Pierson made demand on them for payment in full. He stated that if there was any evidence of payment that they could submit, he would consider it.[38]

Frank W. Matthews responded on April 13, 1961, noting that the due dates on the notes were "not until December of this year, and as far as the purported payments, they are not purported but actually fact." He said that their records for 1960, including transactions with Long, were in the hands of their auditors, and any information would have to come from them. He concluded, "As far as you considering evidence, this is not of any importance to us as the note balance as set out is reflected through the transactions as above mentioned and as the due date is in the future we are disregarding your demand."[39] The notes had provided that "we owe Earl Long [with the amount in numbers and written out]. Interest paid for six months. At the end of six months we promise to repay; if not to start paying interest at six per cent for which Note will be extended for one year."[40]

When the case went to trial, Frank Matthews submitted a copy of a check for $1,000, dated August 26, 1960, payable to the "Earl K. Long Pol. Fund"; a receipt for a Western Union Money Order for $2,000 sent by Ruth Matthews at Mansfield to the Rapides Bank & Trust Co. for deposit to the Earl K. Long Political Fund on July 21, 1960; the August 1, 1960, receipt signed by Jay Chevalier for $5,000 in cash for Earl K. Long; and a list of payments made that included those items plus a number of others for a total of $63,988.28. There was no documentation for payments claimed to have been made for $40,000 on July 21, $6,000 on August 11, $9,000 on August 19, $6,000 on August 20, $11,000 on August 26, and $10,000 on August 28.[41]

Five years later, on July 11, 1966, the case was finally resolved with payment by Frank Matthews of $133,514.29 in satisfaction of a judgment read and signed September 20, 1965. In addition, $66,708.33 were paid in satisfaction of a second judgment in the same matter, for the interest due.[42]

It is a mystery how Earl Long had $160,000 in cash to loan to the Matthews family in mid-June 1960. He was complaining about how hard it was to raise money throughout the campaign, and he said that he had sold property and emptied his safe deposit box to put his hands on every nickel he could. Mr. and Mrs. Matthews were supposedly wealthy, which raises the question of why they needed to borrow money from him. Their notes were dated at the height of the campaign, and it is puzzling that he had that much cash available then. One can surmise that since he was under investigation by the IRS that he did not want it to discover a large amount of cash through subpoenas or otherwise and that the loan took the money out of his hands, with the notes, the only evidence of it, stashed away by him.

Bill Dodd thought Long had left the money with the Matthews for "safekeeping" rather than as a loan, and they returned it during the campaign. He did not think they intended to spend it but were only holding it for Long, with the notes serving as receipts for it. However, Blanche found the notes in Earl's papers and the Matthews could not provide receipts to show they had paid. Dodd wrote that "the money was campaign dollars, and I personally saw the Matthews deliver many thousands of dollars to Earl during the period they claimed Earl got his money back. I was riding in Earl's auto at Pleasant Hill in the presence of Earl's public relations man, Robert Gentry, plus David Bell and Albert Fredericks when Frank Matthews handed Earl $10,000.00 in a paper sack, which Earl acknowledged came from the money Frank was holding for him." Dodd said that Blanche did what anyone else who found notes that had not been cancelled would do; they indicated Mr. and Mrs. Matthews owed her late husband $160,000 so she presented the notes for proof they had been paid, and when it was not forthcoming, she sued to collect them. Dodd also said that most of the money Long spent in the election was his own, "which proves to me that Frank Matthews had given Earl most of the $160,000.00 which Earl had put in Frank's safe, and which after Earl died, Mrs. Long forced Frank to pay back to her. She had demand notes and collected the money. Frank had to pay twice."[43]

The Matthews notes were the most significant assets of the Earl K. Long Estate. They represented virtually all of the cash that he may have had.

His opponents were no doubt disappointed that there were not big bank accounts and lockboxes filled with cash. A 1959 article in *LOOK* magazine said that "Governor Long's salary is $18,000 a year, but responsible sources say his income is closer to $1 million a year."[44] As in other instances, sources were not named and no proof was submitted, only rumors and allegations by opponents that even some of them dismissed as false. Despite his efforts to destroy Long, Willie Rainach, who was in the legislature for both of Long's full terms, said that "one of Earl's good qualities was that he wanted everybody in his administration to be honest. He did not permit any level beneath him taking money and he conducted a relatively honest administration."[45]

Governor John McKeithen, who got his start with Long and was his candidate for lieutenant governor on the Spaht ticket in 1952, said that he caught Earl's eye when he came to the house as a freshman in 1948. "I'm going to make you a floor leader," he said "Mr. Earl" told him. "Now, I want to give you a little advice. Watch out for that whiskey. It's ruined a lot of good men who had come here and had a future. Leave women alone. You ever read over the vows a man takes when he gets married? Well, you leave them women alone. Don't take nobody's money. Keep yourself where you can look any son of a bitch in the eye."[46]

Adras Laborde, the Alexandria *Town Talk* editor for over forty years, who wrote ten thousand Talk of the Town columns about politics, said that "Earl didn't take a dime that didn't belong to him. I'm convinced of that. He and I didn't get along worth a damn. He was a boor and everything else, but as far as dishonest, no. Earl, if he had to do something, get something under the table, it was to help somebody else, not to help Earl Long. That was one of his weaknesses. He was probably the most honest of the Longs."[47]

Long maintained that he was the most investigated man in the history of Louisiana. He was never tied to any wrongdoing in the Scandals, despite the best efforts of the Crime Commission that Governor

Jones established, and he had Senator Overton publish his tax returns in the *Congressional Record* when he announced for governor in 1947. The taxes assessed for 1956–1959 in the settlement his estate made were insignificant in the scheme of things as that was the result of an exhaustive investigation covering four years. He was accused of treating campaign contributions as personal income. Earl maintained that he was running for office year-round, whether in or out of office, so any money he received was a campaign contribution.

While governor, he spent campaign contributions to help allies and to provide "walking around" money for legislative supporters like Sixty Rayburn, who had no salary from his job as a pipefitter at a paper mill when the legislature was in session. Long's handouts took care of hotel rooms and other expenses for needy lieutenants and were typical of the way he operated to help others rather than himself.

18.
MEMORIALIZING EARL KEMP LONG

The stories about Uncle Earl are the stuff of legend.

Ben Bennett recalled that when he was helping Dupre Litton draw up legislation for the governor, Long told him to draft a bill that would take mothers off the welfare rolls if they had more than two children. Bennett's phone rang at 4:00 a.m. one morning, and Long told him to add a provision that if a woman got pregnant out of wedlock through no fault of her own, the proposed law would not apply. Bennett responded that he would add exceptions for victims of rape and incest. "No, I want you to write it up just like I said," Long instructed him. Bennett was perplexed and asked how a woman could get pregnant through no fault of her own other than by rape and incest. "You're a Catholic, aren't you?" Long asked. "You've heard of the Virgin Mary, haven't you?" Bennett said that he had to concede the point.[1]

Jesse Bankston recalled that he was babysitting his son, Dale, one day when Long called to ask him to come to the mansion. Bankston took the boy with him, and Long greeted Dale by giving him a billfold and a dollar bill. He then helped fill the wallet by saying to everyone who came in while they talked, "Give that boy a dollar." Bankston chuckled, "By the time we left, I think he had ten dollars. After that, Dale wanted to go to the Mansion with me every time I did."[2]

Senator Rayburn said, "I've seen him stay up day and night without sleep just to carry his point. He never dreamed of letting his leaders sleep when there was something to be done. He'd telephone you at 3 p.m. or 3 a.m.—it made no difference to him." Rayburn fondly recalled that "Long was a jovial kind of fellow for us who knew him, with a heart bigger than most people will ever know. Long could have been selfish in some of his motives, but he would go out of his way to help a person in need. And he was a man not afraid of anything."[3]

Russell Willie was one of the three state troopers assigned to the mansion in Long's first full term. "I guess Earl liked me because he felt he could trust me," Willie reminisced. "I told him that I didn't want to fool with his horse race betting money because he was always sending people to place his bets. But, I didn't want any of his money. I remember he sent me shopping in New Orleans once and gave me something like $500 to spend to buy a bunch of junk. When I got back to the Mansion, I said here's this and here's that, here's your receipt and here's your change. I guess he was in shock because he really expected me to keep the remaining money. People were stealing from him all the time, but I didn't want his money, and I believe that's when he began to trust me."[4]

Willie, a lieutenant then, was back at the mansion for Earl's final administration. He said during the last year he was with the governor a lot. "I began to spend more and more time with Earl," he said. "I would be at the Mansion late at night and Earl would come down and say let's take a ride. And we'd go out at 11:00 or midnight looking for ice cream or marshmallows or water melons and stuff like that. I spent many an hour just riding and visiting with that man, and you may disagree with me, but I believe he was the best governor Louisiana ever had."[5]

Fondly remembering Long's "roadside shopping deals," Willie said that "if we were going somewhere and he knew we'd be visiting folks in the country for example, he'd first go by the hardware store. He'd buy horse collars, trace chains, stuff like that, things that farmers could use. He'd throw it all in the back of the Cadillac and we'd head out. When he'd pull up to a farmer's house to talk politics or whatever, Earl would notice that the farmer's horse needed a new collar or could use a trace chain, or whatever, and Earl would pull one out and give it to him. Well, you know what that farmer thought of Earl from that day on; hell, he'd kill for him. That farmer was bought off for the rest of his life."[6]

"He was smart like that," Willie said. "I've seen him on the phone and I've heard him talk. I've had three or four people on the line at one time in the Mansion and he'd get some fellows on the phone and say 'how's that old cow?' He'd remember those things. Or, how's that hog, or this or that? He'd ask about everything, the dog, the farm, the last thing he'd ask about was the wife. And that's the honest truth. He wouldn't ask how's your wife and then go after it, he would just ask about the farm and hogs first." Willie said that was because "he knew what was important to the men," but "then again, I've heard people call up, so and so didn't vote for you and he's still got a job with the state. Earl would tell the caller, well, that may be so but that man's got a wife and three kids and they've got to eat and he's going to keep his job. I've heard him do that. It's probably a side that most people never saw or heard."[7]

David Bell noted that "Earl loved Huey dearly. He wasn't jealous of Huey, deep down. He knew he had a hand in making Huey. Earl was always a head-and-head politician. Give him twenty minutes with a local leader and he could almost sell any idea. Huey appealed through oratory and organization. Earl must have died happy because he died after doing what he loved best—politicking." Bell, who had a repertoire of Uncle Earl stories, said the "funniest thing that ever happened in a campaign was at Florien, up in Natchitoches Parish. Sawmill town, and a train was switching there while Earl was speaking. So he had to quit and let the train pass. Just as the train was switching, an old hog went across the track with ten or twelve pigs following her. One of the people in the crowd knew Earl had hogs and hollered, 'Earl there goes your hogs going across the track.' And Earl hollered back, 'How do you know them are mine?' And the fellow said, 'They ain't marked.' In the olden days at home people had hogs in the woods that wasn't marked and people that come across them in the woods, they'd mark them with their own brand. Well, Earl only took himself home one of them hogs. Fresh pork that night!"[8]

Bell said, "Earl sure hated it he never had any children. He wanted children bad. He always kept a bunch of change in his pocket, and if he didn't have any, he'd stop at the first bank we come to and get change. He never did have any money himself, and, if you had some, you better start hiding it. He'd get it from you. He'd get rolls of quarters to give children. He would never give them a nickel. Always more. And he would give money out all day to children."[9]

Reminiscing about the stumping tours, Bell said that

> many times in our campaigning we rented a hotel room just to take a bath and change clothes in. Putting up signs everywhere you get dusty and dirty. Working with Earl was a 24-hours-a-day job because he needed very little sleep. He could get enough in an automobile to keep him up all night and not need any more. Eating was done wherever a sandwich could be bought and mostly while waiting for Earl to speak. Earl ate his while waiting for other speakers

> to get through and give him his turn on the platform. Earl tried to keep it to six or seven speeches a day, but sometimes he made it ten. We were always strictly on the move. Earl was country himself and proud of it. He knew as much about farming and cattle raising as anybody I have ever known. He loved every day, every minute at Pea Patch farm. If he was gone from there, like if we were out of the state four or five weeks, he couldn't wait to get back on the Pea Patch and under the tin roof. I can hear him now, "Let's go home," and he didn't mean after a while. He was ready to go then.

Describing the campaigning, Bell said "I enjoyed every phase of politicking, particularly the speaking at the little towns and villages where Earl went. And I don't think there is a post office in Louisiana that me and him haven't been to at one time or another. Even along the bayou where we had to get to them by pirogue. We went in boats and everything else. Wherever we could find a crowd that is where we went. And Earl got them votes up and down those bayous too!"[10]

Journalist Iris Kelso of New Orleans described Earl Long as "irascible, unpredictable, earthy, brilliant in his deliberately rural ways, a terror on the campaign trail, a master of ridicule. There was no pretense about Earl, especially when he poked fun at politics and reformers. After Louisiana got voting machines, Earl laughed: 'Just give me five commissioners and I'll show you how to make those voting machines play 'Home, Sweet Home.'"[11]

Crowley City Court Judge Edmund Reggie said that Long promised to remove a tax for one of Reggie's clients if they supported him. Reggie asked him to put it in writing and he did. When Reggie found his bill blocked in committee, he suspected that Long was behind that. Earl was reading a racing form when Reggie came to ask, "Now, Governor, didn't you promise me you would take this tax off if I campaigned for you?" "That's right," Long replied. "And didn't you sign a letter promising these people you would take it off?" Reggie asked. "That's right," Long again responded. "Well, what am I going to tell these people, Governor?" Reggie asked. Long replied, "Just tell them I lied, Reggie. Just tell them I lied."[12]

Reggie was thirty years old when he hooked up with Long in the 1956 campaign. "Who else could make eight to ten campaign speeches a day for four months running and draw a cheering crowd at every stop?" he asked. "Who else could detour off the highway down a little dirt road to a plain clapboard house to bring a couple there two pounds of coffee, ask by name about a dozen neighbors, and leave with the neighborhood sewed up for election day?"[13]

"Politics was the fiber of his being," Reggie said. "He and his wife had no children and that void was filled to overflowing by his political appetite. There remains no one who knew the political picture in Louisiana in such minute, personal detail. He could recite comparative election returns by ward, not only by parishes."[14]

Raymond Strother, who became a nationally known political consultant after managing races in Louisiana, wrote Robert Gentry in 2004 that "in a day of professionally dressed, blow-dried, debate-coached, television-trained, poll-directed candidates who become the CEOs of a large organization to raise money and raise profile, Earl Long could not exist. His talents would have never surfaced. His ability would have never been tested. He was indeed the Last of the Red Hot Poppas. And his style, even in 1960, when a young John Kennedy was being groomed to be President, was at least a decade behind the times. Television demands a cool candidate. Hand gestures and loud speechifying don't work when it is pumped into the living room and compressed into a tiny picture tube. A candidate must act the part. A candidate must look the part."[15]

Strother said that "Earl was perhaps the last politician in America to come out of the red dirt with a core that drove him instead of advisors and polls. His fuel was whisky, a love of people, and sweat. He looked wrong, he talked wrong, but he was part of the fabric of the people who voted for him and loved him. If people had to draw a picture of Louisiana in the forties and fifties it would look like Governor Long.

"There were no fence straddlers for Uncle Earl. There were Longs and anti-Longs. His personality was so dynamic and he was so forthright that modern politicians pale in comparison. I long for the days of real men with determination and grit in their belly. I would rather have politicians with dirt under their fingernails but pure driven wanna-do in their hearts. Sure, I remember Uncle Earl."[16]

The Earl K. Long Memorial Park in Winnfield honors the memory of the three-time governor. Its facilities include a pavilion, brick walkways, and a bronze statue of Long. The city of Winnfield has noted that the park is a favorite setting for weddings, picnics, and city celebrations. A state historical marker identifies the location as the "Long Home Site. Home of Huey Pierce Long, Sr. and Caledonia Tison Long. Birthplace of: United States Senator Huey Pierce Long-Congressman George Shannon Long-Governor Earl Kemp Long."

A memorial service for Long was held on Labor Day, September 4, 1961, at which the granite base for the statue was presented to the city by the State Parks and Recreation Commission. The program for the ceremony noted that

> Earl K. Long, thrice Governor of Louisiana, died on Labor Day, 1960, at the age of 65. There is deep poignancy in the fact that the last, great campaign of this political warrior ended on a day so symbolic of everything for which he, himself, had labored. For Earl K. Long was destined to champion the cause of the common man, the needy, the aged, the underprivileged, and the worker. Realizing this, his keen perception dictated that the attainment of this goal called for the holding of high office. He knew that all too often the seats of the mighty had been reserved for those who cared little indeed for the common man. His unconquerable spirit opened the door to this goal. He, alone, could claim the unprecedented record of serving three times as Governor of Louisiana, once as Lieutenant-Governor; then, in the closing hours of his life, perhaps the sweetest yet saddest victory of all, election to the United States Congress as representative from his beloved 8th Congressional District. Earl K. Long brought to the political arena of Louisiana a brand of fearlessness, confidence, and giant-killing energy which, for more than thirty years, was the awe and consternation of his adversaries in all walks of political life. His every political endeavor was both provocative and profound. And the tremendous strength of the man was surpassed by nothing short of the grand scope of his ceaseless drive to better the lot of his fellow man.[17]

Small statues of two dogs guard the rear entrance to the park, though as Clem Huffman noted, they are not the Catahoula Curs that Uncle Earl loved. One of the six benches flanking the statue is engraved with the words of "In the Garden," Long's favorite hymn.

The statue, for which Arthur Morgan was sculptor, depicts Earl K. Long with his right arm raised, as if greeting a crowd. It is mounted on several levels of marble supports, with the base chiseled "Earl Kemp

Long" and adorned with the state seal and his August 26, 1895, date of birth and September 5, 1960, date of death.

The right side of the monument is engraved, "This Native Son of Winn Parish Made Political History for a Quarter of a Century. Earl Kemp Long took the Oath as Governor Three Times. At His Death He Was the Democratic Nominee to the Congress of the United States From the 8th District. Governor of Louisiana: 1939–1940 - 1948–1952 - 1956–1960. Lieutenant Governor 1936–1939. Democratic National Committeeman 1950–1952. Democratic Nominee to the Congress of the United States August 27, 1960."

The left side is engraved, "Earl Kemp Long Worked with Dauntless Courage, Incredible Energy, and Sincere Determination to Serve the People of Louisiana. He Spoke With Wisdom, Wit and Humor Saying With Candor Those Things Which Others Feared to Say. He Loved His Fellow Men and They Loved and Followed Him as He Walked Unafraid Through the Crowd. His Deeds Will Live Long After Him In the Hearts and Minds of Men and Women and Children Throughout the Length and Breadth of His Beloved Louisiana."

Following Long's death, the legislature authorized creation of the Earl K. Long Memorial Commission. Governor Jimmie Davis named as its members Blanche Revere Long, Clara Long Knott, Judge Harwell L. Allen, State Representative W. K. Brown, and Mayor Mary W. "Doc" Allen of Winnfield, and funds were appropriated to develop the park and erect the monument. The rear of the monument is engraved, "This Park Site Donated to the State of Louisiana By Earl Kemp Long and His Wife Blanche Revere Long In Loving Memory of His Mother and Father Caledonia Tison and Huey Pierce Long, Senior. It Was His Request That He Be Buried Here At His Birthplace Near the Home He Loved."

Blanche Long was listed as a donor of the property because Earl's act of donation to the city had not yet been formally accepted by the city council when he died. A new deed was executed, as with his death she became a part owner of the property. Mayor Allen said that Blanche, as his heir, had advised the city that the requirements that the property revert to the original owners if grass was not cut and the land maintained and that a forty-by-one-hundred square foot area be reserved for burial of family members would not be included in the new deed from the estate and no other members of the Long family would be buried there. She said the family wanted the property to be a shrine to the memory of Earl Kemp Long.[18]

The statue was dedicated on July 4, 1963. The Earl K. Long Memorial Foundation, created by friends before the state Memorial Commission was established, used the funds it had collected to build a "shelter house" or pavilion to be used for band concerts, political meetings, "and all of the unpretentious gatherings so dear to his heart."

Judge Cas D. Moss, who swore Long in at the 1948 inauguration, was master of ceremonies for the dedication of the statue and the pavilion. The guest speaker was John S. Hunt, Earl's nephew, who later served on the Public Service Commission in the seat that Huey once held. The statue was unveiled by Mrs. Earl K. Long, and Blanche posed for photographers in front of it afterward.[19]

The Winnfield newspaper said that one thousand people attended the ceremony. Among the many political figures were US Senator Russell Long, Congressman Gillis Long, and State Senator Speedy Long.[20]

Carolyn Phillips, executive director of the Louisiana Political Museum and Hall of Fame in Winnfield, said in 2005 that the park remains a favorite place for weddings, family reunions, and picnics, with many people enjoying their lunch there. Mrs. Phillips said that according to local lore, Long wanted to be buried under his mother's kitchen table, but that since the house burned down in the 1920s, no one was quite sure where that was. The park is used for city celebrations, and the inaugurations of municipal officials are held there. She said the Earl K. Long Memorial Park is being used and enjoyed just the way he wanted it to be, and that his eight-foot statue is waving to those who drop by.[21]

◆ ◆ ◆

Earl K. Long was congressman-elect when he died, as no Republican had filed for the general election. It fell to the members of the Democratic State Central Committee for the district to name a replacement as the Democratic nominee, and after some squabbling, particularly by those who thought Speedy should be named, they certified McSween by a seven-to-five vote at their third meeting; with no opponent in the general election, he was then declared the winner. McSween said he accepted with some reluctance as he was disgusted with politics and felt the strain that having to be in Washington placed on his family. It was logical for him to be named the nominee simply because he finished in second place, whereas another nominee would not have been the choice of any voters in the runoff.[22]

Despite his pronouncements against civil rights in his race against Long and targeting him as "soft" on segregation, in January 1961 McSween voted with a scant 217–212 majority that increased the House Rules Committee membership so that Speaker Sam Rayburn could add additional, more liberal members to it to break the committee's refusal to send civil rights legislation to the floor. A commentator said that McSween "angered conservatives in both parties" and "the enlargement of the committee led to passage of the Civil Rights Act of 1964, which struck down segregation in most situations in the United States."[23]

In 1962, more comfortable in Congress after four years, McSween sought another term but was ousted by Gillis William Long, a distant cousin of Earl.[24] Gillis, whose mentor was Senator Russell Long, had worked in Washington for fourteen years as an attorney and as counsel for committees of Congress before coming home to challenge McSween. Gillis was born in Winnfield and, like Russell, had been elected student body president at LSU. He was supported in his race against McSween by Speedy Long, who was gearing up for a campaign for governor. In 1963, Speedy was first to declare, but he was soon followed by Gillis, who sought the governorship after only one year in Congress. Speedy pulled out of the race for governor and ran for insurance commissioner on the ticket of John J. McKeithen. He did not win, but McKeithen did, and the governor then backed Speedy's challenge to Gillis when he came up for reelection. Speedy attacked Gillis as a "Washington Long" and portrayed himself as a "Jena Long." The old Long people in the district went overwhelmingly for Speedy. Russell Long issued a perfunctory endorsement of Gillis, but the only person of note to support Gillis was McSween.[25]

McSween sought no further office but instead practiced law and served as president of the Rapides Savings and Loan Association. He was convicted of taking kickbacks for approving loans and was given a three-year suspended sentence by a federal court and placed on five years' probation. His probation officer, Tim Harrison, recalled that McSween would never come into the office in the federal building in Alexandria, but instead "would literally sail any paperwork across the room to avoid walking through the door." One day Harrison found McSween outside his office and asked why he avoided coming in. "This is my old office from when I was a Congressman," Harrison said McSween told him, and "it was eating him up that he had to come in and report to me there as a convicted felon."[26]

McSween enjoyed writing and had a number of essays published on literature and politics. The *Virginia Quarterly Review* published "T. Harry Williams: A Remembrance," in 2000; "How to Succeed in Washington Without Really Trying," in 1996; "Earl Long, 1895–1960: Voting Rights Advocate of Political Incorrectness," in 1995; and "Huey Long at His Centenary," in 1993.[27]

After a lengthy illness, Harold McSween died at the VA Medical Center in Alexandria on January 12, 2002, at the age of seventy-four. He had expected to recover and was following an exercise program to regain strength following heart failure.[28]

Ben F. Holt served only a single term in the Louisiana House of Representatives, from 1956 to 1960. Holt said he led the move to immediately adjourn Earl Long's postwestern trip special session in 1959 because he felt Long's intent to remove Theo Cangelosi from the LSU Board of Supervisors for political reasons would hurt the university's national image. He did not seek reelection in the 1959 primary but prepared to challenge Congressman Harold McSween in 1960. Holt, residing in Pineville, was a member of the Rapides Democratic State Central Committee and, after endorsing McSween against Long, sat with committee members from other parishes in the Eighth Congressional District to certify a nominee following Long's death. He supported McSween, the nominee chosen by the committee. A conservative, Holt supported a slate of unpledged electors organized by Leander Perez against the Kennedy-Johnson national ticket in 1960, but state party loyalists rebuffed them. They then organized the Louisiana States' Rights Party, with Holt joining Perez, Willie Rainach, John Garrett, and David Treen as its leaders. Kennedy carried Louisiana in the presidential election. Holt did not take an active or influential role in politics afterward but practiced law until his death at age seventy in 1995.[29]

Willie Rainach, Earl's nemesis, was rumored to have suffered a nervous breakdown himself after failing to make the runoff in the 1959 race for governor, which he had expected to win. One story was that he actually believed he had been elected governor and was ranting and raving so badly that his family locked him up for several days to keep him away from the press. Regardless, he endorsed and supported Jimmie Davis in the runoff against Chep Morrison in return for Davis's promise to create a State Sovereignty Commission and make him its chairman. Davis made good on his promise. The legislation that the commission, under Rainach's leadership, drew up to make voter registration even more complicated for blacks was thrown out by the federal courts. Rainach subsequently disappeared from the public stage. According to a biographical sketch, he was born Willie Odom in 1913. After his mother's death in 1917 from the influenza epidemic that began in 1915 and continued with many more fatalities in the following three years, his father placed his three sons in the Baptist orphanage in Lake Charles. Willie was adopted by Mr. and Mrs. Albert Rainach of Summerfield in Claiborne Parish and took their name. After attending several schools, he started an electric cooperative and later a butane company and prospered. He served in the Louisiana legislature for a total of twenty years, but after completing his final term in 1960, he never sought public office again.[30] In 1978, in declining health, he walked from his home into its backyard, pressed a revolver to his head, and shot himself. He was sixty-five years old, the same age as his old enemy Earl Long was when he died quietly in an Alexandria hospital.[31]

Speedy O. Long served four terms in Congress. By 1972 he had tired of Washington and did not seek reelection that year. Redistricting following the 1970 Census enlarged his district to include several Acadiana parishes and put his own parish, Sabine, in another district. With a more liberal constituency, Gillis Long won back the seat that he had lost to Speedy eight years before. Speedy ran for governor in 1971, finishing far behind Edwin W. Edwards, J. Bennett Johnston, Gillis Long, and Jimmie Davis. Speedy won election as district attorney for the Twenty-Eighth Judicial District in 1973 and served until 1985. He made a last campaign for governor in 1987, polling only one percent of the statewide vote. Speedy practiced law in Jena from 1985 until 2005; he served briefly as Twenty-Eighth Judicial District judge by appointment from the state supreme court until an election could be held to fill that seat. He died in 2006 at age seventy-eight. Speedy said that he had been "raised to regard Huey as God Almighty, Earl as Jesus Christ, and George as St. Peter."[32]

Gillis W. Long represented the Eighth District in Congress between 1963 and 1965 and again from 1973 until his death in 1985. He and McSween became good friends, and McSween endorsed him for governor in the 1971 primary. After his defeat by Speedy in the 1964 election, he was appointed assistant secretary of the Office of Economic Opportunity by President Lyndon B. Johnson, serving the War on Poverty for two years. Returning to Congress in 1973 after Speedy did not seek reelection in the redrawn district, and with a more liberal constituency, he won successive reelections. Following his death from heart failure at age sixty-one, his widow, Catherine Small Long, won a special election as his successor. She completed his term but did not seek reelection to a full term.[33]

Robert Gentry, who said he was "Uncle Earl's P.R. man" at the age of nineteen, earned a degree in journalism from Northwestern State University, working his way through college as a reporter for several newspapers. He was named editor of the Sabine *Index,* which he later bought and operated as its publisher and editor. He did public relations work in campaigns for Harold McSween, Gillis W. Long, and Bill Dodd and served as chairman of the ninety-ninth and one hundredth Jimmie Davis Birthday Celebrations. He was given the Friend of Earl K. Long Award by the Louisiana Political Museum and Hall of Fame in Winnfield. Gentry sold his newspaper but remains a wonderful resource for information and anecdotes about Louisiana politics over a span of fifty years.[34]

Richard A. "Dick" Davis's betrayal of Earl Long, it turned out, had begun before the Eighth District election and involved Theodore Cangelosi, an attorney and onetime close friend of Long's whom Long had appointed to the LSU Board of Supervisors. Long had called Cangelosi to his side in Galveston to represent him, but Cangelosi did not follow through. Cangelosi later said in an oral history interview that he "went to see the Federal Judge in Texas and got him to appoint two top-flight criminal lawyers to represent him and they are the ones who filed the *habeas corpus.*" Since Long's case was in Galveston County District Court, there was no federal judge involved. The Galveston judge appointed two lawyers to represent Long.[35]

Long said that Cangelosi was siding with Blanche, and after he won release and returned from his western trip, he included in his call for the abortive special session a measure concerning membership on state boards and commissions. Earl intended to have the legislature remove

Cangelosi from the LSU Board by addressing him out of office through a declaration that the seat he held was vacant. Long lobbied legislators for Cangelosi's removal and told the press that "there never has been a man who misused and unduly abused my confidence like Cangelosi. If he hadn't done me like he done, and rubbed it in, I might forgive him, but that long-legged sapsucker made more money than any man I ever knew." He attacked Cangelosi for collecting hundreds of thousands of dollars as bond counsel for the Baton Rouge Port Commission and claimed that Cangelosi pocketed the proceeds of a $40,000 mortgage the Longs made on the house Blanche built on Capitol Lake.[36]

Cangelosi was determined to fight his ouster, if only as a matter of pride so that his descendants would not have to hear how the legislature impeached him. To this end, he put together a broad base of legislative supporters in anticipation of the special session.[37]

In the interview, Cangelosi said that Long "was meeting with legislators in various groups all over the state. And, very frankly, I was real lucky. You know this fellow Davis that lives in Lecompte? He was driving Earl at this particular time. And he was a close friend of Camille Gravel who was on my side." Long, Cangelosi said, would "meet with these little groups of legislators throughout the state. He'd meet with a few around Alexandria and that area, and a few around Monroe, a few around Oakdale, a few around Lake Charles—he dedicated himself to getting the votes. And Davis was driving him at that time, and whenever he went to bed at night, Davis, who had been my friend but who was really Camille Gravel's man, and Camille was helping me—would call me every night, anywhere from 2:30 to 4:00 in the morning and tell me what the various legislators said and what Earl told them. That was a great help." Cangelosi said he would then follow up on Dick Davis's intelligence reports without letting the subjects know what Davis told him "and I ran into some first class liars."[38]

Cangelosi said Davis was "quite a fellow." Asked to explain why Davis helped him rather than being loyal to Long, Cangelosi said, "Well, he liked me, number one, but he was Camille's Man Friday so to speak in Alexandria, Lecompte, middle of Louisiana area, in the automobile business. And so, he became my good friend, because of Camille primarily. He acted as a spy. He knew Earl was sick. Earl trusted him and liked him, too. Let me tell you something—those were rough times."[39]

Despite his treachery, in 1988, when news stories said that Ron Shelton's movie *Blaze* would feature the striptease artist's relationship with Long, with Paul Newman playing Earl, Davis publicly claimed that he was closer to the governor than anyone else during his last several years and "he was Long's only personal aide at the time of the Blaze Starr affair, that anyone who wanted to see the Governor had to go through him." He gave the impression that he had been loyal to the very end.[40]

Davis kept his hand in state politics in the years that followed. He supported State Senator Edwin W. Edwards of Crowley in his first campaign for the US House of Representatives in 1965. Edwards told a friend that Governor John McKeithen sent Davis to help in the campaign. After Edwards took office, he put Davis on his congressional staff, working out of district offices in Crowley and Opelousas. Two years later they had differences and Davis left the Edwards staff.[41] Dick Davis died in 1990.[42]

Blanche Revere Long died of dementia at age ninety-three on May 11, 1998, in the Heritage Manor nursing home in Mandeville. She is buried in a Revere family tomb in Lake Lawn Cemetery in Metairie. She would have been pleased with her *New York Times* obituary that recognized her as a "Louisiana Legend."[43] The obituary described her as "an indispensable political asset" for her husband Earl, saying they were "a formidable, if somewhat mismatched, political couple. She was a self-described city girl, a native of Covington who grew up across the lake in New Orleans where she acquired a taste for elegance and refinement in a household whose only concession to politics was voting. He was as country as they come and political to the bone, a rough-hewn, rough-talking product of the family pea patch in the piney woods of north-central Louisiana and the brawling baby brother of Huey P. Long." She ran Earl's campaign headquarters in all but his last campaign.

After Earl's death, Blanche emerged as a significant political power in her own right. In 1963, when Russell Long and his mother, Rose McConnel Long, backed Gillis Long for governor, she supported Public Service Commissioner John McKeithen. Russell and Mrs. Huey P. Long endorsed Gillis in a statewide television broadcast. Blanche Long and Speedy Long campaigned for McKeithen, who beat Gillis Long for a place in the runoff, where he won an upset victory over New Orleans mayor Chep Morrison. McKeithen joked, "I beat his Longs with my

Longs." McKeithen appointed Blanche chairman of the State Tax Commission, and she continued to keep her hand in state politics.[44]

After serving on the State Tax Commission, Blanche eventually left Baton Rouge to return to the New Orleans area. She purchased two small condominiums in Metairie Towers on September 1, 1982, where she and her sister moved in next door to each other.[45]

Blanche Long enjoyed attending functions, and I spoke with her in 1987 at a gala the Times-Picayune Publishing Company held to celebrate its 150th anniversary. Russell Long told me that after he retired from the US Senate, he spent several weeks traveling in Louisiana, visiting old friends and family members, making a final pilgrimage to Winnfield, and in his own words, "taking a farewell tour as my own mortality became heavier upon me."

Russell said that on his final visit with his aunt, she did not know who he was. He thought that she was doing fine, he recalled, until she told him that she was "so sorry that Earl isn't home, but he had to go out for a while on some errands." As he was leaving, she said, "You know, young man, you look just like Russell Long." Smiling, holding her hand, he told her, "Well, Aunt Blanche, that's because I am Russell Long." Blanche replied, "Earl will be sorry he missed seeing you."

Blanche was interdicted by her niece and nephews when she could no longer manage her own affairs. When they could no longer take care of her, she was placed in the nursing home in Mandeville.

Her will left $5,000 each to her nephews Robert David Revere and Jack Warren Harang. The balance of her estate went to her niece Diane Blanche Simon. The only other assets enumerated were five fur stoles and jackets valued at $4,100 and a bank account and other funds with a total of $5,801.81. The total assets, after paying off a mortgage balance in the sale of the units, were $98,209.80. The liabilities, including a hospital bill, funeral expenses, and administrative and attorney's fees were $30,021.36. The net estate of Blanche Revere Long was $68,188.44.[46]

Russell Long remained in the Senate until retirement in January 1987. He was an expert on tax law, serving as chairman of the Senate Finance Committee from 1965 until Republicans gained control of the Senate in 1981. The *Wall Street Journal*, acknowledging his enormous power, called him "the fourth branch of government." He practiced law in Washington after leaving the Senate, was an influential lobbyist, and sat on the board of the New York Stock Exchange. He died in 2003.[47] His services were held at a Baton Rouge funeral home in accord with his wishes; if his family had wanted him to lie in state in Memorial Hall of the capitol, as his father and uncle had, that honor would surely have been accorded him by Governor Kathleen Blanco. He was the only person in US history who followed both his father and mother in the Senate, his mother, Rose McConnell Long, having been appointed to complete the remaining months of Huey's term.

Russell Long was urged by many to seek the governorship in 1988 to cap his storied career, and he probably would have had other candidates deferred to him and not run; however, Edwin Edwards, Buddy Roemer, Bob Livingston, Jim Brown, and Billy Tauzin were not about to give him a clear field, and he was unwilling to fight for it. He said that he was not going to subject himself to a campaign in Louisiana in the summer heat. In 1995, he did not attend the celebration of the one hundredth anniversary of the birth of Earl K. Long in Winnfield on August 26 because of the heat. He told this writer that he did not come home to Louisiana in the summer, preferring his Watergate apartment in Washington and his cabin in the Blue Ridge Mountains.[48]

He sent a message to the anniversary event that stated, "Uncle Earl and my father, Huey P. Long, had a parting of the ways in 1931 when Earl insisted on running for lieutenant governor although Huey had committed himself to support someone else. Earl lost and there were some hard feelings for awhile, but I am happy to report that they made up their differences and Earl was decidedly in Huey's corner at the time of Huey's death in 1935."[49]

"Earl persuaded me to support him for Governor in 1947," Russell wrote. "That was the first state campaign in which I discussed the issues. Earl was very grateful to me for my part in his election, and he did a lot to help me in the years that followed. His experience and advice meant a lot to me, and he did much to help finance my first campaign for the U.S. Senate and thereafter. I shall forever be grateful. In many respects, Earl was a second father to me and I will always love his memory."[50]

Russell Long wrote a foreword to this writer's book, *Uncle Earl Deserved Better: Critical Analyses of Blaze, a Film Written and Directed by Ron Shelton and Earl K. Long: The Saga of Uncle Earl and Louisiana*

Politics, by Michael Kurtz and Morgan Peoples, With Further Commentary on The Last of the Red-Hot Papas, published in a limited edition in 1995. I was incensed by the portrayal of Long in the movie and by the numerous errors in the book, so I made a compilation of them without expecting to publish the manuscript. That changed when I saw Bob Mann, who had been Russell Long's press secretary, and mentioned what I was doing. He asked to see the manuscript and after reading it said he wanted Senator Long to see it. That was of course fine with me, and after a careful reading, Senator Long called me. In a lengthy conversation, he said he had long ago given up trying to correct the misrepresentations, mistakes, and lies about his father and uncle, but he had a different view concerning my manuscript. He said it should be published and offered to write a foreword for it. As I have said on many occasions, the book is for political junkies only, as general readers on Louisiana politics would probably not welcome such detail. However, Mike Stagg, a good friend and junkie like me, happened to own a printing company then, and he published it.[51]

In his Foreword, Russell Long said

> I highly recommend Mr. McGuire's painstaking research to any scholar with an honest desire for truth about my family. Throughout the years, many myths and half truths about my father and uncle—and other members of the Long family—have found their way into print. That information, if unchallenged, may well become the accepted "truths" which future historians will use to formulate their interpretations of Louisiana's political history. Jack McGuire's exhaustive study sets the record straight. It is well written and thoroughly researched. Most of all, it is fair and accurate. I would be the last to claim that I or any member of my family has lived a flawless life. Only one person has ever achieved perfection this side of heaven. Perfection, however, should not be the standard by which we assess our public servants. My Uncle Earl was as mortal as any man. And yet I believe that he stands head and shoulders above the vast majority of men who have occupied the governor's office since Louisiana became a state. To my knowledge, no one ever proved that he was anything other than what he said he was—a sincere man of the people.

Big Bad Bill Dodd passed away on November 20, 1991, at age eighty-two. He was elected state representative in 1940 and reelected while overseas in the army in 1944. He was Earl Long's ticket mate for lieutenant governor in 1948. Breaking with Long, whose support he had expected, he ran for governor in 1951 but failed to make the runoff. He was elected state auditor on the Long ticket in 1956 and in 1959 again failed to make the runoff for governor, as did Long's candidate, Jimmy Noe. Dodd was elected to the State Board of Education in 1960 and to be state superintendent of education in 1964 and again in 1968. When he ran second for reelection in 1972, he withdrew from the runoff and returned to his law practice.[52] Dodd wrote his memoirs in *Peapatch Politics: The Earl Long Era in Louisiana Politics by Earl's Lieutenant Governor, William J. Dodd.*

The manager of the Pea Patch Farm, Clem Huffman, took a job with the Brand and Livestock Inspection Commission when Long returned to office in 1956 and held it until retiring in 1984. He died on April 1, 2007, at age ninety.[53] His daughter, Linda Huffman Cox, Long's beloved Shug, lives in Texas but returns to Winnfield and tries not to miss the Annual Induction Banquet of the Louisiana Political Hall of Fame. At the 2012 banquet, she received the Friend of Earl K. Long Award. She said that "Mr. Earl" treated her like an "adopted daughter or granddaughter" and was generous with gifts to her during her childhood and at her high school graduation. She said that when she was little, he would place a gift on top of his dresser, pull out the drawers, and enjoy watching her use the drawers as steps to climb up to claim her prize.[54] She recalled that she "never had a birthday or special event that I did not get a card and a gift from Mister Earl. He never took a trip that he didn't send me cards and presents."

Ellis Littleton died on November 18, 2005, at age seventy-five. Easy Money, or Easy, was presented the Friend of Earl K. Long Award by the Louisiana Political Museum and Hall of Fame in 2001. After Long's death he held several public jobs, and at his retirement he was supervisor of the Alexandria animal shelter. He treasured the memories of his years with "Mr. Earl" and loved to tell stories about him.[55]

Joseph Arthur Sims continued his involvement in state politics after Long's death and practiced law as the senior partner of Sims and Mack in Hammond. In 1972, he was appointed assistant attorney general by the incoming attorney general, William J. Guste Jr., whom he had supported. He died on May 20, 1973, at age fifty-eight.[56]

W. K. Brown served Grant and Rapides Parishes in the Louisiana House of Representatives from 1960 until 1972. He held a master's degree in elementary education from LSU and taught school in Pollock for several years. W. K. died on July 13, 2011, at age eighty-eight, the last surviving of twelve children. He served in the navy during World War II and owned an insurance agency in Alexandria while in the legislature. He worked for the Rapides Parish Police Jury and was a special assistant to the state superintendent of education until retirement in 1984.[57] In 1998, he received the Friend of Earl K. Long Award from the Louisiana Political Hall of Fame. He was proud that he delivered Long's eulogy before the legislature and sponsored the legislation for the statue at the park in Winnfield.[58]

Wilma Lockhart, Long's devoted secretary, died August 4, 1984. She served with him in both full administrations and worked for Congressman George Long in between them. Earl appointed her a member of the State Tax Commission in 1959; she continued there until 1966, when Governor John McKeithen declined to reappoint her because of opposition by parish tax assessors, who were against her proposals to equalize assessments. He named her executive director of the Highway Safety Committee, and she served in that position until retiring in 1976. When she was asked if there was a lot of money in a safe deposit box she kept for Long, she smiled and said there was not a single dollar, only treasured letters from people thanking him for their old age pensions and other benefits.[59]

Benjamin Buras Rayburn died at age ninety-one in 2008. B. B. Rayburn, or Sixty as he was known, served on the Washington Parish Police Jury and was elected to the Louisiana house in 1948 and to the state senate in 1951. He had a trade school education and was a pipe fitter, but he knew where every dollar was buried in the state budget during his many years as chairman of the Senate Finance Committee. In 1995, he was acquitted on charges of bribery but was narrowly defeated for reelection after forty-eight years in the legislature. He disputed Long's crack that his nickname came from the highest score he made on a test or his seat number in the classroom, saying that 60 was his ballot number when he first sought public office in 1944 and campaigned on the slogan "Vote for 60." He and Long were kindred spirits. "He was just my type of person,"

Rayburn remarked. "He was down to earth. He liked hogs, cattle, and people."[60]

Camille Gravel, who served as executive counsel for three governors and enjoyed a colorful career, died December 23, 2005, at age ninety, in an Alexandria nursing home. He will be remembered for the support he gave to the civil rights struggle when that was unpopular. "Purely as a moral proposition, I think segregation is wrong," he said in 1959.[61]

Dupre Litton, executive counsel to Long, died on January 20, 1992.[62] After extensive service in state government as counsel to the legislature and various state departments, he had a law practice in Opelousas and Baton Rouge. His book *The Wizard of Winnfield* is a wonderful contribution to Earl Long lore.

Jesse Bankston died at age 103 on Thanksgiving Day in 2010. He was an elected member of the State Board of Elementary and Secondary Education for twenty-eight years and was the longest-serving member of the Democratic State Central Committee, having served fifty years, from election in 1960 until his death. A populist deeply concerned about working people, Bankston—as chairman of the Louisiana Democratic Party after Edwin W. Edwards was elected governor in 1972—helped steer the party into the mainstream. While articles about him noted that Long had fired him as director of the State Hospitals Department to gain release from Southeast Louisiana Hospital, they failed to note that Long offered the job back to him. Bankston declined, but they remained friends. He had a long career as a health care consultant and wrote a book about his experiences with Long, titled *Earl Kemp Long: The Inside Story of the Governor as I Knew Him.*[63]

◆ ◆ ◆

From the day he joined his brother Huey's campaign for railroad commissioner in 1918 until the day he died as the Democratic nominee for Louisiana's Eighth District congressional seat in 1960, Earl Kemp Long was a force of nature in Louisiana politics. He brought a fierceness to life and to politics that was both compelling and magnetic. He was a candidate in every state election but one between his first campaign for lieutenant governor in 1932 and his final race for the same office in 1959. Politics was his life, and he drew energy from the people that he drew into the process. Nowhere was that more evident than in his last campaign.

It was a race that most thought he could not win and some believed he could not survive. The tumultuous events of 1959 would have ended the careers of most politicians. But Earl was no mere politician, and he knew how to cure what ailed him. He needed a campaign. He decided to run to unseat Harold McSween in what he sensed might be his final campaign, his last hurrah, in his old home district in the red clay hills and piney woods of north central Louisiana where his life in politics had started.

Earl knew that whatever the risks the campaign posed to his health, he could not live without politics. He also knew that he had no future in politics if he did not redeem himself from the humiliations and defeats of 1959. Earl campaigned with a desperation that betrayed a stark recognition of the stakes. It was all or nothing. He was all in. Earl was campaigning for his life. He was going to win this race or die trying.

He did both.

The Starting Field
In poor health, recently defeated in a statewide election, still reeling from a year of public humiliation and ridicule about his mental health, no one gave Earl Long much of a chance when he joined the field in the Democratic Party's Eighth District congressional primary. Former Long legislative ally Ben Holt from Rapides Parish (center) had already qualified to run against incumbent Harold McSween (right) by the time Earl qualified while recovering from surgery.

Robert Gentry—The P.R. Man
Robert Gentry wrote for the Natchitoches *Enterprise* before joining up with Earl Long's congressional campaign, where he wrote articles and took photographs that were submitted to small town newspapers throughout the district. Courtesy Robert Gentry.

Ellis Littleton—The Driver
Ellis Littleton served as driver and confidante to Earl Long in the 1960 campaign. He's shown here with his wife Bertie after being awarded the Friend of Earl K. Long Award from the Louisiana Political Hall of Fame in 2004. Courtesy Robert Gentry.

RALLY

Earl K. Long CANDIDATE FOR CONGRESS

SPEAKERS

JOE ARTHUR SIMS
Attorney from Hammond and Governor Long's personal Attorney

WILLARD RAMBO
Former Representative of Grant Parish

A. O. RAPPELET
State Senator of Lafourche, Terrebonne, Assumption Parishes

SENATOR F. E. COLE AND A. A. FREDERICKS

BEST MUSICIANS, HILLBILLY BAND, GOOD SINGING, PIANO PLAYING

FRIDAY, JULY 15, 1960

MARTHAVILLE . . . . 4:00 P.M.
NATCHITOCHES

ANACOCO . . . . 5:30 P.M.
VERNON

PITKIN . . . . 7:30 P.M.
VERNON
Hams, Bacon, Groceries and Other Gifts Given Away
Gifts Furnished by Well Wishers

SATURDAY, JULY 16, 1960

LEESVILLE . . . . 9:00 A.M.
VERNON
Hams, Bacon, Groceries and Other Gifts Given Away
Gifts Furnished by Well Wishers

MANY . . . . 10:45 A.M.
SABINE

NATCHITOCHES . . . . 1:15 P.M.
NATCHITOCHES
Hams, Bacon, Groceries and Other Gifts Given Away
Gifts Furnished by Well Wishers

MONTGOMERY . . . . 2:45 P.M.
GRANT
Hams, Bacon, Groceries and Other Gifts Given Away
Gifts Furnished by Well Wishers

EVERGREEN . . . . 4:45 P.M.
AVOYELLES

BUNKIE . . . . 6:15 P.M.
AVOYELLES
Hams, Bacon, Groceries and Other Gifts Given Away
Gifts Furnished by Well Wishers

ALEXANDRIA . . . . 7:45 P.M.
CITY HALL SQUARE
Hams, Bacon, Groceries and Other Gifts Given Away
Gifts Furnished by Well Wishers

SUNDAY, JULY 17, 1960

CLOUTIERVILLE . . . . 10:10 A.M.
NATCHITOCHES

ECHO . . . . 1:15 P.M.
RAPIDES

DUPONT . . . . 2:30 P.M.
AVOYELLES

GOUDEAU . . . . 3:50 P.M.
AVOYELLES

COTTONPORT . . . . 5:15 P.M.
Hams, Bacon, Groceries and Other Gifts Given Away
Gifts Furnished by Well Wishers

MOREAUVILLE . . . . 6:30 P.M.
AVOYELLES
MUSIC AND PRIZES

MARKSVILLE . . . . 7:50 P.M.
AVOYELLES

PLENTY OF CANDY FOR ALL THE CHILDREN

Brutal Summer Schedule Earl Long's weekend campaign schedule through the predominantly rural Eighth Congressional District taxed the stamina of even the young men working for him. Six or seven stops per day were the norm, as this schedule from the middle of July attests.

Big Deal in Small Towns Earl Long's campaign stops were big deals in the small towns and rural communities that comprised the Eighth Congressional District. He brought entertainment, gifts, and speakers to communities where grocery stores were still centers of commerce and gossip.

Something for Everyone
Earl Long's campaign stops included drawings for hams, sacks of flour, and buckets of lard. There was music and singing, along with cold drinks and a layer cake for every lady.

Growing the Circle
This was the start to a typical Earl Long rally. A station wagon sound truck with big speakers mounted on top would draw the crowd. There'd be local speakers and some of Earl's advance crew before he arrived from an earlier stop. Note the ladder on the roof of the sound car in the lower right. That enabled Long's workers to nail signs high enough on poles to prevent opponents from tearing them down.

Snap in His Suspenders
No matter the strength of the warmup speakers or how late he was in arriving, Earl Long's speech was always the highlight of his caravan's stop. He was the best retail politician in Louisiana history. He spoke with passion and wit. He relentlessly attacked his opponents. People knew where he stood. He stood with them, and in the end, they stood with him.

Quarters for the Kids
After his speeches, Earl always gave away quarters to the children who came up to the speaker's platform (in this case, the bed of a pickup truck) after he had spoken. He always made sure he had bags of quarters with him when he started out on the trail each day. Photo by John Curtis Guillet, courtesy the Guillet Family.

Dick Davis's Inside Job
Dick Davis (left, holding a towel) played an evolving role in Earl's life dating back to Long's release from Southeast Louisiana Hospital. He betrayed Long's confidence by serving as a conduit for information to McSween's campaign. He also publicly broke with Long in the runoff. Courtesy Northwestern State University of Louisiana, Watson Memorial Library, Cammie G. Henry Research Center, Joseph Uhrbach Collection.

Black Supporters
Earl Long's final term in office was marked by a protracted fight against segregationists who were intent on purging black voters from the voting rolls across the state. The strain of that fight contributed to his outbursts during the 1959 legislative session, which led to his forced hospitalization. On the campaign trail in 1960, Earl continued to openly court the support of black voters while trying to retain the support of whites. Everyone was welcome at his campaign stops. Photo by John Curtis Guillet, courtesy the Guillet Family.

The Battle of Florien
In the runoff election against Harold McSween, the two campaigns collided in the Sabine Parish community of Florien. The Battle of Florien occurred when McSween arrived for his own town hall meeting in the small community while Earl was still speaking. Standing within feet of each other, the two candidates verbally attacked one another in an exchange of invective that was both jarring and entertaining. McSween had been drawn into a game Earl had long ago mastered. Courtesy Jim Smilie, *The Town Talk*, Alexandria, Louisiana.

Bill Dodd Rallies to Earl's Side

Bill Dodd was the first major political figure to rally to Earl Long's side during the congressional campaign. Dodd is shown here speaking at a Long rally on the banks of the Cane River in Natchitoches in mid-August during the runoff against McSween. Photo by John Curtis Guillet, courtesy the Guillet Family.

Hospital Band

Earl Long left a hospital bed in New Orleans, where he had been recovering from prostate surgery, to open his campaign for Congress with eight stump appearances over the first weekend of the contest. With a Baptist Hospital ID bracelet still on his left wrist, he promised not to throw mud at his opponents unless they started in on him. Photo courtesy the Louisiana Political Museum and Hall of Fame, Winnfield, Louisiana.

Campaign Strain
The strain of an intense campaign carried on through the heat of summer began to show on Earl Long's sixty-five-year-old body.

Birthday Morning
Friday, August 26, 1960, was Earl Long's sixty-fifth birthday and runoff election eve. He had suffered a heart attack on Thursday but put out the story that he had gotten food poisoning. Instead of a hospital, he took to his bed in the Bentley Hotel in Alexandria, fearing that if news of his true condition got out, it would cost him votes. He met with the press in his hotel room on Friday morning, then went under an oxygen tent as soon as the reporters left.

Election Day
The oxygen tent was disassembled and reporters were let into Earl's hotel room on Election Day, Saturday, August 27. He repeated the food poisoning story and read telegrams from well-wishers. Later that night, after being proclaimed the election winner, Long finally was admitted into a hospital.

Earl's Three Sisters

Earl Long surrounded by his three surviving sisters at a Long family reunion in 1960. From left, Clara Long Knott, Lucille Long Hunt, Earl, and Olive Long Cooper. Earl had his sisters Lucille and Clara make his victory statement to supporters at an Alexandria television station on election night. Courtesy Raymond Carpenter, Winnfield, Louisiana.

Back To Winnfield

The hearse carrying Earl Long's body to Winnfield from Baton Rouge. He was buried on September 8, 1960, twenty-five years to the day after his brother Huey was shot.

NOTES

INTRODUCTION

1. Public Affairs Research Council of Louisiana, "20 Years of Louisiana Politics," *Bulletin No. 168*, Baton Rouge (1970). 7. Originally quoted in *Time*, May 18, 1959, Jack B. McGuire Political Collection in the David R. McGuire Jr. Memorial Collection, Louisiana Research Collection, Tulane University Library, New Orleans. Hereafter, McGuire Collection.

2. Jack B. McGuire, "Earl Long," unpublished manuscript, McGuire Collection.

3. G. Dupre Litton, *The Wizard of Winnfield* (New York: Carlton Press, 1982), 35.

4. Baton Rouge *Morning Advocate*, November 7, 1990, McGuire Collection.

5. *Times-Picayune*, August 16, 1968, McGuire Collection.

6. Lake Charles *American Press*, September 24, 1988, McGuire Collection; Jack B. McGuire, *Uncle Earl Deserved Better: Critical Analyses of Blaze, a Film Written and Directed by Ron Shelton and Earl K. Long—The Saga of Uncle Earl and Louisiana Politics, by Michael Kurtz and Morgan Peoples, With Further Commentary on The Last of the Red-Hot Papas* (New Orleans: Good Reading Books, 1995), 72.

7. "Earl Long," Notes by Jack McGuire, McGuire Collection.

8. *Time*, September 19, 1960, Jack B. McGuire, Notes, McGuire Collection.

9. Thomas Martin, *Dynasty: The Longs of Louisiana* (New York: G. P. Putnam's, 1960), 174.

10. Brooks Read and Bud Hebert, *Earl Long: Last of the Red-Hot Papas—The Voice of Earl Long* (Baton Rouge: News Records, 1961), McGuire Collection.

11. Marshall Frady, *Southerners: A Journalist's Odyssey* (New York: New American Library, 1980), 28–29.

12. Ibid.

13. Jack B. McGuire, Notes, McGuire Collection.

14. Jack B. McGuire to Michael S. Martin, August 18, 1999, McGuire Collection.

15. "The Winnfield Frog," *Time*, August 30, 1948, McGuire Collection.

16. Earl K. Long to Mr. and Mrs. K. D. McCoy, March 10, 1949, McGuire Collection.

17. Richard B. McCaughan, *Socks on a Rooster: Louisiana's Earl K. Long* (Baton Rouge: Claitor's Book Store, 1967).

18. McGuire, "Earl Long," unpublished manuscript, McGuire Collection.

19. McGuire, *Uncle Earl Deserved Better*, 188.

20. New Orleans *Times-Picayune*, August 6, 1984.

21. Iris Kelso, "Uncle Earl Still Lives in Louisiana Politics," New Orleans *Times-Picayune*, August 16, 1988, McGuire Collection; "The Gospel According to Earl," McGuire Collection.

22. Jack B. McGuire to Walter Cowan, March 27, 1996, McGuire Collection.

1. THE LONGS: A POLITICAL FAMILY

1. T. Harry Williams, *Huey Long* (New York: Alfred A. Knopf, 1969), 10.

2. Ibid., 20–21.

3. Ibid., 21–22.

4. Ibid., 22–23.

5. Ibid., 13, 23.

6. Martin, *Dynasty: The Longs of Louisiana, 118.*

7. Winn Parish *Enterprise News-American*, September 12, 1963.

8. See http://www.findgrave.com, "Charlotte Arabella Long Davis."

9. Winn Parish *Enterprise News-American*, March 6, 1985, McGuire Collection.

10. Ibid., January 20, 1982, McGuire Collection.

11. Sabine *Index*, February 1, 1973, McGuire Collection.

12. Williams, *Huey Long*, 14–15.

13. Ibid., 15

14. Ibid., 13–14.

15. Ibid., 16.

16. Ibid., 27–28, 315; Walter Greaves Cowan and Jack B. McGuire, *Louisiana Governors: Rulers, Rascals and Reformers* (Jackson: University Press of Mississippi, 2008), 201.

17. Cowan and McGuire, *Louisiana Governors*, 202; McGuire, Notes, McGuire Collection; "The Gospel According to Earl," McGuire Collection.

18. McGuire, Notes, McGuire Collection. Huey told the same story before Earl. See Williams, *Huey Long*, 3.

19. Baton Rouge *Advocate*, August 27, 1988, McGuire Collection.

20. Alexandria *Daily Town Talk*, March 14, 1976, McGuire Collection.

21. Ibid.

22. James Ronald Skains, "Linda Huffman Tells of Life with 'Uncle Earl,'" *Piney Woods Journal* (September 2009), McGuire Collection.

23. Ibid.

24. Ibid.

25. New Orleans *Times-Picayune*, January 20, 23, 1957, McGuire Collection.

26. Linda Huffman Cox told this story to Jack B. McGuire, n.d. Huffman continued to work with the Brand and Livestock Inspection Commission until retiring in 1984.

27. James Ronald Skains, "Linda Was Uncle Earl's Protégé," *Piney Woods Journal* (October 2009), McGuire Collection.

28. Alexandria *Daily Town Talk*, June 11, 1957, McGuire Collection.

29. Ibid.

30. Skains, "Linda Huffman."

31. McCaughan, *Socks on a Rooster*, 244.

32. James Ronald Skains, "Linda Huffman," *Piney Woods Journal* (November 2009), McGuire Collection.

33. Ibid.

34. Ibid.

35. Ibid.

36. Ibid.

37. Ibid.

38. Ibid.

39. Ibid.

40. Ibid.

41. Alexandria *Daily Town Talk*, June 23, 1974, McGuire Collection.

42. "Ellis Littleton, Gentry Notes of Interview," McGuire Collection; Jack B. McGuire, notes, conversation with Ellis Littleton, McGuire Collection, n.d.

43. Bill Carter, "Earl Long's Wife Blocks Parting Gifts," Alexandria *Daily Town Talk*, December 17, 1989, McGuire Collection.

2. EARL KEMP LONG: A POLITICAL LIFE

1. Williams, *Huey Long*, 315–16.

2. Cowan and McGuire, *Louisiana Governors*, 202.

3. Baton Rouge *Morning Advocate*, September 6, 1960, McGuire Collection.

4. Margaret Dixon, "Dixon—Earl Long," typescript of 1948 article for the Baton Rouge *Morning Advocate*, McGuire Collection.

5. McGuire, *Uncle Earl Deserved Better*, 128.

6. Williams, *Huey Long*, 27–28.

7. Litton, *Wizard of Winnfield*, 12.

8. Cowan and McGuire, *Louisiana Governors*, 202.

9. McGuire, *Uncle Earl Deserved Better*, 99.

10. Ibid., 100–101, 107–8; Cowan and McGuire, *Louisiana Governors*, 203. Frank Murphy, United States attorney general, said that "in all of the investigations that we have conducted in the state of Louisiana, not a single lead has carried us to the doorway of Earl Long." McGuire, "Earl Long," 19.

11. Cowan and McGuire, *Louisiana Governors*, 203.

12. New Orleans *Times-Picayune*, December 7, 1947.

13. Jack B. McGuire, Notes for "Earl Long," McGuire Collection.

14. Allan P. Sindler, *Huey Long's Louisiana: State Politics, 1920–1952* (Baltimore: Johns Hopkins Press, 1971), 146.

15. Cowan and McGuire, *Louisiana Governors*, 203–4.

16. Sindler, *Huey Long's Louisiana*, 185–86, 189; Cowan and McGuire, *Louisiana Governors*, 204.

3. EARL LONG'S FIRST FULL TERM AS GOVERNOR: 1948–1952

1. Martin, *Dynasty*, 181.

2. Russell B. Long, "Why I Am for Earl Long," circular, McGuire Collection.

3. Cowan and McGuire, *Louisiana Governors*, 204–5.

4. Ibid., 205.

5. *Time*, August 30, 1948, McGuire Collection; McCaughan, *Socks on a Rooster*, 117.

6. Sindler, *Huey Long's Louisiana*, 181.

7. Cowan and McGuire, *Louisiana Governors*, 205.

8. Martin, *Dynasty*, 185–86; Robert Mann, *Legacy to Power: Senator Russell Long of Louisiana* (New York: Paragon House, 1992), 82–83.

9. Sindler, *Huey Long's Louisiana*, 181.

10. Cowan and McGuire, *Louisiana Governors*, 205.

11. Ibid., 205–6; McGuire, *Uncle Earl Deserved Better*, 111, 113, 115–16.

12. McGuire, *Uncle Earl Deserved Better*, 65, 115–16; Martin, *Dynasty*, 187.

13. Cowan and McGuire, *Louisiana Governors*, 206.

14. Sindler, *Huey Long's Louisiana*, 207, 233.

15. Ibid., 233.

4. THE 1951 ELECTION

1. Cowan and McGuire, *Louisiana Governors*, 206.

2. Ibid.; Jack B. McGuire, conversation with Carlos Spaht; Baton Rouge *Morning Advocate*, May 27, 1998. See also Jack B. McGuire to Carlos Spaht, July 6, 1998, McGuire Collection, and Cowan and McGuire, *Louisiana Governors*, 238.

3. McGuire, Notes for "Earl Long," McGuire Collection.

4. Ibid.

5. Cowan and McGuire, *Louisiana Governors*, 206.

6. Ibid.; McGuire, Notes for "Earl Long," McGuire Collection.

7. McGuire, *Uncle Earl Deserved Better*, 175.

8. McCaughan, *Socks on a Rooster*, 85.

9. Morgan D. Peoples, "Earl Kemp Long: The Man from Pea Patch Farm," *Louisiana History* 17, no. 4 (Fall 1976): 365.

10. Martin, *Dynasty*, 283–84.

5. PEAK EARL: 1956

1. Earl K. Long to E. E. Gentry, May 10, 1955, McGuire Collection.

2. McGuire, *Uncle Earl Deserved Better,* 80.

3. Cowan and McGuire, *Louisiana Governors,* 207.

4. "The Gospel According to Earl Long," McGuire Collection; Iris Kelso, "Uncle Earl Still Lives in Louisiana Politics," *Times-Picayune,* August 16, 1988; McGuire, Notes for "Earl Long," McGuire Collection.

5. Skains, "Linda Huffman."

6. Cowan and McGuire, *Louisiana Governors,* 207.

7. Baton Rouge *Morning Advocate,* January 1, 1956.

8. Cowan and McGuire, *Louisiana Governors,* 207–8.

9. New Orleans *Times-Picayune,* May 17, 1956.

10. *Time,* January 30, 1956.

11. Ibid., July 2, 1956; McGuire, Notes for "Earl Long,"McGuire Collection. In 1983, the Plaquemines Parish Council sued Perez's heirs to recover $80 million of oil royalties received by Delta Development, Inc., between 1936 and 1983. In 1987, the suit was settled, with the parish receiving $10 million and control of the leases of parish lands secretly acquired by Perez, which were expected to yield $3 million annually. Perez had acquired the leases from parish levee boards he controlled and represented as district attorney. According to news accounts of the settlement, his sons—former Commission Council president Chalin O. Perez and former district attorney Leander Perez Jr.—"continued to hide the family's stake in parish lands" following the judge's death in 1969. New Orleans *Times-Picayune,* December 11, 1987.

12. *Time,* July 2, 1956.

13. Cowan and McGuire, *Louisiana Governors,* 208.

14. Read and Hebert, "Last of the Red-Hot Papas," McGuire Collection.

6. THE EIGHTH CONGRESSIONAL DISTRICT FORESHADOWING: 1958

1. Speedy O. Long, conversation with Jack B. McGuire, 1995. Speedy said that he was so small at birth his mother kept him in a shoe box.

2. "Speedy Long," *Biographical Dictionary of the United States Congress,* online edition.

3. Harold B. McSween to Jack B. McGuire, May 14, 1998, McGuire Collection.

4. McGuire, *Uncle Earl Deserved Better,* 177.

5. Ibid.

6. Alexandria *Daily Town Talk,* August 25, 1958, McGuire Collection.

7. Harold B. McSween to Jack B. McGuire, April 12, 1999, January 29, 2001, McGuire Collection.

8. Bill Carter, "Last Wager," Alexandria *Daily Town Talk*, April 7, 1989, McGuire Collection.

9. Ibid.

10. Harold B. McSween to Jack B. McGuire, January 29, 2001, McGuire Collection.

11. Joe Manguno, "Blanche Long: Last of the Red Hot Mamas," *New Orleans Magazine* (September 1977), McGuire Collection.

12. Reggie was indicted on several counts for bank fraud in 1989; pleading to one count, he was convicted. He faced up to ten years in prison and $500,000 in fines but was sentenced by a federal judge to 120 days of home confinement and a $30,000 fine. He obtained thirty-four years of Tulane University scholarships from legislators for family members between 1971 and 1989. His daughter Victoria married Senator Ted Kennedy, New Orleans *Times-Picayune*, April 15, 1995; "Judge Edmund M. Reggie, Former Tulane Board Member," http://www.tulanelink.com/tulanelink/reggie blog; "Lester Gauthier Interviews Camile Gravel on Law Talk," September 5, 1990, Acadiana Open Channel, video posted on YouTube, August 27, 2013, Notes, McGuire Collection.

13. New Orleans *Times-Picayune*, September 6, 1960, McGuire Collection; Baton Rouge *Morning Advocate*, September 6, 1960, McGuire Collection.

14. Natchitoches *Enterprise-American*, July 2, 1959, McGuire Collection.

7. RACE, RAGE, AND RAINACH

1. New Orleans *Times-Picayune*, September 5, 2008, October 10, 2008; McGuire, *Uncle Earl Deserved Better*, 189.

2. New Orleans *Times-Picayune*, October 10, 2008, McGuire Collection.

3. McGuire, *Uncle Earl Deserved Better*, 190.

4. New Orleans *Times-Picayune*, July 19, 2003, McGuire Collection.

5. Ibid., February 25, 1959. See Jack B. McGuire, Letter to the Editor, New Orleans *Times-Picayune*, May 3, 1959.

6. Litton, *Wizard of Winnfield*, 128; McGuire, Notes, McGuire Collection.

7. Sindler, *Huey Long's Louisiana*, 225.

8. Ibid., 34.

9. Perry Howard, *Political Tendencies in Louisiana* (Baton Rouge: Louisiana State University, 1977), 277; *Louisiana v. United States*, 380 U.S. 145, 1965, McGuire Collection.

10. Adam Fairclough, *Race and Democracy: The Civil Rights Struggle in Louisiana: 1915–1972* (Athens: University of Georgia Press, 1995), 180.

11. Notes of Conversations with voters, 1959–1960, McGuire Papers, McGuire Collection.

12. Adam Fairclough, "A Political Coup d'Etat: How the Enemies of Earl Long Overwhelmed Racial Moderation in Louisiana," in *Massive Resistance: Southern Opposition to the Second Reconstruction*, ed. Clive Webb (Oxford: Oxford University Press, 2005,) n.p.

13. Ibid.

14. "Willie Rainach," KnowLA: The Encyclopedia of Louisiana History, Culture and Community, online reference guide, McGuire Collection.

15. Fairclough, "A Political Coup d'Etat."

16. Ibid.

17. Ibid.

18. Fairclough, *Race and Democracy*, 205.

19. Ibid.

20. Ibid.

21. Ibid.

22. Ibid.

23. Ibid.

24. McGuire, "Earl Long."

25. Fairclough, *Race and Democracy*, 181, 207.

26. Ibid.

27. Ibid.

28. Ibid., 207.

29. Ibid., 228.

30. McGuire, "Earl Long," 89.

31. "Willie Rainach," KnowLA, McGuire Collection.

32. Ibid.

33. Notes, McGuire Papers, McGuire Collection.

34. Howard, "*Political Tendencies in Louisiana*," 277.

35. *Louisiana v. United States*, 280 U.S. 145, 1965, McGuire Collection.

36. Fairclough, *Race and Democracy*, 228.

37. T. Harry Williams, foreword to *The Earl of Louisiana*, by A. J. Liebling (Baton Rouge: Louisiana State University Press, 1970), 4–5.

38. Ibid.

39. Natchitoches *Enterprise*, April 30, 1959.

40. Ibid.

41. Ibid.

42. Ibid.

43. Ibid.

44. Ibid.

45. McGuire, *Uncle Earl Deserved Better*, 18; Jack McGuire to Rick Smith, Louisiana Public Broadcasting, July 16, 1985, McGuire Collection.

46. Litton, *Wizard of Winnfield*, 36.

47. McCaughan, *Socks on a Rooster*, 89–90; McGuire, *Uncle Earl Deserved Better*, 237–38; *American Progress*, February 2, 1940, McGuire Collection.

48. McGuire, "Earl Long," 72; McGuire, *Uncle Earl Deserved Better*, 128, 135.

49. Martin, *Dynasty*, 203.

8. UNCLE EARL'S VERY PUBLIC FALL

1. New Orleans *Times-Picayune,* May 18, 1959; McGuire, "Earl Long," 107; McGuire, *Uncle Earl Deserved Better,* 135.

2. McGuire, "Earl Long," 111, McGuire Collection.

3. McGuire, *Uncle Earl Deserved Better,* 135–36.

4. Ibid.

5. Williams, foreword to *Earl of Louisiana,* 5.

6. *Time,* June 15, 1959.

7. Ibid.

8. Martin, *Dynasty,* 213.

9. *Time,* June 15, 1959.

10. Martin, *Dynasty,* 211–13; McGuire, *Uncle Earl Deserved Better,* 136.

11. McGuire, "Earl Long," 126, 136.

12. Williams, foreword to *The Earl of Louisiana,* 5–6.

13. Blanche R. Long, "His Wife's Story of the Commitment," *Life,* June 15, 1959, McGuire Collection.

14. Ibid.

15. Ibid.

16. Ibid.

17. Ibid.

18. Ellis Littleton told the author this story.N.d.

19. Cowan and McGuire, *Louisiana Governors,* 210; McGuire, *Uncle Earl Deserved Better,* 67–68.

20. McGuire, *Uncle Earl Deserved Better,* 67–68.

21. Ibid.

22. T. Harry Williams, *Romance and Realism in Southern Politics* (Baton Rouge: Louisiana State University, 1966), 83.

23. Undated news clipping, from an untitled Galveston newspaper, McGuire Collection.

24. *Shreveport Times,* May 8, 1989, McGuire Collection.

25. Blanche R. Long to Mr. and Mrs. A. A. Fredericks, June 11, 1959, McGuire Collection.

26. Fairclough, *Race and Democracy,* 229.

27. Baton Rouge *Morning Advocate,* June 14, 1959.

28. Blanche R. Long, "His Wife's Story."

29. Martin, *Dynasty,* 230–31; McCaughan, *Socks on a Rooster,* 172–73.

30. See Special Agent in Charge, New Orleans, to Director, re: Governor Earl K. Long, June 2, 1959; A. Rosen to the Director, Subject: "Call from Senator Russell Long relative to Governor Earl Long," June 13, 1959: SAC New Orleans to Director, June 17, 1959. All in The F.B.I. File on Earl K. Long, McGuire Collection. Other than reporting Russell's call that Long was ill and that this was "a family matter," most of the reports from the New Orleans office to Hoover quoted news stories. Typical of so much of the

F.B.I. file on Long, consisting of rumor and innuendo, unverified third-party claims, and acknowledgment that the veracity of informants could not be substantiated, was a hurried report to Hoover from the Detroit office on June 24, 1959, reporting that a confidential informant had advised that "the Teamsters Union has plans all made to kidnap Governor Earl K. Long of Louisiana long enough to have him sign legislation in that state favorable to the Union and for him to sign pardons for a number of their members who are in prison." Long was confined at the Southeast Louisiana Hospital in Mandeville when this was sent. Incredibly, Hoover took such a bizarre report seriously enough so that he noted it to "discreetly advise La. State Police." SAC Detroit to Director, June 24, 1959, McGuire Collection.

31. Mann, *Legacy to Power*, 239–40.

32. *Time*, June 15, 1959, McGuire Collection.

33. McCaughan, *Socks on a Rooster*, 175.

34. McGuire, "Earl Long," 147.

35. Cowan and McGuire, *Louisiana Governors*, 210–11.

36. Petition of Blanche R. Long, June 18, 1959, McGuire Collection.

37. Warrant and Order to Sheriff and Coroner, June 18, 1959, McGuire Collection.

38. *Time*, June 29, 1959, McGuire Collection.

39. McGuire, "Earl Long," McGuire Collection.

40. Ibid.

41. Certificate of Coroner and Physician, June 18, 1950, McGuire Collection.

42. Application of Blanche R. Long, June 18, 1959, McGuire Collection.

43. Ibid.

44. "In the Matter of the Mental Illness of Earl K. Long," certified by Sparkman Wyatt, M.D., and Chester A. Williams Jr., Coroner, McGuire Collection.

45. McCaughan, *Socks on a Rooster*, 210–11.

46. McGuire, "Earl Long"; Cowan and McGuire, *Louisiana Governors*, 211; *New York Times*, November 22, 2013; Baton Rouge *Advocate*, February 13, 2015, McGuire Collection.

47. *Time*, June 29, 1959, McGuire Collection.

48. Gary Cangelosi, "A Tiger on Your Back," oral history interview of Theo Cangelosi by his grandson, McGuire Collection.

49. Ibid.

50. State of Louisiana ex rel Earl K. Long, Petition for Writ of Habeas Corpus of Earl K. Long, June 22, 1959, McGuire Collection.

51. Ibid.

52. Ibid.

53. Ibid.

54. Ibid.

55. Ibid.

56. Ibid.

57. Writ of Habeas Corpus Order, 22nd Judicial District Court, June 22, 1959, McGuire Collection.

58. Motion and Order to Summons [sic]Witnesses, 22nd Judicial District Court, June 23, 1959, McGuire Collection.

59. McGuire, Notes for "Earl Long," McGuire Collection.

60. Jesse Bankston to Jack B. McGuire, November 18, 2002, McGuire Collection.

61. Petition of Earl K. Long, June 25, 1959, McGuire Collection.

62. Ibid.

63. Ibid.

64. Baton Rouge *Morning Advocate*, September 6, 1960, McGuire Collection.

65. Many years later, Bankston wrote the author that

> the night before I was fired, I met with the Lieutenant Governor [Frazar], Bill Cleveland [senate president pro tem], Bob Angelle [speaker of the house], and Wilma Lockhart [Long's secretary]. I told them that since I was following the physician's advice that I could not order the Governor's discharge. I was told that if I did not that the board would be asked to fire me. I told them that the only person who had authority was the Lieutenant Governor, that the Governor had the authority to appoint me and that I was serving at the pleasure of the Governor. They told me, as I recall, that the legal counsel for the Governor told them otherwise. And I suggested that they should check again with Joe Arthur Sims. I guess that they wanted to be sure and that is possibly what happened.
>
> I was prepared to be fired at that meeting the night before and often wondered why the Lieutenant Governor did not do it at that meeting. A few days later, A.R. Johnson, chairman of the hospital board invited me to meet with him at Bob and Jake's Restaurant and he told me about the signatures. He said that the reason for all the signatures was at the insistence of the attorney, and he and some of the members of the board were reluctant to sign. He may have told me that to make me feel better. I did not know that Governor Long signed it. It is interesting that I was well fired.

66. *Time*, July 6, 1959, McGuire Collection.

67. Hammond *Daily Star*, March 22, 1999, McGuire Collection.

68. *Time*, July 6, 1959, McGuire Collection.

69. McGuire, *Uncle Earl Deserved Better*, 139.

70. Martin, *Dynasty*, 261–62.

71. McCaughan, *Socks on a Roster*, 178–80.

72. McGuire, *Uncle Earl Deserved Better*, 140; McGuire, "Earl Long," 161–62.

73. McGuire, "Earl Long," 162.

74. Ibid.

75. Martin, *Dynasty*, 265.

76. Ibid.

77. William J. Dodd, *Peapatch Politics: The Earl Long Era in Louisiana Politics, by Earl's Lieutenant Governor, William J. Dodd* (Baton Rouge: Claitor's Publishing, 1991), 39, 44.

78. Ted Jones, a dear friend, told the author this story in 2012.

79. McGuire, *Uncle Earl Deserved Better*, 6–8, 16–17, 25–26, 35–44.

80. New Orleans *Times-Picayune*, January 21, 1990, McGuire Collection.

81. Ellis Littleton, conversation with Jack B. McGuire, Notes, McGuire Collection.

82. Baton Rouge *State-Times*, December 1989, McGuire Collection.

83. New Orleans *Times-Picayune*, April 12, 1989, McGuire Collection.

84. Ibid., December 15, 1989, McGuire Collection.

85. Blanche R. Long, Answer and Re-conventional Demand, June 30, 1959, McGuire Papers, McGuire Collection.

86. Ibid.

87. Ibid.

88. Blanche R. Long, Motion to Discontinue Inventory, June 30, 1959, McGuire Collection.

89. Baton Rouge *State-Times*, July 2, 1959, McGuire Collection.

90. Ibid.

91. McCaughan, *Socks on a Rooster*, 217.

92. Natchitoches *Enterprise-News American*, July 2, 1959, McGuire Collection.

93. Ibid.

94. Ibid.

95. Ibid.

96. McGuire, "Earl Long," 182–85; Martin, *Dynasty*, 282.

97. McGuire, "Earl Long," 160–63.

98. Ibid.

99. Ibid.

100. Ibid.

101. Ibid.

102. Harry S. Truman to Honorable David D. Lloyd, July 27, 1959, McGuire Collection.

103. Harry S. Truman to Honorable Earl Long, July 27, 1959, McGuire Collection.

104. Harry S. Truman to Brooks Read, January 31, 1962, McGuire Collection.

105. Litton, *Wizard of Winnfield*, 72–76.

106. Skains, "Linda Huffman."

107. McGuire, "Earl Long," 181–82, McGuire Collection.

9. RUNNING FOR LIEUTENANT GOVERNOR: 1959–1960

1. McGuire, "Earl Long," McGuire Collection.

2. Martin, *Dynasty*, 284.

3. "Come Out and Hear the Truth!" Earl Long circular. 1959. McGuire Collection.

4. Ibid.

5. Ibid.

6. Ibid.

7. Ibid.

8. McGuire, *Uncle Earl Deserved Better*, 148.

9. McCaughan, *Socks on a Rooster*, 219.

10. Ibid.; Martin, *Dynasty*, 292–93; Litton, *Wizard of Winnfield*, 106–7.

11. Martin, *Dynasty*, 293–95; McCaughan, *Socks on a Rooster*, 219–33.

12. Baton Rouge *Morning Advocate*, November 15, 1959.

13. Judge Benjamin Bennett, who was the ticket candidate for attorney general, told this to the author. N.d.

14. Jack McGuire, "Earl K. Long between the 1959 First Primary and the Jimmie Davis Inauguration," memorandum, McGuire Collection.

15. McCaughan, *Socks on a Rooster*, 239.

16. When a National Guard sergeant said they were ready to go, and the gurney Long was strapped onto was rolled toward the cargo bay of the Air National Guard plane, Long told Hufft that he was dismissed as adjutant general and announced that he was promoting the sergeant to the rank. Long, however, was fond of Major General Hufft, who was Louisiana's most decorated soldier in World War II, and he later forgave Hufft and kept him on as adjutant general.

17. McGuire, "Earl K. Long between the 1959 first Primary."

18. McCaughan, *Socks on a Rooster*, 235–36; Martin, *Dynasty*, 296–97.

19. Earl K. Long to Jack B. McGuire, December 9, 1959, McGuire Collection.

10. "I WOULD RATHER WIN AND DIE THAN LOSE AND LIVE": 1960

1. Neal Pierce, *The Deep South States of America* (New York: W. W. Norton, 1974), 315.

11. UNCLE EARL'S LAST HURRAH

1. McGuire, *Uncle Earl Deserved Better*, 175.

2. Ibid.; "Earl K. Long, Farewell Address," typescript, McGuire Collection.

3. "Earl K. Long, Farewell Address." Long referred to de Gaulle's visit to New Orleans, during which Mayor Morrison and a citizen's committee slighted him. No one introduced him to the general and his wife on a reviewing stand in front of St. Louis Cathedral, so he introduced himself to them. At a civic luncheon, when Morrison seated him at the end of the table with several reporters and admonished him to keep his remarks short, Long welcomed de Gaulle and then put on his hat and strolled from the ballroom.

4. Ibid.

5. Ibid.

6. McGuire, *Uncle Earl Deserved Better*, 176.

7. Ibid.

8. Ibid.

9. New Orleans *States-Item*, May 3, 1960, McGuire Collection.

10. New Orleans *Times-Picayune*, June 2, 1960, McGuire Collection.

11. Undated newclipping, newspaper unknown, McGuire Collection; McSween ad in the Natchitoches *Times*, August 25, 1960, McGuire Collection.

12. Baton Rouge *Morning Advocate*, June 1, 1960, McGuire Collection.

13. Ibid.

14. Ibid. The failure to disclose the nature of the surgery caused rumors about his condition to circulate. Morgan Peoples, who coauthored a biography of Long, said that Long was impotent and had prostate surgery. There was, however, no indication of prostate cancer in the medical records when he was hospitalized in Alexandria after winning the congressional election, and it is unlikely that he had a radical prostatectomy to remove the prostate to deal with a cancer and prevent its spread. Prostate surgery was a lengthy procedure requiring several hours, and it would not have been possible for Long to recover from that in two days and take the stump. He probably had surgery for an enlarged prostate, which is a one-hour procedure from which he would have recovered quickly. The fact that the procedure was to correct a problem that had bothered him for a long time also tends to point the finger to an enlarged prostate, which causes discomfort with urination, rather than surgery to remove a cancerous prostate.

When he was lambasted by his opponents in the congressional race for chasing strippers, Long responded, "What would I do if I caught one? Sixty-four years of age and I just had one of the worst operations a man can have." In *The Earl of Louisiana*, A. J. Liebling described a news conference at the mansion during the state election campaign. Long said that when he collapsed at the legislature, he was not feeling well and had put off an operation he needed. When a female reporter asked what type of surgery was involved, the governor glanced down and said it was on his "lower parts" and that he would have the procedure in the near future. Jack B. McGuire to Jesse H. Bankston, June 10, 2002, McGuire Collection.

Enemies circulated ugly stories that Long was treated at Baptist Hospital for syphilis or gonorrhea and that he had contracted the sexual diseases from Blaze Starr. There has never been any report to substantiate those rumors; surgery would not have been necessary, as syphilis is treated with massive doses of antibiotics, and gonorrhea is not treatable. The detailed medical records from his final illness, from the blood work done, also indicated that he had never had those diseases. Dr. Willoughby, who performed the surgery, died of a heart attack at a young age in 1966. Thirty-seven years later, his widow said that he was an excellent urologist and any procedure he performed on Long would have involved his specialty, but she had no information on it. Jack B. McGuire to Dr. R. M. Willoughby, August 28, 2003, McGuire Collection; telephone conversation with Mrs. Willoughby August 29, 2003; Earl K. Long Medical Records, Baptist Hospital, Alexandria, LA, McGuire Collection.

15. Baton Rouge *Morning Advocate*, June 3, 1960; Alexandria *Daily Town Talk*, June 2, 1960, McGuire Collection.

16. *Shreveport Times*, June 5, 1960, McGuire Collection.

17. Alexandria *Daily Town Talk*, June 3, 1960, McGuire Collection.

18. Litton, *Wizard of Winnfield*, 120–21.

19. Baton Rouge *Morning Advocate*, June 4, 1960.

20. Martin, *Dynasty*, 194–95; Winn Parish *Enterprise–News American*, January 9, 1969, McGuire Collection.

21. In 1998, McSween said at a symposium at Louisiana College in Pineville that at first he did not take Long's candidacy seriously because he thought that health problems would prevent his making an all-out campaign. McSween believed that after his collapse at the 1959 legislative session, hospitalization, adverse publicity about the western trip, adjournment of his planned special session, and the loss for lieutenant governor, Long would not be able to put a campaign together or withstand the rigors of one. Jack B. McGuire to Harold B. McSween, May 5, 1960, McGuire Collection.

In a "personal and confidential" letter to this writer in 1998, elaborating on his comments at the symposium and that he asked not be made public until after his death, McSween wrote that "I did not take Mr. Earl's candidacy with seriousness at first, because for one thing among others three reputable physicians who had examined him in recent months had conveyed through an intermediary that—if he did run—he could not last more than 60 days of stump campaigning in the summer heat. He was allotted 90+ days. Otherwise I'd have been re-nominated by default, in the second if not the first Democratic primary." McSween acknowledged that Dr. R. U. Parrott, who was married to Long's niece, Charlotte Davis Parrott, daughter of Long's sister Charlotte Long Davis, known as Lottie, was a source through the "medical grapevine" for the statement that Long's weakened heart would not be able to stand the stress of a campaign. McSween said, "I didn't expect him to live until the first primary." Harold B. McSween to Jack B. McGuire, May 14, 1998; Jack B. McGuire, conversation with Harold B. McSween, 1998;Charlotte Davis Parrott to Jack B. McGuire, April 1, 2003, McGuire Collection.

22. Alexandria *Daily Town Talk*, January 13, 2002, McGuire Collection.

23. *Biographical Dictionary of the United States Congress*, online edition.

24. Alexandria *Daily Town Talk*, August 1, 1956.

25. Baton Rouge *Morning Advocate*, June 5, 1960.

26. New Orleans *Times-Picayune*, June 1, 1960.

27. *Shreveport Times*, June 5, 1960, McGuire Collection. The Boston Club is an elite men's social club in New Orleans.

28. "Earl K. Long, Candidate for Congress," McGuire Collection.

29. Alexandria *Daily Town Talk*, June 6, 1960, McGuire Collection.

30. Ibid.

31. Ibid.

32. *Shreveport Times*, July 22, 1960, McGuire Collection.

33. Jack B. McGuire to Ray J. Ellington, April 11, 2003, McGuire Collection.

34. *Shreveport Times*, July 24, 1960, McGuire Collection.

35. New Orleans *Times-Picayune*, June 15, 1960.

36. Ibid. The police report said Long was driving a 1955 Cadillac. Trial on the charges was set for August 18, 1960, but Judge Bucaro again continued it until after the August 27 runoff. See New Orleans Police Department, Motor Vehicle Accident Report, June 14, 1960, McGuire Collection;New Orleans *States-Item*, August 18, 1960, McGuire Collection.

37. Litton, *Wizard of Winnfield*, 111.

38. Baton Rouge *State-Times*, September 7, 1960, McGuire Collection.

39. Ellis Littleton told the author this story. N.d.

40. McCaughan, *Socks on a Rooster*, 68.

41. William C. Havard, Rudolf Heberle, and Perry H. Howard, *The Louisiana Elections of 1960*, Louisiana State University Studies, Social Science Series no. 9 (Baton Rouge: Louisiana State University Press, 1963), 37.

42. Stan Opotowsky, *The Longs of Louisiana* (New York: E. P. Dutton, 1960), 164–65.

43. McGuire, "Earl Long," unpublished manuscript, McGuire Collection.

44. A. J. Liebling, *The Earl of Louisiana* (New York: Simon and Schuster, 1961), 120.

45. Opotowsky, *Longs of Louisiana*, 165.

46. Williams, *Huey Long*, 316.

47. Undated clipping, McGuire Collection.

48. Litton, *Wizard of Winnfield*, 111.

49. Notes, W. K. Brown, McGuire Collection.

50. Alexandria *Daily Town Talk*, September 21, 1998, McGuire Collection.

51. Long appointed Dugas to the LSU Board of Supervisors at the start of his term in 1948, and Dugas served until 1963. He died in 1989 at age ninety-one. Baton Rouge *Advocate*, December 3, 1989, McGuire Collection.

52. Edgar Coco's nephew, Benjamin Clyde Bennett, who had been a legislative assistant to Long during sessions and was the Noe-Long candidate for attorney general in 1959, wrote that "Earl Long liked Edgar and they enjoyed a close and personal relationship beyond politics. Edgar was a fun-loving person and taken to doing unexpected things. Once Earl offered us tickets to an LSU football game to sit with him in the governor's box. I had tickets and declined with thanks. Edgar took four of the six tickets. During the game, strangers were sitting in the box with the Governor and Earl turned to Edgar and said "'Coco, it looks like you hawked those tickets.' He had." Benjamin C. Bennett, draft of a memoir, "Edgar, Leo and Earl," McGuire Collection. Bennett said that he and his wife were in their car when he heard over the radio that Long had announced the Noe-Long ticket in 1959. He said he was put on it for attorney general without any consultation with him. Bennett later served as a state District Court judge for many years.

There were many humorous stories about Edgar and his cousin, Leo Coco, a prosperous businessman in Marksville. Bennett said that "Earl Long loved to tweak Leo. During the time that Earl was confined in Galveston, Leo went to see him." Leo sat in the jury box as a spectator during the habeas corpus hearing, where "Earl approached him and told Leo he needed $500.00, which Leo produced." After he was released from Southeast Louisiana Hospital, Long heard that Leo "boastfully told everyone who would listen that Earl owed him $500.00. By this time, Earl had announced the formation of the Noe-Long ticket on which Edgar was running for insurance commissioner. Earl called Leo to come to Baton Rouge. 'Bring Edgar with you,'" Long said. They were ushered into the office and seated in front of Long's desk; the governor produced five one hundred dollar bills and said, "Here, Leo, I want to pay you what I owe you." Bennett wrote that "he put it in front of Leo and without removing his hand, pushed the bills over to Edgar's side of the desk and said, 'Now you're giving this to Edgar for his campaign.' Leo and Edgar rode back to Marksville in silence." Ibid.

53. Jack B. McGuire to Michael D. Wynne, May 16, 2003, McGuire Collection.

54. New Orleans *Times-Picayune*, October 10, 1993, McGuire Collection.

55. Jay Chevalier told this story to the author in 2002.

56. Alexandria *Daily Town Talk*, September 21, 1988, McGuire Collection.

57. Robert Gentry, "Notes on Earl K. Long," McGuire Collection.

58. Robert Gentry, "Speech, Winn Parish Chamber of Commerce Banquet, November 16, 2004," McGuire Collection.

59. Jack B. McGuire to Michael D. Wynne, October 27, 2006, McGuire Collection.

60. Jack B. McGuire to Judge Benjamin C. Bennett, April 6, 2003, McGuire Collection.

61. Gentry, "Speech, Winn Parish."

62. "Ellis Littleton, Gentry Interview Notes," McGuire Collection; McGuire, conversation with Ellis Littleton.

63. "Joe Arthur Sims," Notes, McGuire Collection.

64. Robert Gentry, "The Afternoon I Met Earl K. Long," McGuire Collection.

65. Robert Gentry, "Notes on Earl K. Long," McGuire Collection.

66. Ibid.

67. Ibid. Gentry recalled that one Sunday morning, they were approaching Alexandria from Winnfield, going up a bypass when they came behind a slow-moving car. "Pass him," Long bellowed. "I can't," Gentry replied. "Why not?" Long demanded. "Because there might be something coming," Gentry answered as a car in the other lane "whipped over the top of the overpass." Long was unmoved by their near miss, remarking, "You'll never get ahead in life unless you take chances." Gentry, "Notes on Earl K. Long."

On another occasion, Gentry was driving them from Marksville to Alexandria at night. Long complained about Gentry's driving, saying he was going too slowly, so Gentry told him to drive. Long took over and ran them off the highway; Gentry said "Long grunted all the way to Alec" after taking the wheel again. Robert Gentry, "Earl K. Long, Notes by Robert Gentry," McGuire Collection.

68. Ibid.

69. Robert Gentry, "Earl K. Long," McGuire Collection.

70. Ibid.

71. Gentry, "Speech, Winn Parish." Long was also known to take his teeth out and rinse them in a water glass at the table after dining.

72. Ibid.

73. Gentry, "Notes on Earl K. Long."

74. Ibid.
75. Ibid.
76. Gentry, "Speech, Winn Parish."
77. Ibid.
78. Ellis Littleton told the author this story. N.d.
79. Robert Gentry "Speech, Winn Parish."
80. Ibid.
81. Ibid.
82. Ibid.
83. "Earl K. Long. Notes by Robert Gentry," McGuire Collection.
84. *Shreveport Times*, June 19, 1960, McGuire Collection.
85. Ibid., June 18, 1960, McGuire Collection.
86. Natchitoches *Enterprise*, June 23, 1960, McGuire Collection.
87. Alexandria *Daily Town Talk*, July 9, 1960, McGuire Collection.
88. Ibid.
89. Alexandria *Daily Town Talk*, July 2, 1960, McGuire Collection.
90. Ibid., July 4, 1960, McGuire Collection.
91. Ibid.
92. Ibid.
93. Alexandria *Daily Town Talk*, August 2, 1960, McGuire Collection.
94. Ibid., June 20, 1960, McGuire Collection.
95. Ibid.
96. *Shreveport Times*, June 23, 1960, McGuire Collection.
97. Alexandria *Daily Town Talk*, June 27, 1960, McGuire Collection.
98. Natchitoches *Times*, June 30, 1960, McGuire Collection.
99. Ibid.
100. Natchitoches *Enterprise*, July 7, 1960, McGuire Collection.
101. Alexandria *Daily Town Talk*, July 16, 1960, McGuire Collection.
102. Ibid., August 1, 1960, McGuire Collection.
103. *Shreveport Times*, July 8, 1960, McGuire Collection.
104. Natchitoches *Times*, July 14, 1960, McGuire Collection.
105. *Shreveport Times*, June 30, 1960, McGuire Collection.
106. Natchitoches *Times*, July 7, 1960, McGuire Collection.
107. Ibid., June 30, 1960, McGuire Collection.
108. Ibid., July 7, 1960, McGuire Collection.
109. Ibid., July 2, 1960, McGuire Collection.
110. *Shreveport Times*, July 7, 1960, McGuire Collection.
111. Earl K. Long to My Dear Friend, July 8, 1960, McGuire Collection.
112. Ibid. Mary Evelyn Parker was, for a time, editor of the Oakdale *Journal* and a friend of Bill Dodd, who also hailed from that Oakdale, in Allen Parish. She began her political career when Long asked her to narrate his radio speeches in the 1948 campaign for governor. Earl appointed her executive director of the Department of Commerce and Industry and, when he returned to office in 1956, named her Commissioner of

Welfare. A political strategist for Long, she was Democratic National Committeewoman during his 1948–1952 term and ran for register of the State Land Office on the Spaht-McKeithen ticket. She supported John McKeithen for governor in 1963 and took a position in his administration when he won election. She was elected state treasurer in 1967 and held that office until retiring in 1987. She died in Baton Rouge on January 17, 2015, at the age of ninety-four. New Orleans *Advocate*, January 18, 2015.

113. *Shreveport Times*, July 9, 1960, McGuire Collection.

114. Alexandria *Daily Town Talk*, July 11, 1960, McGuire Collection.

115. Natchitoches *Enterprise*, July 21, 1960, McGuire Collection.

116. Alexandria *Daily Town Talk*, July 11, 1960, McGuire Collection.

117. *Shreveport Times*, July 24, 1960, McGuire Collection.

118. Natchitoches *Enterprise*, July 21, 1960, McGuire Collection.

119. *Shreveport Times*, July 15, 1960, McGuire Collection.

120. Ibid.; "Earl K. Long Speaks," handbill, McGuire Collection

121. Alexandria *Daily Town Talk*, July 14, 1960.

122. *Shreveport Times*, July 24, 1960, McGuire Collection.

123. Quoted in McGuire, *Uncle Earl Deserved Better*, 177.

124. Earl K. Long to Honorable Alvin Stumpf, August 12, 1960, McGuire Collection.

125. Earl K. Long to George Woodard, McGuire Collection. Note on the outside of an envelope.

126. Jesse Bankston, *Earl Kemp Long: The Inside Story of the Governor as I Knew Him* (Baker, LA: Art-Write Associates, 2002), 47–48, 90–91.

127. McGuire, *Uncle Earl Deserved Better*, 177.

128. Sabine *Index*, July 15, 1960, McGuire Collection.

129. Ibid.

130. Ibid.

131. "Earl K. Long for Congress" circular, McGuire Collection.

132. Natchitoches *Times*, July 21, 1960, McGuire Collection.

133. "The Louisiana Maneuvers (1940–41)," Mark Perry, Military History Magazine, online, November 25, 2008, http://www.militaryhistorymagazine.com.

134. Angela Houser, "Fort Polk Museum Tells History of Installation," Leesville *Daily Leader*, March 3, 2013. Troops were trained there until 1943, when some of the thousands of wooden barracks built for the exercises were used to house German prisoners of war from the Afrika Corps. Troops were trained for the Korean War and Operation Sagebrush (a 1955 exercise with eighty-five thousand troops preparing for war in a nuclear environment) after a brief closing. In 1959, the base was closed again and did not reopen until 1961, during the Berlin Crisis. Troops trained there for Vietnam with over one million soldiers passing through its Tiger Land recreation of Vietnamese villages there. Later, troops destined for Iraq and Afghanistan went through similar training programs. It is presently a combat training center, but its future is again uncertain.

135. Natchitoches *Times*, July 21, 1960, McGuire Collection.

136. Jack McGuire to Ray J. Ellington, May 14, 2003, McGuire Collection; Conversation with Ellis "Easy Money" Littleton, 2004.

137. Litton, *Wizard of Winnfield*, 122–23.

138. Alexandria *Daily Town Talk*, July 22, 1960, McGuire Collection.

139. Natchitoches *Enterprise*, July 21, 1960, McGuire Collection.

140. Ibid.

141. Natchitoches *Enterprise*, July 18, 1960.

142. Alexandria *Daily Town Talk*, July 18, 1960, McGuire Collection.

143. Ibid.

144. Alexandria *Daily Town Talk*, July 19, 1960, McGuire Collection.

145. *Shreveport Times*, July 18, 1960, McGuire Collection.

146. Alexandria *Daily Town Talk*, July 22, 1960, McGuire Collection.

147. *Shreveport Times*, July 22, 1960, McGuire Collection.

148. Natchitoches *Enterprise*, July 21, 1960, McGuire Collection.

149. *Shreveport Times*, July 24, 1960, McGuire Collection.

12. THE RUNOFF CAMPAIGN: ALL IN

1. *Shreveport Times*, July 30, 1960, McGuire Collection.

2. Ibid., July 31, 1960.

3. Natchitoches *Enterprise*, August 4, 1960, McGuire Collection.

4. *Shreveport Times*, August 2, 1960, McGuire Collection.

5. Ibid.

6. Ibid., August 4, 1960, McGuire Collection.

7. Alexandria *Daily Town Talk*, August 5, 1960, McGuire Collection.

8. Natchitoches *Times*, August 4, 1960, McGuire Collection.

9. Alexandria *Daily Town Talk*, August 2, 1960, McGuire Collection.

10. New Orleans *States-Item*, August 4, 1960, McGuire Collection.

11. Alexandria *Daily Town Talk*, August 5, 1960, McGuire Collection.

12. Sabine *Index*, August 5, 1960, McGuire Collection.

13. Alexandria *Daily Town Talk*, August 2, 1960, McGuire Collection.

14. *Shreveport Times*, August 6, 1960, McGuire Collection.

15. Jack McGuire to Judge Benjamin C. Bennett Jr., April 11, 2002, McGuire Collection.

16. Alexandria *Daily Town Talk*, August 6, 1960, McGuire Collection.

17. Natchitoches *Times*, August 4, 1960, McGuire Collection.

18. *Shreveport Times*, August 7, 1960, McGuire Collection.

19. Jack McGuire to Harold McSween, January 29, 2001, McGuire Collection.

20. *Shreveport Times*, August 7, 1960, McGuire Collection.

21. Ibid.

22. Natchitoches *Enterprise*, August 11, 1960, McGuire Collection; McGuire, *Uncle Earl Deserved Better*, 178.

23. *Shreveport Times*, August 10, 1960, McGuire Collection.

24. Sabine *Index*, August 12, 1960, McGuire Collection.

25. "Do Not Reward Such Conduct," advertisement, n.d., McGuire Collection 26. Ibid.

27. "Earl K. Long for Congress," circular, August 12, 1960, McGuire Collection.

28. Ibid.

29. Ibid.

30. Jay Chevalier, *Earl K. Long and Jay Chevalier: "When the Music Stopped"* (Natchitoches, LA: Southern Legacies Press, 2003), 131.

31. Long circular, August 12, 1960, McGuire Collection.

32. McGuire, *Uncle Earl Deserved Better*, 178.

33. Ibid., 179.

34. Natchitoches *Times*, August 11 and 18, 1960, McGuire Collection.

35. *Shreveport Times*, August 16, 1960, McGuire Collection.

36. Alexandria *Daily Town Talk*, August 15, 1960, McGuire Collection.

37. Harold McSween to Jack McGuire, April 12, 1999, McGuire Collection.

38. Ibid. Earl said that Huey never called him Kangaroo and that Francis Grevemberg, a candidate for governor in 1956, was the first person to call him that. In the 1940 campaign against Jones, Long said his opponents were calling him Kangaroo Slickum Long. The Reverend Gerald L. K. Smith had headed the Share Our Wealth Clubs for Huey and delivered the eulogy at his funeral. He later became a notorious anti-Semite.

39. Ibid. The "meat" referred to was the hams and slabs of bacon that Earl gave away.

40. Natchitoches *Enterprise*, August 18, 1960.

41. Ibid.

42. *Shreveport Times*, August 16, 1960, McGuire Collection.

43. Jack McGuire to Judge Benjamin C. Bennett Jr., April 11, 2002, McGuire Collection.

44. New Orleans *Times-Picayune*, July 17, 1991, McGuire Collection.

45. Natchitoches *Times*, August 18, 1960.

46. Benjamin Clyde Bennett Jr. to Jack McGuire, May 4, 2002, McGuire Collection.

47. New Orleans *States-Item*, August 16, 1960.

48. Jack McGuire, notes on Long speech, August 1960, McGuire Collection.

49. Natchitoches *Times*, August 18, 1960, McGuire Collection.

50. Ibid.

51. Ibid.

52. Ibid.

53. Natchitoches *Enterprise*, August 25, 1960, McGuire Collection.

54. *Shreveport Times*, August 19 and 20, 1960, McGuire Collection.

55. Ibid., August 24, 1960. McGuire Collection.

56. Ibid.

57. Natchitoches *Enterprise*, August 25, 1960.

58. Ibid.

59. Bennett obviously meant "drivers" for Long. Benjamin Clyde Bennett Jr. to Michael D. Wynne, March 23, 2002, McGuire Collection.

60. Ibid.

61. Ibid. Sugar teats were small cloths with sugar in them, twisted closed, and put in a baby's mouth for the baby to suck on so it would be quiet.

62. Alexandria *Daily Town Talk*, August 18, 1960, McGuire Collection.

63. Ibid., August 19, 1960, McGuire Collection.

64. *Shreveport Times*, August 23, 1960, McGuire Collection.

65. Jack B. McGuire to Harold B. McSween, May 3, 1999; Alexandria *Daily Town Talk*, August 22, 1960, McGuire Collection. A similar exchange between Long and Gravel occurred when Long spoke in Alexandria during his abortive stump tour for governor in 1959.

66. Bill Carter, "Trying to Regroup," Alexandria *Daily Town Talk*, April 6, 1989, McGuire Collection.

67. "Law Talk with Lester Gauthier," September 5, 1990, Acadiana Open Channel, video posted on YouTube 08/27/13.

68. Alexandria *Daily Town Talk*, August 22, 1960, McGuire Collection.

69. Ibid.

70. Ibid.; Baton Rouge *Morning Advocate*, August 21, 1960, McGuire Collection.

71. Baton Rouge *Morning Advocate*, August 21, 1960, McGuire Collection.

72. Alexandria *Daily Town Talk*, August 13, 1960, McGuire Collection.

73. Ibid., August 22 and 26, 1960, McGuire Collection.

74. Ibid.

75. Gentry, "Earl Long," McGuire Collection.

76. Alexandria *Daily Town Talk*, August 22, 1960, McGuire Collection.

77. McGuire, *Uncle Earl Deserved Better*, 180.

78. Alexandria *Daily Town Talk*, August 22, 1960, McGuire Collection.

79. Ibid.

80. Ibid.

81. Harold B. McSween, conversation with Jack McGuire, 2001. McSween asked McGuire to hold this in confidence until after he, McSween, had passed on.

82. Alexandria *Daily Town Talk*, August 22, 1960, McGuire Collection.

83. Ibid.

84. Winn Parish *Enterprise*, August 23, 1960, McGuire Collection.

85. Gentry, "Earl Long"; Gentry "Speech, Winn Parish."

86. Winn Parish *Enterprise*, August 23, 1960, McGuire Collection.

87. Baton Rouge *Morning Advocate*, August 24, 1960, McGuire Collection.

88. Ibid.

89. Ibid.; *Shreveport Times*, August 24, 1960, McGuire Collection.

90. New Orleans *States-Item*, August 25, 1960, McGuire Collection.

91. *Shreveport Times*, August 25, 1960, McGuire Collection.

92. Baton Rouge *Morning Advocate*, August 24, 1960, McGuire Collection.

93. Alexandria *Daily Town Talk*, August 26, 1960, McGuire Collection.

94. Baton Rouge *Morning Advocate*, August 25, 1960, McGuire Collection.

95. Alexandria *Daily Town Talk*, August 25, 1960, McGuire Collection.

96. Natchitoches *Times*, August 25, 1960, McGuire Collection.

97. Baton Rouge *Morning Advocate*, August 24, 1960, McGuire Collection.

98. *Shreveport Times*, August 27, 1960, McGuire Collection.

99. Ibid.

100. Ibid.

101. Natchitoches *Times*, August 25, 1960, McGuire Collection.

102. Baton Rouge *Morning Advocate*, August 24, 1960, McGuire Collection.

103. McGuire, *Uncle Earl Deserved Better*, 181.

104. Littleton, "Gentry Notes of Interview."

105. W. K. Brown to Jack B. McGuire, May 25, 1998, McGuire Collection; Alexandria *Daily Town Talk*, August 27, 1995, McGuire Collection.

106. Littleton, "Gentry Notes of Interview"; Alexandria *Daily Town Talk*, December 15, 1989, McGuire Collection.

107. Earl K. Long's Medical Records, Baptist Hospital, Personal History, Dr. R. U. Parrott, McGuire Collection.

108. McGuire, *Uncle Earl Deserved Better*, 181.

109. Alexandria *Daily Town Talk*, December 15, 1989, McGuire Collection.

110. Baton Rouge *Morning Advocate*, August 27, 1960, McGuire Collection.

111. New Orleans *States-Item*, August 27, 1960, McGuire Collection.

112. McGuire, *Uncle Earl Deserved Better*, 181–82 113. Alexandria *Daily Town Talk*, August 27, 1960, McGuire Collection.

114. Ibid., December 15, 1989, McGuire Collection.

115. Baton Rouge *Morning Advocate*, August 28, 1960, McGuire Collection.

116. *Shreveport Times*, August 29, 1960, McGuire Collection.

117. W. K. Brown to Jack B. McGuire, May 25, 1998, McGuire Collection.

118. Alexandria *Daily Town Talk*, June 23, 1974, McGuire Collection.

119. *Shreveport Times*, September 1, 1960, McGuire Collection.

120. "Ellis Littleton, Gentry Notes of Interview"; "Earl K. Long's Medical Records, Dr. Parrott's Notes, Baptist Hospital," McGuire Collection. Dr. John A. Worley was a cardiologist.

121. Baton Rouge *Morning Advocate*, August 28, 1960, McGuire Collection.

122. Harold B. McSween to Jack B. McGuire, April 12, 1999, McGuire Collection.

123. Ibid.

124. Ibid.

125. McSween, conversation with Jack B. McGuire, 2001.

126. Alexandria *Daily Town Talk*, August 28, 1960, McGuire Collection.

127. *Shreveport Times*, August 29, 1960, McGuire Collection.

128. Stuart Symington to Earl K. Long, McGuire Collection; Littleton, conversation with Jack B. McGuire, 2002.

129. Baton Rouge *Morning Advocate*, August 29, 1960, McGuire Collection.

130. William J. Dodd to Mr. and Mrs. Albert A. Fredericks, August 31, 1960, McGuire Collection.

131. Ibid.

132. Baton Rouge *Advocate*, November 21, 2002, McGuire Collection.

133. "Ellis Littleton, Gentry Notes of Interview."

134. Ibid.

135. Ibid.

136. Bill Carter, "Long's Last Wager," Alexandria *Town Talk*, April 7, 1989, McGuire Collection.

137. *Shreveport Times*, August 30, 1960, McGuire Collection.

138. Ibid., September 1, 1960, McGuire Collection.

139. Baton Rouge *Morning Advocate*, September 1, 1960, McGuire Collection.

140. Alexandria *Daily Town Talk*, September 3, 1960, McGuire Collection.

141. *Shreveport Times*, September 4, 1960, McGuire Collection.

142. Ibid.

143. Ibid.

144. Gentry, "Earl K. Long, Notes by Robert Gentry."

145. Manguno, "Blanche Long."

146. *Winnfield News-American*, April 19, 1989, McGuire Collection.

147. W. K. Brown to Jack B. McGuire, May 25, 1998, McGuire Collection; McSween, conversation with Jack B. McGuire, 2001. McSween told this writer that he was at the hospital checking on a friend and went to Long's room to congratulate him and wish him a quick and full recovery. He said W. K. Brown came to the door when he knocked lightly and told him Long was sleeping and could not be disturbed because the doctors wanted him to rest. McSween said he asked Brown to tell Long he had come by and that he was later told that Long was very disappointed that Brown had not awakened him.

148. Alexandria *Daily Town Talk*, June 23, 1974, McGuire Collection.

149. New Orleans *Times-Picayune*, September 6, 1960, McGuire Collection.

150. "Ellis Littleton, Gentry Notes of Interview."

151. Alexandria *Daily Town Talk*, June 23, 1974, McGuire Collection.

152. "Earl K. Long Medical Records."

153. New Orleans *Times-Picayune*, September 6, 1960, McGuire Collection.

154. Alexandria *Daily Town Talk*, September 5, 1960.

155. *Winn Parish Enterprise*, September 8, 1960, McGuire Collection; *Winnfield News-American*, September 8, 1960, McGuire Collection.

156. Joy Hollis, Director, Medical Records Department, Rapides Medical Center, To Whom It May Concern, September 22, 1993, McGuire Collection.

157. Jay Chevalier, conversation with Jack McGuire, 2008.

158. Alexandria *Daily Town Talk*, September 7, 1960, McGuire Collection.

159. Baton Rouge *State-Times*, September 9, 1960, McGuire Collection.

13. IN UNCLE EARL'S WAKE

1. *Winn Parish Enterprise*, September 8, 1960, McGuire Collection; *Winnfield News-American*, September 8, 1960, McGuire Collection; New Orleans *States-Item*, September 6, 1960, McGuire Collection.

2. McCaughan, *Socks on a Rooster*, 263.

3. *Shreveport Times*, September 5, 1960, McGuire Collection; New Orleans *States-Item*, September 6, 1960, McGuire Collection.

4. Baton Rouge *Morning Advocate*, September 7, 1960, McGuire Collection.

5. McGuire, *Uncle Earl Deserved Better*, 183; Baton Rouge *Morning Advocate*, September 6, 1960, McGuire Collection.

6. Baton Rouge *Morning Advocate*, September 6, 1960, McGuire Collection.

7. Alexandria *Daily Town Talk*, September 7, 1960, McGuire Collection.

8. Baton Rouge *Morning Advocate*, September 6, 1960, McGuire Collection.

9. New Orleans *Times-Picayune*, September 8, 1960, McGuire Collection. Long filled out a membership card in the First Baptist Church of Baton Rouge on July 10, 1955, professing his faith and requesting that he be baptized. He was baptized during a service on October 5, 1955. Burn Page, Senior Pastor, First Baptist Church of Baton Rouge to Robert Gentry, March 8, 2004, McGuire Collection.

10. Baton Rouge *Morning Advocate*, September 8, 1960, McGuire Collection.

11. Ibid.

12. *Winn Parish Enterprise and Winnfield News-American*, September 8, 1960, McGuire Collection.

13. Ibid.

14. Litton, *Wizard of Winnfield*, 128.

15. *Winn Parish Enterprise and Winnfield News-American*, September 8, 1960, July 15, 1963, McGuire Collection.

16. *Shreveport Times*, September 9, 1960, McGuire Collection.

17. Baton Rouge *State-Times*, September 8, 1960, McGuire Collection.

18. Baton Rouge *Morning Advocate*, September 6, 1960, McGuire Collection.

19. W. K. Brown to Jack B. McGuire, May 25, 1998.

14. LOUISIANA REACTS

1. Baton Rouge *Morning Advocate*, September 6, 1960, McGuire Collection.

2. Ibid.

3. Ibid.

4. Ibid.

5. "Earl Long: Last of the Red Hot Papas—The Voice of Earl Long," McGuire Collection.

6. Williams, foreword to *The Earl of Louisiana*.

7. Baton Rouge *Morning Advocate*, September 7, 1960, McGuire Collection.

8. Ibid.

9. Ibid.

10. Ibid.

11. Baton Rouge *State-Times*, September 6, 1960, McGuire Collection.

12. Ibid.

13. Ibid.
14. Skains, *Piney Woods Journal*, November 2009, McGuire Collection.
15. Ibid.
16. Baton Rouge *Morning Advocate*, September 7, 1960, McGuire Collection.
17. Baton Rouge *State-Times*, September 6, 1960, McGuire Collection.
18. Ibid.
19. W. K. Brown to Jack B. McGuire, May 25, 1998, McGuire Collection.

15. LOUISIANA EDITORIAL REACTIONS TO EARL LONG'S DEATH

1. New Orleans *States-Item*, September 5, 1960, McGuire Collection.
2. Ibid.
3. Baton Rouge *State-Times*, September 5, 1960, McGuire Collection.
4. New Orleans *Times-Picayune*, September 6, 1960, McGuire Collection.
5. New Orleans *States-Item*, September 6, 1960, McGuire Collection.
6. *Shreveport Times*, September 6, 1960, McGuire Collection.
7. Ibid., September 11, 1960, McGuire Collection.

16. NATIONAL EDITORIAL REACTION

1. *Shreveport Times*, September 11, 1960, McGuire Collection.
2. Ibid.
3. Ibid.
4. Ibid.
5. Ibid.
6. Ibid.
7. Ibid.
8. Ibid.
9. Ibid.
10. Ibid.

17. SETTLING UNCLE EARL'S ESTATE

1. Bill Carter, "Long's Last Wager," Alexandria *Daily Town Talk*, April 7, 1989, McGuire Collection.

2. Jack B. McGuire to Robert Wagner, August 12, 2003, McGuire Collection; Alexandria *Daily Town Talk*, December 17, 1989, McGuire Collection; Littleton, conversation with Jack B. McGuire, 2002.

3. Littleton, conversation with Jack McGuire, 2002.

4. Alexandria *Daily Town Talk*, June 23, 1974, McGuire Collection.

5. Littleton, conversation with Jack B. McGuire, 2002; Succession of Earl Kemp Long, McGuire Collection.

6. Succession of Earl Kemp Long, McGuire Collection.

7. Alexandria *Daily Town Talk*, July 13, 1961, McGuire Collection.

8. Order and Proces-Verbal, H. L. Allen, Judge, Eighth Judicial District Court, September 12, 1960, McGuire Collection. Blanche evidently kept the original will after Earl executed it.

9. Ibid.

10. Ibid.

11. Inventory, October 20, 1960, McGuire Collection.

12. Ibid.

13. Ibid.

14. Ibid.

15. Ibid.

16. Ibid.

17. Ibid.

18. Petition of Executrix to Sell Stocks and Bonds at Private Sale, Succession of Earl Kemp Long, May 17, 1962, McGuire Collection.

19. News clippings, paper not identified, March 15, May 3 and 10, 1962, McGuire Collection.

20. Estate of Earl K. Long to Leroy Chandler, September 18, 1961, McGuire Collection.

21. Estate of Earl K. Long to J. D. Harkins, McGuire Collection.

22. C. J. Ellington versus Mrs. Blanche Revere Long as Administrator of the Succession of Earl K. Long, July 12, 1961, and Answer of Mrs. Blanche Revere Long, July 19, 1961, McGuire Collection.

23. Probate Suite No. 1409, Eighth Judicial District Court in and for the Parish of Winn, Succession of Earl K. Long, Recorded July 19, 1963, McGuire Collection. It is not known whether he and other claimants were paid. Dr. Parrott was killed in an accident on the Red River Bridge in Alexandria in 1966 when a trailer being towed by another vehicle broke loose and hit his car head-on. His wife, Long's niece, died in 2006. Alexandria *Daily Town Talk*, January 19, 2006, McGuire Collection; Jack B. McGuire to Jay Chevalier, May 14, 2003, McGuire Collection.

24. Alexandria *Daily Town Talk*, July 13, 1961, McGuire Collection.

25. Petition, Succession of Earl K. Long, No. 1409, Eighth Judicial District, McGuire Collection. David C. Treen, a partner in the law firm representing the Longs, later served in Congress and for one term as governor.

26. Undated news clipping courtesy of Robert Gentry, McGuire Collection. The home, now known as Longview House, is the office and Baton Rouge residence of lobbyist Randy K. Haynie.

27. Cash Sale, July 7, 1958, Mrs. Irene R. Simon to Earl Kemp Long and Mrs. Blanche R. Long, McGuire Collection.

28. Cash Sale, North Baton Rouge Development Company, Inc., to Earl Kemp Long and Blanche Revere Long, August 25, 1958, McGuire Collection.

29. *Shreveport Times*, June 10, 1960, McGuire Collection.

30. Cash Sale, Earl Kemp Long and Blanche Revere Long to G. Harold King, June 8, 1960, McGuire Collection.

31. *Governor Earl K. Long v. Blanche Revere Long*, Order, Baton Rouge, June 9, 1960, McGuire Collection.

32. Cash sale, G. Harold King to Blanche Revere Long, Parish of East Baton Rouge, June 9, 1960, McGuire Collection.

33. Instrument, Earl K. Long, Appearer, Parish of East Baton Rouge, Declaration and Acknowledgment by Earl Kemp Long, June 29, 1960, McGuire Collection.

34. Undated clippings, file about the lawsuit, McGuire Collection.

35. "Estate of Earl K. Long vs. Mr. and Mrs. Frank Matthews," memorandum by Jack McGuire, McGuire Collection.

36. Clint L. Pierson, Attorney for Mrs. Blanche Revere Long, to Mr. Frank Matthews, December 15, 1960, McGuire Collection.

37. Ibid.

38. Clint L. Pierson to Mr. Frank Matthews, April 6, 1961, McGuire Collection.

39. Frank W. Matthews to Clint L. Pierson, April 13, 1961, McGuire Collection.

40. Copies of Notes, McGuire Collection.

41. "Analysis of Notes, Earl K. Long," McGuire Collection.

42. "Satisfaction" receipt for payment by Mrs. Blanche Revere Long, July 11, 1966, McGuire Collection.

43. Dodd, *Peapatch Politics*, 53–53, 251.

44. Robert Wool, "The Louisiana Story: Clowns, Complacency, Corruption," *LOOK*, December 8, 1959, McGuire Collection.

45. McGuire, *Uncle Earl Deserved Better*, 151.

46. Jack Bass, and Walter DeVries, *The Transformation of Southern Politics: Social Change and Political Consequences since 1945* (Athens: University of Georgia Press, 1995), 171.

47. Ibid., 158–59.

18. MEMORIALIZING EARL KEMP LONG

1. Baton Rouge *Advocate*, September 20, 1998, McGuire Collection.

2. Ibid.

3. Ibid.

4. Louisiana State Police—75th Anniversary, "Feature Interview: Russell Willie," in The Louisiana Trooper, n.d., http://www.lsp.org/images/75th/history_Willie.

5. Ibid.

6. Ibid.

7. Ibid.

8. *Shreveport Times*, May 8, 1989, McGuire Collection. At that time, many farmers raised hogs as free-range animals and put notches in their ears to mark them; their ear notches were registered in the clerk of court's offices to prove ownership. Hogs with no notches were fair game for whoever got them.

9. Ibid.

10. Ibid.

11. New Orleans *Times-Picayune*, August 16, 1988, McGuire Collection.

12. Edmund M. Reggie to Michael D. Wynne, March 17, 1997, McGuire Collection.

13. Ibid.

14. Ibid.

15. Raymond Strother to Robert Gentry, March 13, 2004, McGuire Collection.

16. Strother also told Gentry this story: "Mary Evelyn Parker told me yet another Long story. Earl was riding down the highway between Natchitoches and Alexandria with a young reporter. Long was ill and frail and had just beaten Silver Spoon McSween. The young reporter expected great wisdom from the wise old legend but all he got was silence as they sat in the back seat and shot gun shacks, porches with leaking sofas on the front porch, hulks of wrecked cars in the yard flashed by the windows. Finally the old man spoke. He waved his hand. 'Son, you see them people?' 'Yes, Sir.' Them's good, honest people.' 'Yes, sir.' 'You know why?' 'No, sir.' 'Never been tempted.' I was too young to vote for Earl Long. But I would have." It's a wonderful story, but Long could not have been riding in a car as described after beating McSween; he was in the hospital. Perhaps this took place during the primary or runoff. Ibid.

17. "Memorial Services for Earl K. Long, Labor Day, September 4, 1961, 11:00 a.m. at Winnfield," McGuire Collection.

18. Photographs of the statue and park, McGuire Collection; Winn Parish *Enterprise News-American*, September 8, 1960, McGuire Collection.

19. "Unveiling of Bronze Statue of Earl K. Long, July 4, 1963, 11:00 a.m., at Winnfield," program, McGuire Collection; Winnfield *Enterprise*, July 11, 1963, McGuire Collection.

20. Winnfield *Enterprise*, July 11, 1963, McGuire Collection.

21. Alexandria *Daily Town Talk*, March 5, 2005.

22. McSween discussed this in a conversation with Jack McGuire, 1998.

23. Harold B. McSween, conversations with Jack McGuire, 1996, 1998, 2000.

24. New Orleans *Times-Picayune*, January 14, 2002.

25. McSween explained the "Long versus Long" race to Jack B. McGuire in conversations, 1996, 1998, 2000.

26. Alexandria *Daily Town Talk*, August 25, 2003, McGuire Collection.

27. Harold B. McSween, "Harold Barnett McSween: Writings," McGuire Collection. In his essay on Earl Long, McSween paid tribute to his opponent on the centennial of Long's birth, remarking that "I had observed Earl Long's rousing first campaign for governor in 1940 when a high school freshman, never dreaming I would ever go up against him myself. It's still frightening to think about this, 35 years later. Writing about Mr. Earl comes easier than tangling with him. He can't talk back, but is entitled to his due as one of the incomparables." McSween praised "the indomitable Earl Long" as

an advocate of voting rights for minorities, as a promoter of increased voter registration by blacks in his 1948–1952 administration that saw a fivefold increase in black registrants, and regarding the circumstances of his breakdown while fighting purges of blacks from voter registration rolls. McSween concluded that Long was "alone among contemporary Southern governors of the 1940's and 1950's as a voting rights champion for African Americans." Harold B. McSween, "Earl Long, 1895–1960: Voting Rights Advocate of Political Incorrectness," *Virginia Quarterly Review* (Summer 1995), McGuire Collection. Admirers of Governor James "Kissing Jim" Folsom of Alabama would argue that he was no racist and that he was similar to Long in his attitude and efforts.

28. Jack McGuire to Harold McSween, December 10, 2001, McGuire Collection.

29. Ruston *Daily Leader*, July 28, 1959; Baton Rouge *State-Item*, April 12, 1960; Alexandria *Daily Town Talk*, November 7, 1960; undated/unidentified news clipping, 1955, McGuire Collection; Glen Jeansonne, *Leander Perez, Boss of the Delta* (Baton Rouge: Louisiana State University Press, 1977).

30. "Willie Rainach," KnowLA, McGuire Collection.

31. Ibid.

32. *Biographical Dictionary of the United States Congress*, online edition. Dan Cornett, in a eulogy for Speedy, said that he was practicing law in Baton Rouge when Speedy convinced him to come back to Jena to serve as his first assistant district attorney, and when Speedy chose not to run for another term, he won the office with Speedy's support. "Speedy was truly a man of the people, a man for the people," Cornett said. "He had an innate sense of right and wrong and knew how the working man felt about things. He stuck with his word. He made me a better attorney. When he spoke, you listened." Alexandria *Daily Town Talk*, October 10, 2006, McGuire Collection.

33. *New York Times*, January 22, 1965; *Biographical Dictionary of the United States Congress, 1977–present*, online.

34. Robert Gentry to Mrs. Jane Purser, undated memo of notes for introduction of him, McGuire Collection.

35. Cangelosi, "A Tiger on Your Back."

36. Ibid.

37. Ibid.

38. Ibid.

39. Ibid.

40. Baton Rouge *Advocate*, August 27, 1988, McGuire Collection.

41. Edwin W. Edwards to Robert Gentry, March 15, 2004, McGuire Collection.

42. Lecompte, Louisiana, cemetery record, Dick A. Davis, 12/23/1918–12/21/1990, McGuire Collection.

43. *New York Times*, May 18, 1998, McGuire Collection.

44. Ibid.

45. Succession of Blanche Revere Long, Proces [*sic*]Verbal of Inventory, Twenty-Fourth Judicial Court for the Parish of Jefferson, Division "C," No. 524-437, March 10, 1999, McGuire Collection.

46. Succession of Blanche Revere Long, Detailed Descriptive List, Twenty-Fourth Judicial District Court for the Parish of Jefferson, Division "C," No. 524-437, August 24, 2000, McGuire Collection.

47. "Russell B. Long," *New York Times*, May 11, 2003.

48. Russell B. Long, conversations with Jack B. McGuire, 1995, 1996.

49. "To the Long Family Reunion," from Russell B. Long, August 18, 1995, McGuire Collection.

50. Ibid.

51. *Uncle Earl Deserved Better* was published by Good Reading Books in New Orleans. About one thousand copies were printed, but while they were being distributed, the printing plant flooded and several hundred were destroyed. Bob Mann is a professor at Louisiana State University and holds the Manship Chair in Mass Communications and is director of the Reilly Center for Media & Public Affairs. He served as press secretary for Senator Russell Long and his successor, Senator John Breaux, and was communications director for Governor Kathleen Blanco. He has written many journal articles and several books, including *Legacy to Power: Senator Russell Long of Louisiana* (1992); *When Freedom Would Triumph: The Civil Rights Struggle in Congress, 1945–1968* (2007), and *A Grand Delusion: America's Descent into Vietnam* (2001).

52. Zwolle newspaper clipping, unidentified, McGuire Collection; Glen Jeansonne, "Bill Dodd," KnowLA Encyclopedia of Louisiana, online, August 30, 2013.

53. Alexandria *Daily Town Talk*, April 2, 2007.

54. James Ronald Skains, *Piney Woods Journal* (January, 2012).

55. Alexandria *Daily Town Talk*, November 19, 2005.

56. "Joseph Arthur Sims," Baton Rouge *Morning Advocate*, May 21, 1973; New Orleans *Times-Picayune*, May 21, 1973.

57. Baton Rouge *Morning Advocate*, July 15, 2011; Alexandria *Daily Town Talk*, July 17, 2011.

58. Alexandria *Daily Town Talk*, September 12, 1999.

59. New Orleans *Times-Picayune*, August 6, 1984, McGuire Collection.

60. Baton Rouge *Advocate*, March 5, 2008, McGuire Collection; New Orleans *Times-Picayune*, March 6, 2008, McGuire Collection.

61. New Orleans *Times-Picayune*, December 24, 2005, McGuire Collection.

62. Gilbert Dupre Litton, http://www.findgrave.com, McGuire Collection.

63. Baton Rouge *Morning Advocate*, October 8, 2007, November 28, 2010, November 30, 2010, McGuire Collection.

BIBLIOGRAPHY

MANUSCRIPTS

David R. McGuire Memorial Collection. This collection is divided into three series: The David R. McGuire Papers, The Jack B. McGuire Papers, and the Jack B. McGuire Collection of Louisiana Political Materials that includes the Jack B. McGuire Collection of Huey P. Long Papers. Many of the sources cited in the Bibliography and Notes are in these collections. A principal source has been "Earl Long," an unpublished manuscript by Jack B. McGuire, and Jack B. McGuire's notes for *Uncle Earl Deserved Better.*

Tulane University Library, Special Collections Division, Louisiana Research Collection, New Orleans, Louisiana.

RECORDING

Read, Brooks, and Bud Hebert. *Earl Long: "Last of the Red Hot Papas," The Voice of Earl Long.* Baton Rouge: News Records, 1961.

NEWSPAPERS

Alexandria *Daily Town Talk*
American Progress
Baton Rouge *Morning Advocate* and *Advocate*
Baton Rouge *State-Times*
Dallas *Daily News*
Hammond *Daily Star*
Lake Charles *American Press*
Natchitoches *Enterprise* and (subsequently) *Enterprise-American*
New Orleans *States-Item*
New Orleans *Times-Picayune*
New York Times
Piney Woods Journal

Ruston *Daily Leader*
Sabine *Index*
Shreveport Times
Winn Parish *Enterprise* and (subsequently) *Winn Parish Enterprise and Winnfield News-American*

PERIODICALS

Life
Look
Newsweek
Times

ARTICLES AND BOOKS

"Back in the Saddle Again." *Time*, May 24, 1948.

Bankston, Jesse. *Earl Kemp Long: The Inside Story of the Governor As I Knew Him*. Baker, LA: Art White Associates, 2002.

Bass, Jack, and Walter DeVries. *The Transformation of Southern Politics: Social Change and Political Consequence since 1945*. Athens: University of Georgia Press, 1995.

Beam, Jim. "Friends Remember Uncle Earl." Lake Charles *American Press*, September 24, 1998.

"Bitin' Man." *Time*, February 2, 1948.

"The Brother." *Time*, September 19, 1960.

Carter, Bill. "Earl Long's Friend to 'Blaze': Humbug!" Alexandria *Town Talk*, December 14, 1989.

———. "Long's Last Wager." Alexandria *Town Talk*, April 17, 1989.

———. "Trying to Regroup." Alexandria *Town Talk*, April 6, 1989.

Chevalier, Jay. *Earl K. Long and Jay Chevalier: "When the Music Stopped."* Natchitoches, LA: Southern Legacies Press, 2003.

Cowan, Walter Greaves, and Jack B. McGuire. *Louisiana Governors: Rulers, Rascals and Reformers*. Jackson: University of Mississippi Press, 2008.

Dodd, William J. *Peapatch Politics: The Earl Long Era in Louisiana Politics, by Earl's Lieutenant Governor, William J. Dodd*. Baton Rouge: Claitor's Publishing, 1991.

"Earl's Whirl." *Time*, May 18, 1959.

Fairclough, Adam. "A Political Coup d'Etat: How the Enemies of Earl Long Overwhelmed Racial Moderation in Louisiana." In *Massive Resistance: Southern Opposition to the Second Reconstruction*. Edited by Clive Webb. Oxford: Oxford University Press, 2005.

———. *Race and Democracy: The Civil Rights Struggle in Louisiana: 1915–1972*. Athens: University of Georgia Press, 1995.

Frady, Marshall. *Southerners: A Journalist's Odyssey*. New York: New American Library, 1980.

Gauthier, Lester. "Lester Gauthier Interviews Camille Gravel on Law Talk." September 5, 1990. Acadiana Open Channel. Video posted on YouTube, 08/27/2013. Transcribed by Jack B. McGuire. Jack B. McGuire Papers.

Gentry, Robert. "The Afternoon I Met Earl K. Long." Jack B. McGuire Papers.

———. "Notes on Earl Long." McGuire Papers.

———. "Speech, Winn Parish Chamber of Commerce Banquet, November 16, 2004." Jack B. McGuire Papers.

"The Governor Goes Home." *Time*, June 29, 1959.

"Happy Days." *Time*, March 8, 1948.

Havard, William C., Rudolf Heberle, and Perry H. Howard. *The Louisiana Elections of 1960*. Louisiana State University Studies, Social Science Series No. 9. Baton Rouge: Louisiana State University Press, Baton Rouge, 1963.

"His Worst Enemy." *Newsweek*, July 20, 1959.

Howard, Perry H. *Political Tendencies in Louisiana*. Baton Rouge: Louisiana State University Press, 1977.

"I'll Shoot 'Em." *Newsweek*, July 27, 1959.

"Invictus." *Time*, July 6, 1959.

Jeansonne, Glen. *Leander Perez: Boss of the Delta*. Baton Rouge: Louisiana State University Press, 1977.

Kelso, Iris. "Recalling an Eventful Summer at a Covington Motel." *New Orleans Times-Picayune*, January 21, 1990.

———. "Uncle Earl Still Lives in La. Politics." New Orleans *Times-Picayune*, August 16, 1988.

"Last of the Red-Hot Poppas." *Time*, July 2, 1956.

Littleton, Ellis. "Gentry Notes of Interview." Jack B. McGuire Papers.

Litton, G. Dupre. *The Wizard of Winnfield*. New York: Carlton Press, 1982.

Long, Blanche R. "His Wife's Story of the Commitment." *Life*, June 15, 1959.

Long, Earl K. "Come Out and Hear the Truth." 1959, McGuire Collection.

———. "Earl K. Long, Farewell Address." 1960, McGuire Collection.

———. "My Dear Friend." July 8, 1960, McGuire Collection.

———. "To the Citizens and Residents of the Eighth Congressional District." August 12, 1960, McGuire Collection.

———. "To the Ladies of the Eighth Congressional District." August 12, 1960, McGuire Collection.

Long, Russell B. "Why I Am for Earl K. Long: The Speech in Which Huey Long's Son Answered the False Charges Made against His Father." 1948, McGuire Collection.

Manguno, Joe. "Blanche Long: Last of the Red Hot Mamas." *New Orleans Magazine*, September 1977.

Mann, Robert, *Legacy to Power: Senator Russell Long of Louisiana*. New York: Paragon House, 1992.

Martin, Thomas. *Dynasty: The Longs of Louisiana*. New York: G. P. Putnam's, 1960.

McCaughan, Richard B. *Socks on a Rooster: Louisiana's Earl K. Long*. Baton Rouge: Claitor's Book Store, 1967.

McGuire, Jack B. "Earl Long." Unpublished manuscript. Jack B. McGuire Papers.

———. *Uncle Earl Deserved Better: Critical Analyses of Blaze a Film Written and Directed by Ron Shelton and Earl K. Long—The Saga of Uncle Earl and Louisiana Politics, by Michael L. Kurtz and Morgan Peoples, With Further Commentary on The Last of the Red-Hot Papas*. New Orleans: Good Reading Books, 1995.

McSween, Harold B. "Harold Barnett McSween: Writings." McGuire Collection.

Miller, Robin. "Uncle Earl: Stories from Friends and Foes." Alexandria *Town Talk*, September 21, 1998.

"Ole Earl." *Time*, June 15, 1959.

Opotowsky, Stan. *The Longs of Louisiana*. New York: E. P. Dutton, 1960.

Peoples, Morgan D. "Earl Kemp Long: The Man from Pea Patch Farm." *Louisiana History: The Journal of the Louisiana Historical Association* 17, no. 4 (Fall 1976).

Perry, Mark, "The Louisiana Maneuvers, 1940–41." *Military History*, November 25, 2008. http://www.historynet.com/louisiana-maneuvers-1940-41.htm.

Pierce, Neal. *The Deep South States of America*. New York: W. W. Norton, 1974.

"The Price of Education." *Time*, July 21, 1950.

Public Affairs Research Council of Louisiana. *20 Years of Louisiana Politics*. Bulletin No. 168. Baton Rouge: Public Affairs Research Council of Louisiana, 1970.

Sindler, Allan P. *Huey Long's Louisiana: State Politics 1920–1952*. Baltimore: Johns Hopkins Press, 1971.

Skains, James Ronald. "Linda Huffman Tells of Life with 'Uncle Earl,'" *Piney Woods Journal*, September 2009. McGuire Collection.

———. "Linda Was Uncle Earl's Protégé." *Piney Woods Journal*, October 2009. McGuire Collection.

Starr, Blaze. *Blaze Starr: My Life As Told to Huey Perry, A Novel By Blaze Starr and Huey Perry*. New York: Pocket Books, 1989.

"Strange Behavior." *Newsweek*, June 8, 1959.

"The Unquenchable Longs." *Newsweek*, August 8, 1960.

"Up and Down." *Time*, December 13, 1948.

Williams, T. Harry. Foreword. *The Earl of Louisiana*. By A. J. Liebling. Baton Rouge: Louisiana State University Press, 1970.

———. *Huey Long*. New York: Alfred A. Knopf, 1969.

———. *Romance and Realism in Southern Politics*. Baton Rouge: Louisiana State University Press, 1966.

Willie, Russell. "Feature Interview: Russell Willie." *Louisiana Trooper*, Louisiana State Police 75th Anniversary, 2011.

"Willie Rainach," KnowLA: The Encyclopedia of Louisiana History, Culture and Community," online reference guide. A project of the Louisiana Endowment for the Humanities. http://knowla.org.

"The Winnfield Frog." *Time*, August 30, 1948.

"With Long in Texas: I'll Shoot 'Em." *Newsweek*, July 27, 1959.

Wool, Robert. "The Louisiana Story: Clowns, Complacency, Corruption." *Look*, December 8, 1959.

"Younger Brother." *Time*, January 30, 1956

INDEX